T0330294

Utility Regulation and Competition Policy

Edited by

Colin Robinson

Editorial Director, Institute of Economic Affairs, London, and Professor of Economics, University of Surrey, UK

In Association with the Institute of Economic Affairs and the London Business School

Edward Elgar

Cheltenham, UK • Northampton, MA, USA

Published by
Edward Elgar Publishing Limited
Glensanda House
Montpellier Parade
Cheltenham
Glos GL50 1UA
UK

Edward Elgar Publishing, Inc.
136 West Street
Suite 202
Northampton
Massachusetts 01060
USA

A catalogue record for this book
is available from the British Library

Library of Congress Cataloguing in Publication Data

Utility regulation and competition policy / edited by Colin Robinson.
    p. cm.
    "In association with the Institute of Economic Affairs and the London Business School."
Includes bibliographical references and index.
    1. Public utilities—Great Britain. 2. Public utilities—Deregulation—Great Britain. 3. Trade regulation—Great Britain. 4. Industrial policy—Great Britain. 5. Competition—Government policy—Great Britain. 6. Public utilities—European Union countries. 7. Public utilities—Deregulation—European Union countries. 8. Trade regulation—European Union countries. 9. Industrial policy—European Union countries. 10. Competition—Government policy—European Union countries. I. Robinson, Colin, 1932- II. Institute of Economic Affairs (Great Britain) III. London Business School.

HD2768.G74 U85 2002
363.6'094—dc21   2001053237

ISBN 1 84064 850 3

Printed and bound in Great Britain by MPG Books Ltd, Bodmin, Cornwall

Contents

List of figures and tables

FIGURES

TABLES

Abbreviations and acronyms

BG	British Gas
BSC	Broadcasting Standards Commission
CAPEX	capital expenditure
CEER	Council of European Electricity Regulators
CTC	compensation for transition to competition
DETR	Department of Environment, Transport and the Regions
DGES	Director General of Electricity Supply
DGFT	Director General of Fair Trading
DGWS	Director General of Water Supply
DSO	distribution system operator
DTI	Department of Trade and Industry
ECHR	European Court of Human Rights
ECJ	European Court of Justice
ECPR	efficient component pricing rule
EMR	European Merger Regulation
ETSO	European Association of TSOs (see below)
FERC	Federal Energy Regulatory Commission (USA)
FTA	Fair Trading Act
ISO	independent system operator
IT	Information Technology
M&A	Mergers and Acquisitions
MALC	market abuse licence condition
MCR	Merger Control Regulation
MMC	Monopolies and Mergers Commission
MS	Member State
NBP	national balancing point
NERA	National Economic Research Associates
NETA	new electricity trading arrangements
NGTA	new gas trading arrangements
nTPA	negotiated third-party access
NTS	national transmission system
OCM	on-the-day commodity market
Ofcom	Office of Communications
Offer	Office of Electricity Regulation
Ofgas	Office of Gas Supply

Ofgem	Office of Gas and Electricity Markets
OFT	Office of Fair Trading
Oftel	Office of Telecommunications
OPEX	operating expenditure
OPRAF	Office of Passenger Rail Franchising
ORR	Office of the Rail Regulator
PSO	public service obligation
RA	Radio Authority
RAB	regulatory asset base
RCAM	Regulated Community Asset Mutual
REC	regional electricity company
RETA	Review of Electricity Trading Arrangements
ROSCO	rolling-stock leasing company
RTO	regional transmission organization
rTPA	regulated third-party access
SBM	single-buyer model
SND	seasonal normal demand
SO	system operator
SPV	special purpose vehicle
SRA	Strategic Rail Authority
TACs	track access charges
TFP	total factor productivity
TOC	train operating company
TPA	third-party access
TSO	transmission system operator
USO	universal service obligation

The authors

Mark Armstrong is Official Fellow in Economics at Nuffield College, Oxford. He was educated at the Universities of Oxford and Cambridge, and until 1997 was Professor of Economic Policy at Southampton University. Much of his research concerns the theory of optimal pricing and tariffing decisions by firms with market power, including various forms of price discrimination, quantity discounts and auctioning schemes. Other, more applied, research interests are to do with regulatory and competition policy, with a special focus on telecommunications and broadcasting; this includes, with Simon Cowan and John Vickers, *Regulatory Reform: Economic Analysis and British Experience* (MIT Press, 1994). He is currently managing editor of the academic journal *Review of Economic Studies*, and has acted as an economic adviser to the Office of Telecommunications (Oftel) and the Office of Fair Trading (OFT).

Ian Charles Rayner Byatt was appointed as the first Director General of Water Services on 1 August 1989. He is an economist and an expert on the regulation of public utilities. His previous post was Deputy Chief Economic Adviser to the Treasury (1978–89).

Ian Byatt (born 1932) was educated at Kirkham Grammar School and St Edmund Hall and Nuffield College, Oxford. He holds a D.Phil. in economics. He also studied at Harvard as a Commonwealth Fund Fellow, and has lectured in economics at both Durham University (1958–62) and the London School of Economics (1964–67).

Byatt joined the Civil Service in 1967 as Senior Economic Adviser to the Department of Education and Science. His career in the Civil Service also included spells at the Ministry of Housing and Local Government and the Department of the Environment, before joining the Treasury in 1972 as Under-Secretary (1972–78); Deputy Chief Economic Adviser (1978–89); Chairman, Economic Policy Committee of the European Communities (1982–85) (Member 1978–89); Member: Board of Management, International Institute of Public Finance (1987–90); Council, Royal Economic Society (1983–90); Vice-President, Strategic Planning Society (1993–). Member of the Council of Management, National Institute of Economic and Social Research (November 1996–). Member: Centre for Management Under Regulation Advisory Board (1996–). Member: Governing Body of Birkbeck College (1997–). President,

The Economics and Business Education Association (1998–). Chairman, Friends of Birmingham Cathedral (1999–). Member: Board of Advisers, St Edmund Hall (1998–). President, Human City Institute (1999–).

He is an Honorary Fellow of the Chartered Institution of Water and Environmental Management. In 1994 he was awarded an honorary doctorate by Brunel University. In 2000 he was awarded an honorary doctorate by University of Central England and a Knighthood in the Queen's Birthday Honours.

Publications include *The British Electrical Industry 1875–1914* (Oxford University Press, 1979).

David Currie is Dean of City University Business School. He was Deputy Dean, Professor of Economics and Governor at London Business School. He has held visiting appointments at the International Monetary Fund, the Bank of England and the European University Institute, and has acted as a consultant to the European Commission and the OECD.

He has published extensively in the fields of forecasting and macro-economic policy, and particularly on economic and monetary union. His work is international in scope, focusing on key policy issues facing the European and international economies and business. Lord Currie is a member of the Management Board of UK energy regulator Ofgem, chairs the Arbitration Panel of the UK Pharmaceutical Price Regulation Scheme and served as a member of the Treasury's Panel of Independent Forecasters (the 'Wise Men') from its inception in 1992 until the end of 1995.

He is a trustee of the Joseph Rowntree Reform Trust, a non-charitable trust that supports a range of organizations and activities across the political spectrum, particularly in the area of constitutional reform. He lives in Islington, where he supports a number of local organizations, including the Almeida Theatre and the Islington Museum Trust.

David Edmonds is Director General of Telecommunications, the independent telecommunications regulator. He held various posts in the Department of the Environment from 1966 to 1984 and was then appointed Chief Executive of the Housing Corporation, which became the major instrument for delivering the government's social housing programme from 1991 to 1997. He was Managing Director, Group Central Services at NatWest Group and a member coordinating work on the Group's preparation for European economic and monetary union. He also chaired the Group's charitable foundations and was responsible for creating the Lothbury Gallery in the City.

Dieter Helm is a fellow in economics at New College, Oxford. He is a director of OXERA (Oxford Economic Research Associates), an associate editor of the *Oxford Review of Economic Policy*, and editor of *The Utilities Journal*. He is a member of the Department of Trade and Industry's (DTI) Energy Advisory Panel and is Chairman of the Department of Environment, Transport and the Regions' (DETR) Academic Panel. He is also a member of the Steering Group of the DTI's UKAEA Review (2000).

His recent publications include: 'British Utility Regulation: Theory, Practice, and Reform', *Oxford Review of Economic Policy,* 1994; *Competition in Regulated Industries* (Oxford University Press, 1998, with T. Jenkinson); 'The Assessment: Environmental Policy – Objectives, Instruments, and Institutions', *Oxford Review of Economic Policy,* 1998; *Environmental Policy: Objectives, Instruments and Implementation* (Oxford University Press, 2000 (ed.)), and 'Making Britain More Competitive: a Critique of Competition and Regulatory Policy', forthcoming in *The Scottish Journal of Political Economy.*

Dieter Helm is Fellow of the Institute of Energy, Fellow of the Royal Society of Arts and Fellow of Winchester College.

He is currently completing a major study of energy policy since 1979, and developing a series of proposals for regulatory reform.

Geoffrey Horton has been an industry regulator, economist and international consultant, and now runs his own firm, Horton 4 Consulting. He works on regulatory issues in a number of industries, including electricity, gas, railways, banking, bus transport and pharmaceuticals.

As Director of Consumer Affairs at the Office of Fair Trading from 1995 to 1998 he was responsible for the half of the office concerned with consumer protection and regulatory work such as credit licensing. From 1992 until 1995 he was an independent electricity regulator, Director General of Electricity Supply for Northern Ireland and Head of Offer (NI). From 1990 to 1995 he was also Director of Regulation and Business Affairs at the UK Office of Electricity Regulation (Offer), where his responsibilities included price controls. From 1990 to 1992 he worked at National Economic Research Associates, directing projects on energy, environment and the like.

He has previously been the Senior Economic Adviser responsible for advice in the Department of Energy when it reorganized the electricity industry, run an international macroeconomics consultancy, coordinated the forecasts at HM Treasury, and lectured at the University of Wales.

He is married with two young children, and holds master's degrees from Oxford and London universities.

Stephen C. Littlechild was Director General of Electricity Supply (DGES), in charge of the Office of Electricity Regulation (Offer), from its foundation in September 1989 to December 1998. Previously he advised ministers on the regulatory regime for British Telecom and the water industry. In 1983 he proposed the RPI–X approach to price controls, which has since been widely adopted for regulating utilities in the UK and overseas. He was a member of the Monopolies and Mergers Commission (MMC) for six years. Before 1989 he acted as a consultant to various public and private sector organizations.

Professor Littlechild graduated as Bachelor of Commerce from the University of Birmingham in 1964. He did postgraduate work at Stanford University 1965-67; Northwestern University 1967-68; the University of Texas in Austin 1968-69, obtaining his Ph.D. there in 1969; and postdoctoral research at UCLA and Northwestern. From 1972 to 1975 he was Professor of Applied Economics at Aston Mangement Centre. He was Professor of Commerce and Head of the Department of Industrial Economics and Business Studies at the University of Birmingham from 1975 to 1989. During 1979-80 he was a visiting professor or research fellow at Stanford University, New York University, University of Chicago, and Virginia Polytechnic and Institute. Since 1994 he has been Honorary Professor in the University of Birmingham Business School.

Professor Littlechild's publications include *Operational Research for Managers* (Philip Allan, 1976), *The Fallacy of the Mixed Economy* (IEA, 1978), *Elements of Telecommunications Economics* (Institute of Electrical Engineers, 1979), *Energy Strategies for the UK* (with K.G. Vaidya) (Allen and Unwin, 1982), *Regulation of British Telecommunications' Profitability* (Department of Industry, 1983), *Economic Regulation of Privatised Water Authorities* (HMSO, 1986) and over 60 articles. Since stepping down as DGES at the end of 1998, Professor Littlechild has engaged in lecturing and consulting for government departments, regulatory bodies, universities, research institutes, regulated companies and international organizations including the World Bank. In May 1999 Stanford University conferred on him the Zale Award for Scholarship and Public Service.

Eileen Marshall worked as a stockbroker in the City of London before becoming a university lecturer, then senior lecturer, in industrial economics. Her research specialism was in energy economics and she acted as consultant to many companies and bodies.

Dr Marshall took up the position of Director of Regulation and Business Affairs with the Office of Electricity Regulation (Offer) in October 1989. In April 1994, she was appointed Chief Economic Adviser and Director of Regulation and Business Affairs at the Office of Gas Supply (Ofgas). Her responsibilities covered the full range of Ofgas policy issues, including the setting of price controls and the introduction of domestic competition. In January 1997, while retaining her previous responsibilities at Ofgas, Dr Marshall became a part-time economic adviser to Offer, and from autumn 1997 led the Review of Electricity Trading Arrangements. In January 1998, she was awarded a CBE for services to regulatory policy. In June 1999, the former regulatory offices, Ofgas and Offer, were merged and renamed the

Office of Gas and Electricity Markets (Ofgem). Dr Marshall took up the new position of Deputy Director General, with particular responsibility for competition and trading arrangements.

Callum McCarthy is the first energy regulator for the UK. He was appointed Director General of Gas Supply on 1 November 1998, and Director General of Electricity Supply on 1 January 1999. Both appointments are effective until 31 October 2003.

A graduate of Oxford University, McCarthy also has a Ph.D. in economics from Stirling University and an MS from the Graduate School of Business at Stanford University (USA), where he was a Sloan Fellow. On graduating in 1965, he joined ICI as an economist and operations researcher. He moved to the Department of Trade and Industry in 1972, where he held a number of posts, including Principal Private Secretary to Roy Hattersley when he was Secretary of State for Prices and Consumer Protection, and to Norman Tebbit when he was Secretary of State for Trade and Industry.

McCarthy left the DTI in 1985, having reached the grade of under-secretary, and joined Kleinwort Benson as Director of Corporate Finance. In 1989, he joined BZW as Managing Director and Deputy Head of Corporate Finance. In 1993, he was appointed Chief Executive Officer of Barclays Bank's operations in Japan, where he served until 1996, when he became responsible for their businesses in North America.

Callum McCarthy is married with three children. His wife has a Ph.D. from Sussex University.

Derek Morris is Chairman of the Competition Commission (formerly the Monopolies and Mergers Commission). He first joined the MMC in 1991 as a member, becoming a deputy chairman in 1995 and chairman in 1998. Having studied politics, philosophy and economics at Oxford from 1964 to 1967, and then for a D.Phil. in economics at Nuffield College, he took up a research fellowship at the Centre for Business and Industrial Studies at Warwick University. Then, from 1970 until 1998, he was fellow and tutor in economics at Oriel College, Oxford.

During this time he wrote numerous books and articles, primarily in the field of industrial economics. Books included *The Economic System in the UK* (Oxford University Press, third edition, 1985); *Unquoted Companies* (Macmillan, 1984); *Industrial Economics and Organisation* (Oxford University Press, second edition, 1991); and *Economic Reform and State Owned Enterprises in China 1979–1987* (Clarendon Press, 1993) (the last three written with D. Hay). Other academic activities included chairmanship of the economics sub-faculty and then social studies faculty at Oxford and editorial board responsibilities for the *Journal of Industrial Economics*, the *Oxford Review of Economic Policy* and *Oxford Economic Papers*, among others.

Other activities have included three years on secondment as Economic Director of the National Economic Development Council, Chairman of Oxford Economic Forecasting Ltd and a Governor of the National Institute of Economic and Social Research. He has also been involved for over 20 years in various types of advisory and consultancy work, initially in the field of competition policy but more recently for the Asian Development Bank, in helping to design and implement economic reform measures in China and Central Asia.

Colin Robinson was educated at the University of Manchester, and then worked for 11 years as a business economist before being appointed to the Chair of Economics at the University of Surrey in 1968.

Professor Robinson has written more than 20 books and monographs and over 150 papers, mainly on energy economics and policy. For the IEA, he has written *A Policy for Fuel?* (IEA Occasional Paper no. 31, 1969); *Competition for Fuel* (Supplement to Occasional Paper no. 31, 1971); *The Energy "Crisis" and British Coal* (IEA Hobart Paper no. 59, 1974); (with Eileen Marshall) *What Future for British Coal?* (IEA Hobart Paper no. 89, 1981) and *Can Coal Be Saved?* (IEA Hobart Paper no. 105, 1985); *Competition in Electricity? The Government's Proposals for Privatising Electricity Supply* (IEA Inquiry no. 2, March 1988); *Making a Market in Energy* (IEA Current Controversies no. 3, December 1992) and *Energy Policy: Errors, Illusions and Market Realities* (IEA Occasional Paper no. 90, October 1993). He has contributed chapters to *Privatisation & Competition* (IEA Hobart Paperback no. 28, 1989) and to four volumes in the *Regulating Utilities* series. His most recent publication for the IEA, written with John Blundell, the Institute's General Director, is *Regulation Without the State* (IEA Occasional Paper no. 109, 1999).

Professor Robinson became a member of the IEA's Advisory Council in 1982 and was appointed its editorial director in 1992. He was appointed a trustee of the Wincott Foundation in 1993. He received the British Institute of Energy Economists' award as 'Economist of the Year 1992' and the 'Outstanding Contribution to the Profession' award in 1998 from the International Association for Energy Economists.

Paul Seabright is Professor of Economics at the University of Toulouse-1, a member of the Institut d'Economie Industrielle and a Research Fellow of the Centre for Economic Policy Research. Previously he was Reader in Economics at the University of Cambridge and a senior research fellow of Churchill College. He is one of the managing editors of the journal *Economic Policy*. He has published widely in theoretical and applied microeconomics, particularly in the fields of regulation and competition policy. Together with Damien Neven and Robin Nuttall, he published *Merger in Daylight* (London, CEPR, 1993), an early study of the operation of the European Merger Regulation, and has since followed this up with studies of other aspects of European competition policy, including vertical restraints and state aids. He has been a consultant to many private and public sector firms and international organizations, and is a member of the European Commission's Academic Advisory Panel on Competition Policy Questions.

Thomas Sharpe QC holds degrees in economics and in law and held a number of university appointments teaching these subjects, latterly at Nuffield College, Oxford. He was part-time Executive Director of the Institute for Fiscal Studies and on the UK board of National Economic Research Associates (NERA). In 1987 he started practice at the bar and became a QC in 1994. His practice mirrors his academic interests, UK and EC competition law and regulation. He has appeared in many competition cases in the High Court and in the European Court, including *Clear Communications* v *NZ Telecom*, *European Night Services* and the *British Sugar/Tate & Lyle* cartel case, and appeared many times in Competition Commission (ex-MMC) inquiries, for example, cars, domestic electrical goods and supermarkets. His regulatory practice consists mainly in such inquiries, including fixing K factors for South West Water, Transco gas transmission prices, number portability and calls to mobiles for BT, and successfully resisting the 'market abuse licence condition' on behalf of a UK energy company. He serves as a member of the advisory board of the Consumer Policy Review; and is a trustee of the Musicians' Benevolent Fund.

Graham Shuttleworth specializes in the electricity and gas industries. His work has two major components: promotion of competition in electricity and gas markets; and the regulation of networks. In 1990, he helped to write the rules for the UK's Electricity Pool and, ever since then, he has advised on the design of electricity markets and power contracts around the world. In 1996, he co-authored the leading book in the field with Sally Hunt, *Competition and Choice in Electricity* (John Wiley and Co., 1996), and has contributed widely to books and journals.

At the same time, he has been actively involved in the development of new regulatory regimes for monopoly networks, particularly where economic analysis lies at the forefront of decision-making. His work has covered estimation and 'benchmarking' of revenue requirements, design of price cap formulae, and dispute resolution.

Clare Spottiswoode is best known for her work as the UK's gas regulator between 1993 and 1998. She spear-headed the world's first introduction of choice and competition all the way down to the domestic level in either the gas or electricity industry, and this experience is now enabling other countries and other industries to emulate what has been done in the UK in ways appropriate to their particular circumstances.

Spottiswoode is Chairman of BuyENERGYonline, a reverse-auction web site for electricity and gas; Billbusters, a consumer-friendly company, getting best-value products across home services; and she is chair of Economatters, a specialist publisher, conference organizer, and consultancy for the gas industry across the world. She is also a non-executive director at Caminus Corp., an energy risk management software and consultancy company based in New York and the UK; and of Advanced Technology Ltd, a company which designs and sells advanced metering products for many areas, but in particular for utilities. Spottiswoode is on the government-sponsored Public Services Productivity Panel, with specific responsibility for the Home Office.

Following on from a degree in mathematics and economics at Clare College Cambridge, and then a Mellon fellow scholarship to do an M.Phil. in economics at Yale University, Spottiswoode started her career as a civil servant in HM Treasury, before becoming an entrepreneur, first in the importing business, and then as founder of a software house, specializing in vertical market software for business.

She is author of two computer books, and editor of two others, all of which were translated into Spanish. She also has an honorary doctorate from Brunel University, and was honoured in the 1999 New Year's Honours with a CBE for services to the gas industry.

Irwin M. Stelzer is a senior fellow and director of Hudson Institute's regulatory studies program. Before joining Hudson Institute in 1998, Stelzer was resident scholar and director of regulatory policy studies at the American Enterprise Institute. He also is the US economic and political columnist for *The Sunday Times* (London) and *The Courier Mail* (Australia), a contributing editor of *The Weekly Standard*, a member of the Publication Committee of *The Public Interest*, and a member of the board of the Regulatory Policy Institute (Oxford).

Stelzer founded National Economic Research Associates, Inc. (NERA) in 1961 and served as its president until a few years after its sale in 1983 to Marsh & McLennan. He also has served as Managing Director of the investment banking firm of Rothschild Inc. and as director of the Energy and Environmental Policy Center at Harvard University.

As a consultant to several US and UK industries with a variety of commercial and policy problems, Stelzer advises on market strategy, pricing and antitrust issues, and regulatory matters.

His academic career includes teaching appointments at Cornell University, the University of Connecticut, and New York University, and an associate membership of Nuffield College, Oxford. He is a former member of the

Litigation and Administrative Practice Faculty of the Practicing Law Institute. He served on the Massachusetts Institute of Technology Visiting Committee for the Department of Economics, and has been a teaching member of Columbia University's Continuing Legal Education Programs.

Stelzer received his bachelor's and master's degrees from New York University and his doctorate in economics from Cornell University. He has written and lectured on economic and policy developments in the USA and the UK. He has written extensively on policy issues such as America's competitive position in the world economy, optimum regulatory policies, the consequences of European integration, and factors affecting and impeding economic growth. He served as economics editor of the *Antitrust Bulletin* from 1970 to 1983 and is the author of *Selected Antitrust Cases: Landmark Decisions* (Richard D. Irwin, seventh edition, 1986) and *The Antitrust Laws: A Primer* (American Enterprise Institute, Washington DC, fourth edition, 2001).

Tom Winsor was appointed Rail Regulator and International Rail Regulator with effect from 5 July 1999.

He was born in 1957 and brought up in Broughty Ferry, Dundee. He was educated at Grove Academy, Broughty Ferry and then at the University of Edinburgh, where he graduated with an LL.B. (Scots Law) in 1979. As a solicitor, he qualified first in Scotland, where he is a Writer to the Signet, and subsequently in England and Wales. After general practice in Dundee, he took a postgraduate qualification in oil and gas law at the Centre for Energy, Petroleum and Mineral Law and Policy of the University of Dundee.

In the course of his legal career, Tom Winsor specialized first in UK and international oil and gas law, later adding electricity, regulation, railways and public law. He joined Denton Hall as a partner in 1991, where he was responsible for the design of the regulatory regime for the electricity industry in Northern Ireland. In 1993 he was seconded to the Office of the Rail Regulator as Chief Legal Adviser and later as General Counsel. He returned to his partnership at Denton Hall in 1995 as head of the railways department, part of the firm's energy and infrastructure practice.

Tom Winsor is an honorary lecturer at the Centre for Energy, Petroleum and Mineral Law and Policy of the University of Dundee, where he directed the UK Oil and Gas Law summer course from 1993 to 1997. He is married, with one daughter, and lives in Kent, travelling daily to his office in London by train.

George Yarrow is Director of the Regulatory Policy Institute, Oxford, and an economic adviser to Ofgem. He is also a visiting professor at the University of Newcastle and an emeritus fellow of Hertford College, Oxford.

After graduating from St John's College, Cambridge, he held appointments at the Universities of Warwick, Newcastle and Oxford. His principal research activities have covered a broad range of issues in the economics of competition and regulation, but he has also written monographs and papers on welfare reform and on aspects of environmental policy.

In addition to his advisory work for Ofgem, he has recently served on expert panels advising on the Communications White Paper and on the regulatory impact assessments now widely used across government departments.

He has previously given lectures in the IEA/LBS series on social obligations in telecoms, progress in gas competition, the Monopolies and Mergers Commission, and economic assessments under the Competition Act.

Introduction

Colin Robinson

In the autumn of 2000 the tenth annual series of Beesley Lectures, named after the late Michael Beesley, took place. Following the example set by Michael, the organizers of the series selected lecturers who would apply economic principles to review some of the most topical issues in utility regulation and competition policy, complementing their papers with comments from regulators and ex-regulators. The combination of papers by independent commentators with remarks from the relevant regulators is a unique feature of the Beesley series. The papers and the comments, revised by their authors, appear as the chapters in this volume.

The first chapter is on one of the most significant and innovative developments in any of the privatized utilities – the introduction of new electricity trading arrangements (NETA) which bring genuine markets into electricity and dispose of most of the remaining central controls left over from nationalization. Professor David Currie, speaking five months before the new arrangements were successfully introduced (in March 2001), makes a powerful case for the changes, arguing that NETA moves electricity much closer to a 'normal market' and also instals a governance structure which 'allows for easy adjustment and change'. NETA is, in his view, a big improvement on the Pool, representing a 'major step advance in the direction of a more competitive and efficient electricity market'.

Callum McCarthy, the electricity and gas regulator, reinforces Currie's emphasis on the importance of the new arrangements, making two principal points. First, he argues that, as the nature of the electricity industry changes, so the main skills required will move away from engineering towards trading. The regulator and the competition authorities will also have to become concerned with contractual as well as physical positions. Second, the links between electricity trading and gas trading will become increasingly significant.

Dr Dieter Helm's chapter discusses rail regulation. His starting point is that the regulatory system for the railways and its institutions is deeply flawed and must be reformed. There is a 'confusion of roles, functions and incentives; performance has been poor; and the cost of capital high'. The integrated transport strategy under New Labour requires an integrated regulatory regime but that has been missing. Helm's main proposal for institutional reform is to merge the Strategic Rail Authority and the Office of Rail Regulation to integrate the periodic review and Railtrack regulation with refranchising and the regulation of franchises. He argues that this would reduce the scope for personal discretion in regulation and thereby bring down the cost of capital.

The rail regulator, Tom Winsor, disagrees with much of Helm's argument. In Winsor's view, an independent regulator is necessary to secure investor confidence, without which required investment will not be forthcoming. There has been no fundamental shift in the regulator's stance towards Railtrack, he says. Moreover, changes he is introducing will reduce perceived regulatory risk. The allowed rate of return for Railtrack is higher than for other utilities not because of regulatory risk but for more substantial reasons.

My chapter considers whether the water industry is so different from other network utilities that competition is not feasible. It begins by assessing the performance of the regulatory regime in water, concluding that the system – centred on competition by comparison and with restrictions on takeovers – has not worked well compared with regulation of the electricity and gas industries. The regime is not sustainable. Reforms should concentrate on introducing competition rather than prescriptive regulation of the whole industry. Entry should be eased, networks should be separated and the powers of environmental regulators should be curbed, with more emphasis on self-regulation.

Sir Ian Byatt agrees that 'the time is ripe for achieving greater competition in the water industry'. He disagrees, however, about the sustainability of the present regime which, he argues, is 'only too sustainable', unattractive as it is with 'detailed regulation driven by politicians and environmental regulators'. He sets out a number of proposals which would ease the transition to competition, including improved common carriage arrangements and competitive bidding for abstraction licences, and he foresees a time when it would be sensible to relax restrictions on takeovers.

The new gas trading arrangements, introduced about eighteen months before the new arrangements in electricity, are discussed by Professor George Yarrow, who stresses their evolutionary nature. An on-the-day commodity market was introduced in October 1999 and the other major reform was the introduction of auctions for primary entry capacity, sold as firm rights. Yarrow also considers system balancing and the reduced role for the system operator as reliance on markets increases, suggesting some trading arrangements which might fit better with markets. He concludes by emphasizing a point made by McCarthy – the likelihood of growing interactions between the gas and electricity networks.

Dr Eileen Marshall, commenting on Yarrow's chapter, says that, by stepping back and examining the new arrangements from first principles, he has provided valuable insights. She points out that Ofgem has consistently argued the need for participants to be exposed to the economic costs of their actions which are best determined through markets. Far-reaching changes still continue in gas, including the sale of storage in the pipes (linepack) to complete the storage reforms and, most important, alignment of the gas and electricity balancing regimes.

A lively review of privatization and regulation experience in the UK is provided by Dr Irwin Stelzer. In his view, that experience shows privatization was a necessary condition for the introduction of 'competition where feasible, and regulation where necessary' and the subsequent efficiency gains in some but not all privatized industries. Irwin criticizes reliance on the RPI–X formula which is at the heart of UK regulation and which raises the problem of how to decide on the value of X. However, he praises the regulators, who have in effect created an 'entirely new branch of government'. In future, regulators should concentrate on getting incentives right, withdrawing from areas where competition is possible and making regulation more transparent.

In commenting on the chapter, Professor Stephen Littlechild says that Stelzer gives insufficient credit to the duty to promote competition which has proved so vital in the transition to competitive markets. Similarly, the RPI–X system has been a more important stimulant to efficiency gains than Stelzer acknowledges. Finally, transparency has been much improved in recent years and it is difficult to see what more could be done. Professor Littlechild also added some comments, at the request of the organizers of the series, on Michael Beesley's contributions to ideas about privatization, competition and regulation, concluding that a 'generation of UK thinking on privatization, competition and regulation is a testament to his influence'. These comments appear immediately after this introduction.

Professor Mark Armstrong's chapter is on convergence in communications and the implications for regulation. He begins by pointing out that, given that different regulatory bodies are associated with different infrastructures, there is a danger of asymmetries and inefficiencies appearing as convergence proceeds. However, he sees benefits as well as disadvantages in having multiple regulators rather than super-regulators with 'too much power concentrated in a single body'. He would like to see the BBC operate under the same regulatory regime as other broadcasters, with an investigation of the licence fee versus alternatives. Armstrong sees asymmetries also in the treatment of BSkyB and the cable companies. Economic regulation of electronic transmission networks should be done by the Office of Communications (Ofcom) but it is not clear that content regulation should be under the same body.

In his comment, David Edmonds argues that the prime task of a new regulatory agency should be to ensure that consumers get the best deal possible. In telecommunications, he sees his job as providing 'an environment in which competition flourishes'. In his view, a harmonized framework for the telecoms and broadcasting sectors is required. There should be a single regulatory agency for electronic communication networks and services, starting from fundamental principles, though it would be a complex world that the new agency would have to address.

Liberalizing European electricity and gas markets has become an important issue, and a contentious one in some EU countries. Graham Shuttleworth addresses it in his chapter, reviewing progress made so far and explaining the principal features of the electricity and gas directives before embarking on a survey of some of the challenges which confront regulators, in unbundling, real-time balancing and cross-border trade. He then looks at ways in which regulators may prevent recovery of certain costs. He concludes that in energy markets regulation is required to promote competition and that regulation of natural monopolies will be permanent. Shuttleworth sees the biggest problem now as designing efficient transmission pricing, and he also urges regulators to be sensitive to the need for future investment, restraining any tendency to behave opportunistically.

Clare Spottiswoode takes, as she says, a 'slightly different view' because of her belief, founded on a dynamic view of competition, in the ability of markets to deliver. She criticizes the EU directives because of their weak separation provisions and the absence of a discrimination clause. Spottiswoode emphasizes the importance of introducing competition for the market in the case of monopolies and the advantages of unbundling, which makes the network easier to manage and to regulate. She argues also that, in the UK, the benefits of introducing competition into gas far outweighed the costs.

The subject addressed by Tom Sharpe QC is 'Concurrency or convergence? Competition and regulation under the Competition Act 1998'. He points out that the Act gives the sector regulators concurrent powers with the Director General of Fair Trading (but within their own spheres) to investigate, make decisions and impose heavy penalties on companies. Sharpe expresses doubts about whether 'regulators should be trusted with the development of competition law' because, he argues, regulation is about structure whereas the Act is about conduct or behaviour. Violence may well be done to the development of competition law as regulators seek to achieve their objectives. He fears also that regulators will be inconsistent in their application of competition laws.

Geoffrey Horton sees less conflict between competition promotion and the application of general competition law than does Sharpe, but he shares his concern about possible abuse by regulators of licence conditions to control anti-competitive conduct. He argues also that Sharpe is too restrained about the dangers of regulators promoting consumer benefits which, they claim, competition would not provide. In general, industry regulators should be 'working hand in hand with competition policy to promote effective competition and regulate monopolies where competition cannot be introduced'.

The final chapter is by Professor Paul Seabright, who examines ten years of European Union merger control which, as he says, 'dwarfs the remainder of its activity in all other areas of competition policy combined'. Moreover, activity has been growing: the number of transactions notified in 1999 was 292 compared with 60 in 1991. The 'sheer productivity of EU merger control' is impressive in terms of 'cases processed, jurisprudence created and major judicial embarrassments avoided'. Nevertheless, Paul raises some broader questions – for example, how the Commission's procedures allow it to identify cases which pose a danger to competition, and whether it is right that the Commission is not obliged to set out its understanding of the business rationale for the transaction under investigation.

Dr Derek Morris agrees, in general, with Seabright's favourable assessment of the EU regime. But he argues that a 'substantial lessening of competition' test is superior to the 'dominance' test applied in EU merger control. He also builds on the points made by Seabright about the significance of intangible assets in mergers. In his view, the UK competition authorities have in recent years paid considerable attention to intangibles, though they face the inevitable dilemma of deciding whether joint control of intangibles results in unacceptable market power or is just part of the normal process of competitive markets.

The chapters in this volume illustrate, once more, the rich variety of issues which arise from the UK's privatization and utility regulation programme and from the attempts of the UK and EU authorities to maintain competition in markets.

As regards the privatized utilities, a clear division seems to have emerged between some industries (for example, gas and electricity), where competition has been successfully introduced and both retail and wholesale markets are now flourishing, and others (such as the railways and perhaps water), where serious problems have arisen and are as yet unsolved. It is unclear whether the competitive solutions which appear to have worked in electricity and gas will be applied to the railways and water, or whether refuge will be sought in more prescriptive regulation and increasing government control. The roles of some of the industry regulators may therefore be about to change. The relationship between industry regulators and the general competition authorities under the new competition regime has also not yet settled down and there may be tensions on the horizon. Moreover, divisions have already appeared among EU members about the extent to which the UK's pioneering efforts should be followed and utility markets should be opened to competition. In future, the UK may find itself more and more affected by competition law and regulatory decisions made by the EU.

As the Beesley Lectures enter their second decade, there are plenty of controversial subjects for discussion.

Michael Beesley's contribution to privatization, competition and regulation

Stephen Littlechild

I have been asked to add some comments on the contributions of Professor Michael Beesley to privatization, competition and regulation.

Everyone here knows how enthusiastic Michael was about privatization, competition and regulation. He spent long hours on these topics, wrote countless memos, and made excited phone calls. Not everyone had the pleasure of receiving these phone calls on Saturday nights and Sunday mornings. But we always took the calls because we knew we would benefit from them, and Michael's enthusiasm was infectious.

What made Michael's contributions so valuable? Certainly he had greater breadth of experience in relevant areas than anyone else. He had been involved in all the utility industries. In the 1960s (when I first met him), he was Reader in Transport Economics at the LSE and Economic Adviser to the Department of Transport. His responsibilities included road, rail, bus and air transport. In the 1980s he advised the Department of Industry on the liberalization of telecommunications, the Department of Transport on bus privatization, and the Department of the Environment on water privatization and regulation. He and I frequently discussed competition in electricity and gas in the 1980s and he formally advised Offer, Ofgas and later Ofgem on these matters in the 1990s. He had previous interests and experience in regional planning and competition policy. He was a consultant to companies as well as to governments, in the USA and Australia as well as in the UK.

Michael's first employment was in the private sector, working in a small engineering company in the jewellery quarter of Birmingham.[1] Small firms were a particular interest. Later he was a part owner of a potential airline, as much as anything to get the experience of entrepreneurship and to see regulation from the perspective of the regulatee.

This background indicates that while Michael saw the need for an appropriate framework of government and regulation, he had a strong underlying sympathy for the free competitive market. Indeed, he once stood as a Liberal candidate on this ticket, and left the party when it no longer seemed committed to a policy descended from Gladstonian liberalism.

No doubt part of his academic upbringing contributed to this perspective. His collected papers are dedicated 'to an inspiring teacher, Arthur Shenfield'. He says that 'Arguments in favour of free markets were implanted in my undergraduate days at Birmingham from 1942 to 1945, by Arthur Shenfield's unfailingly brilliant defence of the competitive paradigm.' Michael was particularly impressed with the ideas of Schumpeter, which 'offered an explanation for the existence of profits as an outcome of innovation: that is, new products, services and production methods'.

This Austrian emphasis on the nature of competition as a dynamic process over time, rather than the neo-classical focus on equilibrium at a point in time, pervaded Michael's thinking. Having previously worked with him primarily on the determinants of car ownership, I was not aware of his long-standing interest in the Austrian approach. I found his insights particularly helpful in the early 1970s, when I was working on the *Fallacy of the Mixed Economy*, which was an Austrian critique of recent economic thinking and policy. 'Remember the marbles in the bowl', he kept saying. Whether you added a few marbles or took a few away, they would always lie at the bottom of the bowl. Similarly, adding a few firms or taking away a few would not fundamentally affect the competitive outcome in any industry: it is not the number of firms that really counts, but the conditions of entry and exit.

Michael was the ideal person to talk to about a possible profit control on BT at the time of its privatization. We debated the alternatives at length. Neither of us liked any of them. I remember him saying one morning that he had considered the situation carefully the night before and come to the conclusion – as indeed I had – that despite its unpalatable nature, a price control was better than a profit control. This was primarily because of its incentive properties. He emphasized that the potential savings from increased productive efficiency improvements were typically an order of magnitude greater than the potential savings in allocative efficiency. In the longer term the savings and benefits from innovation might be greater still. To secure these gains, competition and new entry were of crucial importance where possible. But elsewhere, or until competition was effective, a price control independent of the actions of the companies would give greatest incentive to their efficiency. He was well aware of the X-efficiency literature, referring to unnoticed or unexploited opportunities to reduce the cost curve. Indeed, he had earlier made his own contribution to this literature by arguing for the analogous concept of Y-efficiency – the potential gains from the hitherto unnoticed scope to introduce new products and increase the demand curve.

His own view on the RPI element of the RPI–X concept was interesting. Many argued that the index should better reflect movements in the price of utility inputs. In contrast, Michael argued that, as far as incentive properties were concerned, it did not matter what it reflected. It could just as well reflect the price of bananas, as long as it was independent of the actions of the regulated companies.

Michael was a pioneer of cost–benefit in the UK. This approach required a disciplined laying out of the possible courses of action and the criteria for evaluating them. This permeated his thinking. The matrix in my Report on BT's Profitability, evaluating and ranking the alternative regulatory mechanisms against the criteria set out in the terms of reference, owed much to his insistence on this discipline. We later did the same thing in evaluating alternative organizational structures for a privatized electricity industry, though this was never published, being overtaken by events. I think Michael felt that the discipline of formally ranking alternatives against explicit criteria made the judgements clearer, and provided some protection against the economic adviser being biased or over-ridden by preconception or political enthusiasm.

Some economists are primarily or even exclusively theoreticians; others are mainly gatherers and summarizers of data. Michael was both. Theory and evidence constantly interacted. In exploring data, he found it helpful to start by specifying some initial hypothesis to test. He was not dogmatic about methodology – he simply found that this was a good discipline to organize one's thinking. Conversely, in analysing policy, he was always prepared to trace through the implications of particular assumptions. But he would never go too far without consulting or seeking empirical data. Many's the time at OFFER he advised us that it was time to get some sort of empirical check on what we were debating. He always had more sources of data to propose than we had considered. For example, not only were the flotation prospectuses of the companies a rich source to which he often returned, but he insisted we explore the more informative prospectuses filed for the US flotations. He repeatedly emphasized the relevance of the information provided by the share price performance of the companies. I suspect we should have taken more notice of this.

Michael always had so many ideas that we could not take up all of them. And some of them seemed, at the time, less persuasive than others. He insisted on the importance of future cash flow in setting the price controls, and we did focus on this to some extent. But we never went as far as he would have liked in doing so. My colleagues will remember the lengthy debates as to whether we should accept a regulatory asset base, and the concept of depreciation, which he regarded as somewhat backward-looking, or instead look only to the companies' forward cash flows and financial requirements. I was never entirely sure what the latter approach entailed, or whether it could be presented acceptably to all the interested parties. Focusing too much on what cash the companies needed and had on hand could be a disincentive to prudent operations – there were many commentators urging me to take it away if the companies did not need it. I felt, too, that the implied specification of companies' future dividend policies and maybe even share prices would be too interventionist for a regulator, and that some more explicit and indirect approach would be preferable. In the event, the importance of financial considerations was fully brought home to us. Since a rate-of-return approach has its own problems, as we all know, it may be that Michael's preferred approach will one day command more attention.

Another of Michael's interests was the role of a transmission company. In the early days, perhaps even when the wording of the Electricity Act duties was under consideration, I asked his view of the role of a transmission company. He never initially liked the idea that the profit incentive of the grid should be compromised by a duty to facilitate competition, which he regarded as the proper task of the regulator. What should a transmission company do then? 'Make trouble', he said. By that he meant that it should have an entrepreneurial role, bringing or increasing competition into areas where local generators were offering less favourable terms than newer or more distant ones could. I suspect this was a vision more suited to a network that was less complete than in the UK. But I also suspect that international comparisons will eventually show that the profit incentive of the grid is an important mechanism for securing efficiency and protecting against market power in generation, particularly in balancing the system in real time and removing transmission constraints.

In sum, Michael was always a stimulating colleague, always ready to contribute to policy debates with wise advice and innovative ideas, but ideas that were firmly grounded in how the market really operated. A generation of UK thinking on privatization, competition and regulation is a testament to his influence. The organizers of the Beesley Lecture Series might want to consider a future session devoted to a more thorough exploration of his ideas. They will undoubtedly be the source of much future research.

NOTE

1. M.E. Beesley, Introduction, chapter 1 in his collected papers, *Privatization, Regulation and Deregulation*, 2nd edn, London, Routledge, 1997.

1. The new electricity trading arrangements in England and Wales: a review

David Currie

INTRODUCTION

My aim in this chapter is to review the new electricity trading arrangements (NETA) which will come into force quite soon.[1] This review cannot be that of an objective outsider, since my role has been more that of an insider. Thus, following Stephen Littlechild's invitation, I first served as a special adviser to Offer on RETA (Review of Electricity Trading Arrangements) as it was then called; then following our chairman McCarthy's invitation as a member of the Ofgem Management Board; and then finally before the summer helping to see the Utilities Bill through the Lords, including proposing with Gordon Borrie an amendment which the government became minded to accept to place a limit on the level of fines that the new regulatory authority can impose. I sense that my role is more that of accomplice than objective observer. And the key ringleader, Callum McCarthy, acts as discussant of my chapter. We thus provide an example of collusion that some might think mirrors, but does not attain, the excesses of the Pool arrangement that will soon be consigned to history.

None the less, in this chapter I seek to wear my academic hat. My aim is to step back from the fray and provide an objective account of the new arrangements. How successful I am in that is left to the reader to judge.

To make one final point before plunging into the substance of the chapter, this longstanding lecture series was the brainchild of my late colleague, Professor Michael Beesley, after whom the lecture series is now named. Michael was the grandfather of the British regulatory model, and a major influence on many aspects of its practical operation. He was also an important influence on the reform of electricity trading, serving as Economic Adviser to Ofgem on NETA, working closely with Eileen Marshall and her team who have been the driving force behind NETA. I well remember Michael just a few weeks before his death in animated discussion about the details of the reform.

We shall miss his contribution, but it is apposite that this first lecture in the new Beesley lecture series should be on the reform that was so close to his heart just before his sudden and unexpected death.

The structure of the chapter is as follows. The first part addresses a key issue concerning the Pool arrangement: whether the problem of generator dominance in the Pool arises from the degree of concentration in generation or from the market rules. The former would point to the need for divestment; the latter to that for changing the market rules. I argue that, although both matter, reform of the market rules is crucial to delivering a well-ordered market. I then go on to review some other areas of controversy, both past and continuing. Some of these are issues on which I think the answers are clear-cut; others are ones where we may well need to learn from experience and allow evolution. I also consider those issues that will need to be addressed in the future. Finally, I reflect on two questions: what are the main achievements of the new arrangements relative to the old; and why is it that reform has been pushed through successfully on this occasion, whereas in the past it has been ducked, despite the overwhelming evidence of the need for change?

Two basic ideas, both learnt from Michael Beesley, have underpinned my thinking on NETA since I became involved in electricity trading reform. The first is that, on the whole, market relationships work much better than any form of regulation or administered market, not least in promoting innovation and change. The second is that no system is perfect, so that any system of electricity trading is likely to need periodic adjustment and reform. The major virtues of NETA are twofold: that NETA moves the electricity market much closer to a normal market; and that it puts in place a governance structure that allows for relatively easy adjustment and change. In both respects, it represents a major advance on the Pool.

INDUSTRY STRUCTURE VERSUS MARKET RULES

The deficiencies of the Pool arrangement are well known and require little rehearsing. The arrangement was put in place just before privatization to provide a rudimentary market mechanism whereby a privatized and decentralized electricity industry could operate in a way consistent with the need to maintain balance on the network and subject to the physical laws governing electrical systems. Essentially it consisted of grafting part of the previously centralized control system on to the market system. Generators were required to bid into a centralized market (the Pool), and the system operator (NGC) used the old computer program (GOAL) to schedule generation to match demand in a supposedly efficient manner given the information in the bids.

Those who put this arrangement in place generally saw it as a quick fix to ensure that a privatized and decentralized system could function. They thought it would quite quickly be replaced by a more sophisticated arrangement. However, such change was impeded by the structure for the governance of the Pool arrangement put in place at privatization. This was a mutual structure, relying on near consensus to effect change. I am told that this arrangement was made to give stability to the nascent market, and to preclude too rapid change. If so, it spectacularly overachieved its objective. The obvious difficulty with the arrangement was that reform in the general interest could be blocked by vested interests. In practice, although there was some evolution, as GOAL morphed into Super-GOAL, it was quite limited. This was a severe weakness of the way electricity privatization was effected. In defence, one can perhaps note that few appreciated at the time just how strong would be the vested interests against change.

These vested interests came from the ability of the large portfolio generators to manipulate the Pool price. This has been well documented in a number of places, and requires little reiteration. (See, for example, Armstrong et al., 1994 for an early discussion, as well as Von der Fehr and Harbord, 1993; Wolak and Patrick, 1996; Brealey and Lapuerta, 1997; and Wolfram, 1998.) The interesting question concerns the source of this market power. Two different sources are usually identified: dominant market positions; and the specifics of the Pool rules.

There is clearly much in both views. At privatization, the generation market was dominated by the two big players, National Power and PowerGen. For most of the period since privatization the market shares of these companies have been a source of concern. Now overall market shares are appreciably lower, but the issue remains a live one. That is partly because the big generators continue to have large market shares in the sub-market for mid-merit and peaking plant, which generally determines the uniform Pool price (system marginal price) that all generation is paid. Whether this sub-market dominance would be of such concern if it did not set the overall market price is less clear. Thus the issue of dominance may well be a product of the Pool rules, and this certainly helps to explain why in this market concerns about dominance arise at levels of market share that in other markets would not attract much interest.

This last point is a crucial one, and deserves more discussion. Some commentators have argued that the issue of dominance is the key in respect of generation, and that by focusing on trading arrangements NETA is missing the main target. On this view, it has been the gradual divestment by the large generators that has been key in bringing greater competition to the wholesale market, so that the new trading arrangements are a side-show. I disagree profoundly with this view, because it ignores the important influence that trading arrangements have on the scope for collusion, whether overt or implicit, in price setting. The reason why relatively low market shares in this sector go together with concerns over dominance is that the Pool arrangements have fostered collusion. NETA, by contrast, should discourage it.

Let me develop this point first in the context of the Pool. The essential feature of the Pool is (and I can still use the present tense) that in bidding generators are essentially dealing with a computer program, GOAL or son of GOAL. Of course, the outcome of their transactions depends on how other bidders interact with the same program; but none the less all transactions are mediated through GOAL. Not surprisingly, smart individuals playing repeatedly can hit on strategies (certain to be mixed) that systematically beat GOAL. The benefits of such strategies accrue to generators in the form either of a higher system marginal price or other payments (for example, capacity payments), and the costs fall on customers.

Note that in developing this argument I have said nothing about the particular trading rules within the Pool. I could engage in a long digression on the many different and clever ways in which sophisticated bidders can take GOAL and customers to the cleaners, but I do not propose to do so. For my point is much more general: almost irrespective of the form of rules used by the computer program at the heart of the Pool responsible for scheduling, smart people will learn the optimal way to outwit it. And since all generators are playing with the same program, they will alight on similar types of strategy for winning. In effect, the program acts to coordinate the different players, encouraging and sustaining a form of parallel behaviour to the detriment of customers. Such parallel behaviour is normally banned under the UK Fair Trading Act as a complex monopoly. It greatly amplifies the impact of strategic behaviour. What is certainly undesirable when carried out singly becomes totally unacceptable when generalized.

Now, of course, I have somewhat overstated my case. Those with some knowledge of auction theory may argue that it is possible to devise a set of optimal rules for bidding that elicits the optimal price, and that a Pool that embodies such rules will not suffer from the defect that I have just been discussing. I will come to a key argument against this proposition in a moment. But first note an implication of the current line of argument. Any deviation from the optimal rule is likely to be exploited by bidders to the detriment of customers. In this respect, a compulsory Pool arrangement is unlikely to be robust in its performance.

This is a serious deficiency once one notes the complexity of devising an optimal set of auction rules for electricity. The theoretical models assume, for understandable reasons of theoretical tractability, that electricity is a homogeneous commodity, at least within each period of trade. Yet it is not. Electricity supplied at different points of the grid entails different transmission losses, and more importantly has quite different value because of transmission constraints. Unless the trading period shrinks to an instant, electricity supplied at different moments within the trading period has different value, depending on the demands on the system. Acceptance of generation from one plant for one period of trade may well entail acceptance of supply for adjacent periods because of inflexibilities in turning generation on and off, and these characteristics differ from plant to plant. I am no auction theorist, but I guess that the resulting interdependencies between auction periods greatly complicate the design of optimal auction rules. Resulting suboptimalities in design will then give rise to the problems that I have been discussing.

However, there is another line of argument that reinforces these concerns. The UK's leading auction theorist, Paul Klemperer (who after designing the UK's auction of UMTS licences deserves to be one of the richest economists in the country), notes the greater vulnerability of uniform-price auctions to collusive behaviour (Klemperer, 2000a,b; see also Fabra, 2000). This is especially so in repeated auctions, such as in electricity. The reason for this greater vulnerability is that, with uniform-price auctions, bidders can more freely use their bids to signal their intentions to other players. Thus the knowledge that bidders will receive the same price as everyone else irrespective of how they bid facilitates the use of signalling both cooperative behaviour and threats. This makes covert collusion much easier to establish and enforce. In discriminatory-price auctions, where bidders get what they bid (pay-as-bid), the use of bids for signalling purposes will carry a much higher cost, because the bid may well be accepted. Pay-as-bid removes the guarantee that all will get the same, and thereby increases the cost of signalling and collusive behaviour. The fact that it does not eliminate the scope for such behaviour is a point to which I return.

Though the formal literature followed, it is this line of reasoning that partly motivated the NETA design. The first key element in the design is to eliminate the compulsion to trade through the Pool. This facilitates bilateral, pay-as-bid, trading of the kind normal in most other markets. The intent is that the bulk of electricity will be traded in this way, probably through the power exchanges that are being established by private sector players. The design of such exchanges is for the market to provide, and is therefore not part of the NETA. But the fact that NETA does not specify these exchanges and Ofgem has played no role in getting them established should not obscure their central importance to the new trading arrangements.

In most other markets (for example, financial markets), such bilateral trading suffices. However, the special physical characteristics of an electricity grid entail a balancing mechanism to ensure the physical integrity of the system. As I have said, the design intent is that this will be a residual balancing mechanism, used for achieving balance close to real time, and that the vast bulk of trading will happen through forward trading. But one way of subverting this intent is by making this market susceptible to manipulation and collusion. The decision, controversial in the view of some commentators, to adopt pay-as-bid in the balancing market was motivated by the advantages discussed above of pay-as-bid in reducing the susceptibility to market manipulation and collusion.

There is another, much more down-to-earth, argument for pay-as-bid in the balancing market, which concerns the heterogeneity of electricity supply.[2] It is common to think of electricity as a homogeneous product – after all, all electrons are identical, a key fact that makes possible retail competition in electricity. But in the balancing mechanism, it is not electrons that are traded, but rather bundles of electricity supply, all with very different characteristics. From the perspective of the system operator, there is a world of difference between the plant that needs three and a half hours' notification to supply, and may then need to be ramped down slowly, and capacity that can be turned on ten minutes before (such as pumped storage or partly loaded plant on spinning reserve). Speed of response and different ramp rates all require different rewards, so that there is no common price that can be applied to them all. This heterogeneity undermines the definition of, let alone the case for, a common system marginal price.

DUAL CASH-OUT PRICES

One aspect of the design of the balancing market that provoked much debate has been the adoption of dual cash-out prices, with the price varying depending on whether the bidder is seeking to rectify a short or a long position. It has been suggested that this arrangement of dual cash-out prices is arbitrary and penal. The renewables lobby argued strongly, in debate during the passage through Parliament of the Utilities Bill, for netting, so that supply into and demand from the grid are equally priced.

What is proposed is that cash-out prices will be determined by the prices that the system operator has to pay for buying or selling electricity in the balancing market. Thus in the period from gate closure to real time, the system operator will intervene in the balancing market to secure additional generation for the half-hour period in question. The average of the prices that are paid for additional generation will be the price for cashing out those whose actual supply falls short of contract notification. Similarly the system operator will enter the balancing market to stand-down generation. The average of the prices for these transactions is the price for cashing out those whose actual supply exceeds contract notification.[3]

It is fair to say that this particular formula for determining the dual cash-out prices is somewhat arbitrary, and can be criticized and probably improved in the light of experience. However, the principle that there should be a dual price is entirely defensible. Generators whose actual supply differs from that contracted impose additional costs on the system operator who is required to balance the system in real time. It is important that these costs are charged to the generator concerned, to act as a deterrent to such divergences of supply from plan. This will provide appropriate incentives for ensuring predictability of supply, and will encourage the predictable and reliable plant and deter the unpredictable and unreliable. It may be difficult to judge the actual cost imposed by such unpredictable supply, but to assume that it is zero by adopting a single cash-out price would be even more arbitrary. In all markets, the supply and demand prices diverge by a margin to reflect the costs of market-making, and this should be no different in the balancing market. Indeed, the margin is likely to be larger in this market where the costs of balancing are high, as compared with financial markets where the market-making process is typically lower cost. It may be possible to improve on the formula over time to get it to reflect better the true costs that are imposed on the system, and this development should be encouraged. It is not intended that a mountain of cash should arise from the spread between the two prices (a fear sometimes referred to in the industry as 'beer money'); and if there were indications that the spread was too great in practice, then the formula should be adjusted. But the principle of the spread is appropriate.

One objection to this line of argument is that the cash-out price penalizes divergences between the contracted position and actual metered supply, not the informational deficit, which is the difference between final physical notification and the metered position. If actual metered supply were to match exactly the contracted position, but the generator did not notify, then the cash-out arrangement would impose no penalty. But the generator would then be in breach of the Grid Code, which requires generators to give the system operator accurate notification of their contractual position. Breaches of the Grid Code can attract penalties under the generator's licence. In designing the new trading arrangements, it was decided that a potential double penalty – fines for a licence breach coupled with a cash-out penalty – would be unduly onerous, so the cash-out penalty for the informational deficit was dropped. However, I think this is one of the design features that may be worth reconsidering in the light of experience. Clearly systematic and large-scale discrepancies between the contract position and the notification position can be dealt with via the Grid Code, but it may well be sensible to have a cash-out penalty to discourage both minor and major discrepancies. Since the software functionality for this has been put in place, this is something that can readily be revisited.

More generally, ensuring that costs fall where they should is a key design feature, providing the correct incentives for reliability. This is a feature that has been absent from the current Pool arrangement. Capacity that is unable to perform on the day is not penalized under current arrangements, despite the fact that its unreliability requires the system operator to bring on additional, more expensive plant. Correct incentives should ensure greater reliability, and therefore enhance security of supply. This is a very important feature of the reform that is often ignored, perhaps because of a failure to appreciate the importance of having the right incentives in a market-based system. The indications are that the incentive for reliability is already biting: one of the reasons why so much capacity has been taken off this summer [summer 2000] for maintenance is that generators appreciate the need for more reliable plant under NETA.

This argument about predictability and reliability is one that many agree with except when it comes to renewables. In the debates on the Utilities Bill in the Lords, there were persistent calls for netting for renewables, so that supplies to and demand from the grid would be priced similarly. One can see the attraction of that for renewables, since much existing plant, whether wind, solar or other, is highly variable and unpredictable. Despite my personal interest in renewables, I argued very strongly against netting. If the future is to be renewables, it is very important that we encourage more reliable, more predictable renewables plant. We must establish a premium for reliable renewables, as for all other plant, so as to give an incentive for innovation that improves on reliability or develops effective methods of storage (such as the advances in regenerative fuel cells). It is therefore important that the dual cash-out arrangement applies to all forms of generation.

To encourage renewables in general is a task that lies beyond NETA, with the climate change levy and other forms of incentives for green energy. (I could digress into the limitations of what is currently proposed, the weaknesses of the climate change levy and what should be done instead, but that would be to stray too far from the focus of this chapter.) The right approach is to combine a sharpening of those incentives with the dual cash-out system in NETA, so as to promote renewables in general and reliable and predictable renewables in particular.

EX ANTE VERSUS *EX POST* NOTIFICATION

Another issue that generated a certain amount of heat was the question of whether traded positions should be notified in advance, or whether *ex post* notification should be permitted. I thought this a very peculiar debate and I must confess, one that I found it hard to take very seriously. If notification happens later, then there is nothing to prevent contracts being settled after the event. Now while there are many examples where contracts are set in advance of exchange and others where contracting and exchange happen at the same moment, I can think of no markets where contracts are settled after exchange. To allow *ex post* notification would have encouraged people not to contract forward. It would also have allowed the complete circumvention of the dual cash-out system, the case for which I developed earlier.

AGGREGATION

A much more substantive issue concerns aggregation, where there are serious arguments to be weighed on both sides. Let me put the issue at its simplest and most stark. Imagine a user with variable and unpredictable demand. It will be difficult for that user to contract forward for the unpredictable component of its demand, and it may therefore be forced into the balancing market and thereby suffer the penalty of the dual cash-out arrangement. Since it thereby imposes costs on the system operator, that penalty is appropriate.

Suppose now that there is a flexible generator nearby, who can readily match the peaks and troughs in the user's demand. It would be very simple to write a requirements contract, whereby the two agree that the generator will meet the user's fluctuations in demand. The consequence would be that the user places no unpredictable demand on the grid, so that the system operator is unaware and need not be concerned with the user's fluctuations in demand. It would seem inappropriate to impose any penalty on either the user or the generator. In effect, they are making life easier for the system operator. The proposed contract enhances economic efficiency.

However, such a requirements contract is not permitted under NETA, which rules out the aggregation implicit in the contract just described, except in the very special case where the generator and user lie behind a common meter, so that the generator becomes, in effect, embedded generation. Ruling out aggregation means that the variable demand of the user will be priced in the balancing market at one cash-out price, while the variable supply of the generator will be priced at the other, lower cash price. In effect, the efficient trade is subject to a tax. The trading rules precluding aggregation introduce an inefficiency.

What justification can be given for such an apparently inefficient system? The answer is that we are in the world of second best. (I will return later to the question of how we move closer to first best.) There are three important arguments against allowing aggregation of the type just described: one concerned with market liquidity; the second with market dominance; and the third with transmission constraints.

I see the market liquidity argument as a transitional one. In creating new trading arrangements, it is clearly important that the new markets develop substantial depth, facilitating liquid trade and encouraging the growth of secondary forward and derivative markets. Once they are established, liquidity is unlikely to be a problem. But in the early stages it is probably wise to avoid policies that may drain liquidity from the market. The difficulty with aggregation, if permitted on a large scale, is that it could very easily take a large amount of trade out of markets, inhibiting the development of deep, liquid markets. Vertical integration in the industry adds to this concern, since it facilitates aggregation within a single company.

The second argument concerns the fact that, though there has been considerable divestment, some companies retain appreciable market share. For the reasons that I have given before, I believe that the new trading arrangements will appreciably reduce concern about these market shares, moving the electricity market closer to a much more normal market structure in which it is possible to be relaxed about market shares of around 20 per cent or so. However, as the new trading arrangements bed down, there must be concerns that large players may find opportunities for gaming. In particular, permitting large-scale aggregation would undoubtedly give the larger players greater scope to tie up important parts of the market, and possibly impede the development of a robust and liquid market.

The third argument points to the most obvious type of gaming, namely exploitation of transmission constraints. Let me return to my previous example, and now imagine that a significant transmission constraint lies between the user and the generator. Then permitting the requirements contract through aggregation could well result in an outcome that is highly inefficient. The user and the generator face a common price; but the system operator may have to enter the balancing market on either side of the transmission mechanism, taking off generation on the generator's side and bringing on generation on the user's side. In this case, the aggregated requirements contract yields no efficiencies, only inefficiencies. Since transmission constraints are commonplace, this represents a powerful argument against aggregation.

These arguments reinforce each other. The scope for gaming is enormously increased by the presence of transmission constraints. Thus a large portfolio generator could enter into a requirements contract across a transmission constraint in the expectation that some of its plant will benefit from the actions of the system operator and bidding in the balancing market accordingly. The extreme would be where the presence of the constraint requires the system operator to take off the generator's plant on one side of the constraint and call another of the generator's plant on the other side. The scope for gaming would therefore be appreciable, and it would be the large players who have the most scope to take advantage of it. Ruling out aggregation reduces the scope for this, though by no means eliminates it.

The other key point is that widespread gaming of this type would inhibit the development of broad and liquid markets and of secondary and derivative markets. That is why it is especially important to inhibit such behaviour in the early development stages of the new markets. I return to this point later when I discuss the market abuse condition. But first I shall address one key direction in which I see the new trading arrangements developing, namely towards locational pricing and the explicit pricing of transmission capacity.

LOCATIONAL PRICING

I have just set out what I trust is a convincing second-best argument for ruling out aggregation. A key part of the argument concerned the limited extent of pricing of transmission capacity and therefore of transmission constraints.[4] An important question for the future is whether and how we will see the emergence of the separate pricing of transmission capacity, resulting in locational pricing.

I have no doubt that this will be a necessary evolution of the trading arrangements. The move to a more market-based structure will expose the difficulties that the lack of an explicit market in transmission capacity entails. It will also allow the easing of the constraints on aggregation, since a well-designed system for pricing transmission capacity should eliminate the problems discussed earlier. Indeed one possible evolution towards transmission pricing would be to allow greater aggregation behind key transmission constraints, so that different area prices start to emerge from the resulting market trades.

The advantages of pricing transmission capacity are considerable. It would allow the market to reveal the value of additional capacity, thereby providing robust signals for investment in future capacity in the right parts of the network. It would allow the various interconnectors to be treated within the same framework as the rest of the system, facilitating the creation of both a more integrated UK-wide network and integration within the European market. And it could facilitate the development of a more competitive market in the provision of transmission capacity, moving away from the standard view of the grid as something that can be provided only by the monopoly network operator.

I would not be surprised to see such developments starting within a year or two of the launch of NETA – my discussant will continue to have a very full agenda! But this development needs to be handled with care. There are inevitable political sensitivities to the idea that people in different parts of the country will face different prices for electricity, and these sensitivities need to be managed. There is the related transitional problem that, while the pricing of transmission capacity will incentivize the investment to relieve transmission constraints, the presence of severe transmission constraints could easily throw up very big initial price differences that cause acute discomfort to customers and government: an ill-judged and poorly managed move to a secondary market in transmission rights could risk the problems of California, and promote the spread of ochlocratic tendencies from other parts of the energy market to electricity.[5] Moreover, the technical design of the appropriate market rules for a market in transmission capacity is no simple task, and will need very careful consideration.

MARKET ABUSE CONDITION

One other area of appreciable controversy, recently put to the Competition Commission, has been Ofgem's introduction of the market abuse condition. I think that I have probably said enough about the scope for large players in the market to engage in a variety of forms of gaming to the detriment of the other market participants not to have to dwell on this point at length. The scope for gaming was very considerable in the Pool, and I am confident that it will reduce with the new trading arrangements for reasons that I have discussed. But electricity markets give considerable market power to players, even small ones, close to real time, both because of transmission constraints and because of inflexibility of generation. The need for a fair trading or good behaviour condition seems clear.

What is more difficult is the form that this condition should take. In particular, the new Competition Act gives considerable concurrent powers to the Office of Fair Trading and Ofgem to deal with anti-competitive behaviour. Why are these powers not sufficient?

The key to the application of competition policy is the definition of the appropriate market. From the economist's perspective, the relevant definition of market can be defined in many dimensions, as the Arrow–Debreu framework demonstrates, and in particular is likely to be both time- and state-contingent. But in practice, the adopted definition of market is driven by legal precedent, especially in the European context. Whereas in electricity, small players at particular times and in particular places may have appreciable market power, competition law may not in practice apply. While one generator may have appreciable market power, not to say monopoly, in the market for flexible plant behind a binding transmission constraint ten minutes ahead of real time for delivery of electricity between 19.30 and 20.00 on 10 October 2000, it is highly unlikely that the courts would uphold such a narrow definition of market, relevant though it may be from the perspective of the economics of the case. Certainly there are no precedents in European case law for such an interpretation of market.

It is for these reasons that Ofgem decided that it could not rely on the Competition Act and needed the market abuse condition. Of course, an alternative and more heroic course would have been to test the application of the Competition Act by seeking to extend (or more accurately narrow) the received definition of market. But even if that met with initial success, it would have been challenged all the way through the courts, and the issue would have taken years to resolve. The resulting uncertainty could have been damaging for electricity markets, and could have weakened, or even jeopardized, the launch of the new trading arrangements. Not surprisingly, and rightly in my view, Ofgem chose to safeguard the new arrangements by introducing the market abuse condition.

There is a further and rather different objection to the market abuse condition; namely that its incorporation into licence conditions allows for no formal appeal mechanism against the judgement of the regulator, and that this is against natural justice. Although few are willing overtly to cast our chairman as the enemy of justice, the spectre of a future regulatory ogre is often invoked, with passing reference to one or other current regulator.

It is, of course, true that the regulator cannot establish a formal, *de jure*, appeal mechanism to his or her judgement concerning the breach of a licence condition, and so can establish no appeal route against judgements made under the market abuse condition. This is because the Director General (and the new authority when it is established shortly) cannot delegate or give away its statutory powers given to him, her or it by Parliament. But Ofgem has made every effort to establish a *de facto* review procedure that almost certainly achieves the same result as a formal appeals procedure.[6] Callum McCarthy has established a high-powered Advisory Board, made up of individuals of considerable reputation and independence, to give a judgement on any disputed case resulting from decisions under the market abuse condition. That judgement will be in the public domain. For the regulator or authority to disregard the reasoned judgement of this Advisory Board is very likely to lead to a successful challenge under judicial review. Even if it did not, for the regulator or authority to disregard the Board would result almost certainly in a sharp drop in confidence and reputation. In every conceivable situation, the judgement of the Board will hold sway.

So the *de facto* appeal procedure is as good as a *de jure* one. That leaves the concern that the authority may, at some point in the future, decide to sweep away the appeal process. I think that is an extremely remote possibility.

Since presenting the above discussion, this possibility has become largely irrelevant, since the Competition Commission decided to rule against Ofgem in this matter. (See Competition Commission, 2000.) Ofgem responded promptly and entirely correctly by removing the market abuse condition from those companies that had agreed to its incorporation in their licences. However, I leave the argument to stand, since I believe it has continued validity. I trust that we will not come to regret the Commission's reasoned judgement in this matter.

THE PROCESS OF REFORM

It will be clear from what I have said that I think that the new electricity trading arrangements represent a major advance in the direction of a more competitive and efficient electricity market. They put in place a better structure of governance that will allow the arrangements to evolve organically in the light of experience; and the technical design of the new arrangements is, in my view, well thought through. Although the arrangements will continue to be improved in the light of experience, even in their initial form they will deliver major benefits. Current market signals give the lie to those, including some of my colleagues at London Business School (Bower and Bunn, 1999), who argued that the reforms would drive prices higher. Forward prices some four or five years out are some 20–25 per cent below levels before the reform process. And each whisper of the possibility of delay in introducing NETA pushes forward prices higher.

I conclude by reflecting on the process of reform itself, and why it succeeded now and not before. I would identify four factors, three fundamental and one contingent. First, there was simply the increasing indefensibility of the old trading arrangements. What was acceptable around privatization as a way of making privatization work and obtaining its other benefits became increasingly hard to justify with the passage of time. The pressures for reform grew and became increasingly hard to resist.

Second, there was the increasingly diverse nature of the industry, in contrast to the relatively homogeneous nature of the industry immediately after privatization. This came from changes of industry structure, new entry and the rise of retail competition. This heterogeneity meant that reform proposals met with a much more differentiated response than before. The opponents of reform were still there, but Ofgem and the government found many friends of reform arguing for change. The politics of reform in a diverse market were more manageable.

Third, there were the examples of reform elsewhere. Whereas the UK was at the cutting edge of reform at the start of the decade, the electricity industry had fallen behind change in other countries, and in other sectors in the UK. The growing contrast with the gas industry was increasingly hard to justify.

The contingent factor came from politics. Although I was and continue to be a firm supporter of this New Labour government, I was surprised how readily ministers embraced the reform of electricity trading, an arcane subject devoid of obvious popular appeal. It is a quirk of history, of the kind that makes politics so fascinating, that Geoffrey Robinson's misguided attempt to rescue the coal industry and the débâcle of the ban on new gas-fired power stations created a real determination to push through the reform of electricity trading.

I think that in all of this the industry as whole missed a real chance to initiate reform itself. Mired in the rigidities, politics and sectional interests of the Pool, the industry only saw the need for reform very late in the day and only after the regulator and the government had demonstrated their determination to act. Those interested in virtual history may speculate on what the reformed arrangements might have looked like had the industry been able to take the lead. As it is, we can all watch with keen interest over the next year to see how the new arrangements are working. I am confident both that they will work well and that they will need to evolve. I am sure that future Beesley lectures will return to this fascinating subject.

NOTES

1. This chapter was originally presented as a paper on 10 October 2000, when the NETA reforms were due to be implemented in the November/December 2000 period. The published version was finally edited in early February, when the Go-Live date was scheduled for March 2001.
2. I owe this point to Julian Bagwell.
3. This is a simplified statement of the rules. Additional rules specify what happens if the system operator does not enter one side of the balancing market in the period from gate closure to real time, as well as an algorithm which removes 'arbitrageable' offers and bids and removes offers and bids that are deemed to be due to transmission constraints.
4. Currently NGC transmission charges reflect overall transmission constraints, and therefore vary depending on where generation is located. A key question is how much such charges will affect final consumer bills; transmission is typically 5 per cent to 10 per cent of the total bill, and in general transmission charges will probably not vary enormously, except when the system is under stress.
5. Ochlocracy: government by the mob (*OED*).
6. This is similar to the arrangement adopted by Don Cruickshank at Oftel when he placed a similar fair trading requirement on BT before the introduction of the Competition Act, with a view to reducing more quickly the scope of the price cap imposed on BT.

REFERENCES

Armstrong, Mark, Simon Cowan and John Vickers (1994), *Regulatory Reform*, Cambridge, MA: MIT Press.
Bower, John and Derek Bunn (1999), 'A Model-Based Comparison of Pool and Bilateral Market Mechanisms for Electricity Trading', London Business School, May.

Brealey, Richard and Carlos Lapuerta (1997), 'A Report on Generator Market Power in the Electricity Market of England and Wales', The Brattle Group. Revised 1998.

Competition Commission (2000), *AES and British Energy*, Report No. 453, December.

Fabra, Natalia (2000), 'Uniform Pricing Facilitates Collusion: The Case of Electricity Markets', European University Institute, January, mimeo.

Fehr, N. von der and D. Harbord (1993), 'Spot Market Competition in the UK Electricity Market', *Economic Journal*, **103**, 531–46.

Klemperer, Paul (2000a), 'Why Every Economist Should Learn Some Auction Theory', Nuffield College Oxford, mimeo.

Klemperer, Paul (2000b), 'What Really Matters in Auction Design', Nuffield College, Oxford, mimeo.

Wolak, F. and R. Patrick (1996), 'The Impact of Market Rules and Market Structure on the Price Determination Process in the England and Wales Electricity Market', POWER Working Paper PWP-047, University of California.

Wolfram, C. (1998), 'Strategic Bidding in a Multi-Unit Auction: An Empirical Analysis of Bids to Supply Electricity in England and Wales', *Rand Journal of Economics*, **29**, 4, 703–25.

CHAIRMAN'S COMMENTS

Callum McCarthy

I first mention very briefly Michael Beesley in whose name we are meeting. One of the many pleasures of coming to this job was to meet in the flesh someone whom I had long admired. To meet Michael was to find someone whose contributions were varied; and, once they were deciphered (because sometimes they were so tightly packed that they need deciphering), they were always thought-provoking and stimulating. To see a robust, tough mind in a tough, much-used and quite battered body was always deeply impressive, so it is a great honour to chair the first occasion which is in Michael's name.

When I introduced David Currie I said that critiquing what he had to say was going to be very difficult, not only because I regard him and myself as having been partners, but also because I regard his account as a masterly review of a complex subject. But on all the main issues that he has identified – the importance of divestment to reduce market share versus the changes in market structure being brought in by NETA; the treatment of environmental issues; the emphasis on NETA as a process that will be evolutionary rather than simply 'big bang'; the benefits that come about from a system based on consenting adults contracting willingly between each other, and the need for and the reasonable administration of the market abuse licence condition – on all of those I entirely agree, so I have some difficulty in critiquing. What I would like to do is to extend one or two of the points that David has made.

First, I would like to develop what David said about moving electricity generation in the direction of other commodity markets because I think that the implications of this have not been fully appreciated. It has a specific bearing on the skill sets which will be required in the future. If I can exaggerate to make the point, ten years ago the key skill set of generators was in engineering: how to build power stations; how to ensure that distribution worked; how the turbines ran. Five years on, if not already, the prime skill set will be a trading skill set balancing buy-and-sell obligations. That has profound implications, particularly for the management of the companies concerned, but also for some of the regulatory issues involved. For the management of the companies, questions such as how to deal with credit ratings of counter parties will become an issue of much greater importance than it is at present. Similarly, how to manage and control traders (who will devise increasingly complex derivatives) when the people who are in senior positions in the companies will not have gone through a learning experience in their own careers based on trading, represents a serious question for the management of those companies. And the competition authorities and the regulators will increasingly have to be concerned not only with the physical situation but with contractual positions – and I am not sure that any of us have yet fully thought through the implications of that.

The second point I would like to develop further is the link between electricity trading, which David has been concerned about in his contribution, and gas trading. One result of developments in both electricity and gas will be increased arbitrage between gas as a generating feedstock and gas for other uses; and again I think that neither the companies' management nor those responsible for questions of security of supply have yet thought through fully the implications of the arbitrage that will be made more possible by developments in NETA and the parallel developments which are informed by the same philosophy and approach that are happening in terms of the new gas trading arrangements.

Lastly, I'd like to raise a question. One of the fundamentals of NETA is to incorporate demand signals and demand-side decisions much more fully than they are at present in the Pool, from which they are almost totally absent. It is not clear how many customers will immediately take advantage of this and the question I pose is whether there are other things we can and should do to encourage the demand side as well as the supply side.

2.   A critique of rail regulation*

Dieter Helm

1.   INTRODUCTION

Very few privatizations have been free of teething problems, and all new regulatory bodies have faced criticisms, made mistakes, and had to improvise and adapt with experience. Perfect models and perfect processes are matters of academic debate; practical experience is bound to be less satisfactory.

Rail privatization and regulation, however, stands out from the pack: it has been much more controversial, and its critics have been much more vocal. Whereas the core objectives of the privatizations of the water, electricity, gas, telecoms and airport sectors were widely shared (and now accepted by all the main political parties), those for rail were not. The Conservatives' vision of a subsidy-free rail industry, gradually opened to competition, was quite different from the heady aspirations of Mr Prescott's integrated transport strategy. The differences were carried over to regulation, where the approaches of Tom Winsor and Alistair Morton are very different from those of John Swift and Chris Bolt.

There is, as yet, no sign that the Labour model of the railways has settled down, nor that the service to customers is markedly improved. Some argue that this unsatisfactory state of affairs is inevitable, and that a revitalization of the railways will take time. Things are bound to get worse before they get better.

There is much truth in this claim. I shall, however, argue that the existing regulatory regime and its institutions are fundamentally flawed, and that, without major reform, there is little reason for optimism. At the heart of the rail regulatory regime is a confusion of roles and a personalization of regulatory conduct that is not conducive to the efficient achievement of objectives. The tensions and inherent differences of interest between the Office of the Rail Regulator (ORR) and the Strategic Rail Authority (SRA) are an expensive luxury the railways cannot afford.

I shall argue, too, that the long-term monopolies that will be produced by

*This chapter was written before a serious railway accident at Hatfield in October 2000, with numerous fatalities, which subsequently stimulated a debate about rail safety in Britain, and before Railtrack was placed in administration.

the franchising process currently under way will create significant regulatory difficulties, and that the enforcement regime may prove counterproductive. Fortunately, most of these problems have solutions, but a central argument of this chapter will be that the existing framework is not adequate to address them.

The structure of the chapter is as follows. The next section reviews the Conservative model in order to identify the objectives that the regulatory regime was designed to achieve. This is then contrasted with Labour's integrated transport strategy. Labour's objectives were to be met by the SRA, whose functions are reviewed in section 4. The integrated transport strategy required more money, and section 5 explores how the Treasury became a key player. Section 6 considers the rail regulator's role in setting the track access charges (TACs), and shows how the 'tough' stance taken by Chris Bolt has been weakened in the face of investors' concerns about his successor's approach to the exercise of the personal discretion at the heart of the regulatory regime. Section 7 provides a critique of the regime, focusing on the institutional structure, the franchising and periodic-review processes, and the enforcement regime. Finally, section 8 presents the main conclusions.

2.   THE CONSERVATIVE MODEL

The main objectives of the Conservative government, particularly in the rail industry, were to gradually eliminate the subsidy, to use private borrowing to finance investment, and to improve the efficiency of the industry. The Conservatives did not set out to engineer a switch from roads to railways, or to create an 'integrated transport strategy', but rather to turn British Rail into a 'normal' set of businesses. Although there was a 'great transport debate' and a fuel price escalator, these aspects of transport policy were largely peripheral to rail privatization and regulation.

The structure put in place was reasonably well designed to achieve these objectives: competitive bidding for franchises would bear down on the Treasury burden; an ungeared Railtrack balance sheet provided the financing mechanism; and the introduction of competitive services over time would force the management's attention to shift towards costs and customer services.

There were several reasons why these objectives were not met. In opposition, Labour's threats of renationalization increased the risks of bidding for franchises and of investing in Railtrack. The risk of investing in train operating companies (TOCs) led the government to persuade the regulator to 'moderate' competition. As the political debate hotted up, political necessity soon made privatization *the* objective, rather than a means towards the wider ones listed above.

The immediate post-privatization performance of the industry was widely considered to be dreadful. TOCs set about reducing labour costs. Railtrack played the classic utility monopoly game and failed to tackle the fundamentals of managing a network which had operated within the public sector, and, hence, had paid scant regard to the basics of asset registers, disaggregation of costs, and the management of large capital projects. The rolling-stock leasing companies (ROSCOs) proved embarrassingly profitable, creating the first railway millionaires – another consequence of the hostile position of the Labour opposition towards privatization.

The reasons for these performance failures are much disputed. The initial disaggregated structure has been blamed; the first rail regulator has been accused of not using his full powers; and the management has been criticized. Behind all of these criticisms lie the underlying incentives, and it is important to see how far this poor performance resulted from the incentives created in the initial architecture. For the TOCs, costs substantially comprised the TACs that were fixed – and fixed to ensure that Railtrack's revenue was secure, so that investors would buy its shares even under the threat of renationalization under Labour. Thus, the obvious way in which TOCs could make money in the short term (and before Labour got into office) was to drive down operating costs – primarily drivers and staff – and, hence, quality suffered. Railtrack has had an almost guaranteed income from the TACs and, hence, profits were the difference between that income and costs. Volume was not of much interest – indeed, more passengers and freight could actually make matters worse by increasing costs. Penalties for non-delivery were trivial in comparison to the cost implications of company performance to meet the higher demand. Finally, the ROSCOs were sold competitively, so, if there were few bids at the right prices, that was the fault of government and opposition.

Arguably, the Conservative model could probably have been made to work. The more fragmented structure, contrary to much subsequent criticism over its lack of coordination, in practice follows the trend in network industries. Information technology (IT) has facilitated much more extensive use of markets. In water, Kelda, Hyder, Anglian and others are contracting out services. In telecoms, BT is contemplating separating its network from the retail and other activities. In electricity, the regional electricity companies (RECs) have been formally split, and, in gas, Transco is contemplating breaking itself up.

Contrary to much comment, there is no reason to believe that the rail industry is unique, or that it is immune from the broader trends towards using markets and competition which IT has facilitated. There is little evidence that monolithic companies covering whole industries are likely to be efficient or have much regard for the interests of their customers. In particular, it will be argued that the case for further horizontal and vertical integration is at least economically dubious.

However, the Conservative model, unlike much of the Thatcherite inheritance of privatized industries, was not to survive the change of government without radical modification, and at the heart of this redirection was a fundamental change in the objectives of policy. The question changed, and, not surprisingly, a different answer was needed.

3.   THE WHITE PAPER – A STRATEGY FOR GROWTH

In opposition, Labour had pledged to take Railtrack back into public control (and also not to privatize National Air Traffic Services). The manifesto had to refine this,[1] and made great play of the transformation to the transport sector. Among the ten key points in 'our contract with the people', it pledged to 'safeguard our environment and develop an integrated transport policy to fight congestion and pollution'.[2]

Implementing this manifesto pledge was to prove a much more difficult exercise. In July 1998, a White Paper, *A New Deal for Transport: Better for Everyone*, was published, providing the detailed plans. The central theme of the White Paper was simple and sharp: transport was to be considered as a whole, in an integrated way. The task of government was to encourage a switch from cars to buses and trains. New roads – based on 'predict-and-provide' – were no longer the answer. Instead, the decline of bus and rail services was to be reversed to address the congestion and environmental problems.

This new approach was much more demanding than anything the Conservatives had envisaged when the industry was privatized. While their aim had primarily been efficiency, the White Paper required an *expansion* of the railways. The expansion was to be led by the proposed Strategic Rail Authority, supported by the Commission for Integrated Transport (which would advise on policy), and the rail regulator was to be left to set the charges. It was envisaged in the White Paper that the rail regulator would be *subordinate* to the SRA, as paragraphs 4.22–4.24 made clear, and, indeed, as was to be eventually reflected in the Transport Act 2000.

In many industries, expansion, and the associated investment, is financed through borrowing, backed by expected revenues from customers. Telecoms and the new broadband networks to support the explosion of Internet and other services provide the most recent example. The railways, by contrast, could not be expected to pay their way. The peculiar economics of the industry witnesses its main competitor network – the roads – provided by the state. Road users do not pay TACs, but rather petrol taxes and a fixed licence fee.

Petrol is heavily taxed, but there is no direct reflection in prices of congestion or the long-run marginal costs of providing and maintaining the road infrastructure and supporting services or the costs of the deaths, injury and pollution that road transport causes. Revenue is not hypothecated. There is no 'Roadtrack', no separate regulatory accounts, no explicit rate-of-return requirement on the miles of concrete, and no infrastructure renewals charge reflecting the costs of mending the roads. Ancillary costs (such as the police) are financed separately, and the cost of some 3000 deaths and 5000 injuries per year go unaccounted. Whereas a small number of regrettable deaths in a rail accident at Ladbroke Grove has led to the Secretary of State announcing over £1 billion of extra spending, the daily carnage on the roads has no such cost consequences to the infrastructure. (The reaction to the Hatfield accident was even more extreme, in the context that at least as many people died on the roads on the same day as died in the accident.)

Relative prices, and relative costs to be recovered from customers between road and rail, do not remotely resemble economic reality, and the White Paper's real message was that greater sums of public money would be needed to reverse the decline. But – crucially – the White Paper did not provide concrete commitments on new money: it was all promises on the assumption that the Treasury would deliver.

The Treasury was – rightly – reluctant to give a blank cheque, and preferred first to see how much investment could be squeezed out of the industry. The 'solutions' proposed by the Shadow SRA were to take the industry a long way from the Conservative model – to undermine the sharp structural distinction between network infrastructure and services, and to turn the franchising process into a long-term monopoly model. Both steps have serious regulatory consequences, and both, I shall argue, will significantly reduce the chances of meeting the objectives of the 1998 White Paper.

4. THE CREATION OF THE SRA – OPRAF TRANSFORMS ITSELF INTO A PLAYER

The creation of the SRA, which was eventually legally sanctioned in autumn 2000, was an attempt to take the objectives of policy and translate them into a 'clear, coherent and strategic programme for the development of our railways' (White Paper, paragraph 4.12), so that the SRA became 'the main regulator of passenger network benefits'. It would have unspecified funds to support its activities.

Alastair Morton was appointed its first chairman, and immediately set out his vision based around the slogan 'investment, investment, investment', indicating that some £100 billion might be needed. This vision gradually unfolded through a series of interlocking financial sources – Railtrack's balance sheet, the TOCs' balance sheets, and the Treasury's capital and revenue support (as well, of course, as the farebox).

It was rapidly apparent that Railtrack's balance sheet could not carry all the debt necessary to finance the investment to meet the overall objective. Railtrack's financial limits were set by the underpinning from the TACs, and by investors' confidence in the stability of those charges, reflected in its cost of capital. The institutional problem created by the White Paper framework was that neither the level of charges nor the regulatory risk was in the Shadow SRA's hands, but rather with the ORR. Under the proposals for the first periodic review of the TACs put forward by Chris Bolt, the traditional utility model implied a limited regulatory asset base (RAB) and a tight cost of capital. Investors took fright, and there was a sharp deterioration in Railtrack's share price.

The appointment of Tom Winsor on 5 July 1999 coincided with a further crisis in investor confidence, as Figure 2.1 illustrates. The fall-off in 1999 coincided with wider market developments, as the equity boom of the 1990s began to run out of steam. However, it is important to recognize that utility stock, such as Railtrack (especially whose volume incentives are weak), has much more predictable earnings and an implicit guarantee with regard to the

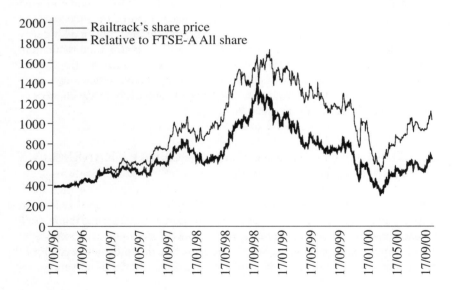

Source: Datastream.

Figure 2.1   Railtrack's share price, May 1996–September 2000

financing of its functions than do conventional companies. Hence, it might have been expected that Railtrack's share price would not have fallen as sharply as the market in 1999. Regulatory risk must be part of the explanation.

Repeated tough public statements, combined with a fines-based approach (see below), put continued pressure on the share price, and, in turn, pushed out further the timing of any rights issue necessary to stretch Railtrack's balance sheet. (Softening the periodic-review parameters provided the counterbalance, notably in the second half of 2000.)

The Shadow SRA's first source of finance for the strategic plan was therefore largely *outside* its control, and apparently going in the wrong direction. It was hardly surprising that this spilled over into a perception that the working relationship between the two key players was less than perfect, and this *perception* did little to improve investor confidence. Contrary to much media comment, it was less the fault of the individuals than the institutional setting within which they found themselves.

If Railtrack's balance sheet was increasingly limited, the Shadow SRA had an alternative to explore – the balance sheets of the TOCs. Given that the SRA was also functioning in shadow form with the powers of OPRAF, and given that this created a day-to-day focus on TOCs and the franchising process, it was natural that Morton's wider investment vision should come together with the detail of the franchising process.

The Shadow SRA's approach to franchising had two parts: first, the limited-period franchises would be renegotiated and turned into longer-term monopolies; and, second, the TOCs would be encouraged to venture into infrastructure activities, and, hence, start an element of vertical integration. Both of these were motivated by the desire to accelerate investment, and, hence, meet the political imperative of letting current customers (and voters) see the benefits sooner rather than later.

The TOCs have consistently argued that the franchise periods were too short to encourage them to invest in new trains and to upgrade services. Not knowing whether they would retain their franchise in future, TOCs, it was argued, would focus on short-term objectives. While a monopolization of TOCs' franchises was very clearly directly in their self-interest, it is important to realize that the TOCs' criticism is one that can be applied to *all* franchising, and it is not surprising that it is a well-researched problem. While any franchisee would, other things being equal, prefer a monopoly, the important distinction is between capital costs that are *fixed* and those that are *sunk*. Sunk costs cannot be recovered on exit – that is, losing the franchise. In the case of TOCs, it is likely that the assets of the incumbent will be taken over by the entrant – that is, there are few, if any, sunk costs. The argument is in this respect, therefore, largely spurious.

Note, too, that the prospect of refranchising exerts a strong incentive on the incumbent to perform. Failure to deliver services in the current period *should* have an impact on the decision to renew, and most incumbents will want to carry on. (None has said it would like to leave the industry at refranchising.) Finally, and crucially, refranchising reveals a great deal of information about costs and services, releasing new ideas and challenging existing practices. Once the long-term franchises are let, what incentives do the incumbents have to perform? Very harsh penalty regimes may be required (to which I return below). Dealing with the sort of performance that some of the TOCs have delivered would be almost impossible faced with an entrenched monopolist.

Selling monopolies – which is what the SRA has, in effect, been doing – does have the merit of getting the monopoly rents *up front*, and the SRA has been encouraging TOCs to promise new investment in exchange for the monopolies. Like the Elizabethans' trade monopolies in the sixteenth century, and later, the monopoly privatizations under the Conservatives in the 1980s, the family silver can always be sold – but only once. Competitions for franchises, however, do at least need to follow fair-competition rules, and it is far from obvious how one bid can be preferred to another unless the criteria are stated. How, for example, are lower subsidies to be traded off against higher ones with differential investment? If there are no clear criteria for bid assessment, and no common investment terms with Railtrack, the SRA runs the risk of judicial review, and possibly even the fate that has befallen the Lottery Commission. The early examples of the Chiltern and East Coast Main Line illustrate the scale of the problems facing the SRA.

The SRA has added a further twist to the refranchising process – it wants TOCs to become involved in infrastructure projects. There were at least two reasons. The first was that it could then add the TOCs' balance sheets to those of Railtrack to raise more of the £100 billion. The second was a core concern that Railtrack lacked the ability to deliver capital projects.

The chosen method appears to be off-balance-sheet financing, through 'special purpose vehicles' (SPVs), created to sit between the TOCs, Railtrack and the SRA. Highly complex structures are envisaged, but ultimately they have to provide answers to simple questions: Who would bear the risk? What would be the supporting revenue streams? What would the cost of capital be? How would disputes be resolved? At the time of writing, these issues have not been resolved and the cost of capital for SPVs would appear high – perhaps very high.

5. ENTER THE TREASURY: THE TEN-YEAR PROGRAMME

Driven partly by the need to bring the various components of the financial structure together, partly by the political necessity of meeting the manifesto commitments by the election, and partly as a fall-out of the Comprehensive Spending Review, the government's eventual contribution took the form of the ten-year plan: *Transport 2010*.

The plan is far from clear. It promises £121 billion of capital investment in the period to 2010, combining public and private contributions. It gives money across all the transport sector, representing a partial retreat from the objective of engendering a switch from road to railways, and, indeed, even resurrecting some road schemes. Rail is to receive £14.7 billion of public money, against an estimated £34.3 billion from the private sector – that is, together, less than half of Morton's £100 billion. However, later in the plan, government spending is put at £29 billion, comprising:

£12 billion	revenue support for passenger and freight train operators
£7 billion	the new Rail Modernization Fund
£4 billion	capital projects for renewals (including the West Coast Main Line)
£5 billion	completion of the Channel Tunnel link and London hub.

In effect, the government intends to halt the decline of the subsidies to TOCs (pumping more money through them to support the new franchise agreements), to pump new money through the SRA, which can then use SPVs or direct grants and support to TOCs and Railtrack, and to support large, discrete projects.

The sums of money are, as with all major public spending, the outcome of a complex web of political, regulatory and economic factors. Underlying all the figures is a headline political necessity – fixing fares to customers (and voters) at RPI–1. There is then a political cap on the revenue stream, with the government monies being the variable designed to make it all add up. The TACs, to be set by the rail regulator, in principle finance Railtrack's functions. However, since a central function is enhancement, the rail regulator needs to be given the SRA's answer before he can set the charges. The SRA fixes this aspect of the functions, and ORR finances them.[3]

This converging of the various components of railway finance around the ten-year plan is, however, far from complete. It remains to be seen whether, in practice, it all adds up, which in part depends on how the industry and the regulators perform. A ten-year plan is no more than a 'plan': experience will depend on how fast and effectively the industry spends the money. That, in turn, depends on the SRA's ability to 'leverage up' the £7 billion fund; on ORR's ability to regulate effectively and ensure that performance is delivered; on keeping the regulatory risk down (and, hence, ensuring that investors'

confidence returns at a reasonable cost of capital); and on Railtrack's and the
TOCs' ability to deliver.

6.   THE PERIODIC REVIEW AND ORR'S ROLE

The rail regulator, and the supporting ORR, were set up by the Conservatives
along the traditional utility regulatory model. The regulator would regulate the
natural monopoly (Railtrack) through a conventional RPI–X-type regime,
supported by a licence. He would also be responsible for encouraging the
growth of competition, as the initial franchise monopolies gave way to
competitive services.

The rail regulator would therefore be 'king' in the regulatory world.
OPRAF was set up as a *contracting* body – to let the franchises, on behalf of
government. It could, eventually, wither away, although, as long as there were
franchises, they would need some oversight.

The flaw in this Conservative model was the failure to recognize that TOCs
would need to be permanently regulated to ensure they delivered on their
franchise contracts, and, most importantly, to deny ORR responsibility for the
interface with customers. Just as in the gas industry, Transco services shippers
who then service customers, so Railtrack's conduct impacts on rail passengers.
Ofgas regulated the full supply chain; ORR did not.

The immediate confusion of roles was reflected in several dimensions – in
attempts to decide whose 'fault' was the evident failures to perform; in trying
to establish coherent and consistent incentives between Railtrack and TOCs;
and in attitudes to competition. Given that the rail regulator had wide
discretionary powers, as did OPRAF, it was inevitable that the differences
would become 'personalized'. The utility regulatory regimes have all suffered
generally from such discretion and personalization: the rail industry suffered
much more because it had *two* potentially conflicting sources. (Indeed, it is a
tribute to John Swift and Roger Salmon, the first head of OPRAF, that they
managed the relationship without the more public problems that were to
follow.) The dual regulatory approach was flawed from the start.

In the early years, under John Swift, the task of ORR was to bear down on
Railtrack and its performance *within* the initial TAC agreement. With very
public criticism of Railtrack's performance, ORR began the long process of
putting flesh on to the initial agreements, which, partly for reasons of the
flotation process, had been unduly ill defined.

ORR began the process that Ofwat had attempted to perform before it in the
water industry of trying to define output measures more precisely, to create a
better understanding of Railtrack's costs, and to provide some definition to the
investment programme. There followed a long-drawn-out set of initiatives,

including licence amendments with regard to information provision, the development of the Network Management Statement, and interventions on specific incidents and topics. On the other side, Railtrack's initial responses to ORR were rather like those of British Gas to Ofgas. Not taking regulators seriously is a fault common to many privatized utilities, but all have learnt the errors of this approach.

In response to very public criticism, and because volumes turned out higher than expected, the early notions of Railtrack managing a static railway network were replaced by a more demanding set of infrastructure renewals and enhancements. Capital expenditure in the first period turned out higher than anticipated, but the vagueness of the original TAC contract left it unclear how this extra spending would be treated, and particularly whether it would go into the RAB.

The absence of information on asset condition, and the lack of much definition in the contracts for maintenance between Railtrack and its main contractors, made the job of both the company and the regulator very difficult in this first period. Criticism of Railtrack's management, in being tardy in grasping the managerial problems, as well as its weakness in project management, was probably justified. The experience with the West Coast Main Line project was not to be a happy one in the latter regard. But it is far from clear that there was much that ORR could do about it, beyond what it did in that period. Suggestions that the first rail regulator was slack in not using the powers he had to impose draconian fines on Railtrack are misplaced, if the intention was to change the actual performance in the short run. It is easy to forget that ORR did achieve a great deal, of which Licence Condition 7 provided the basis on which not only the Network Management Statement, but also much of the subsequent enforcement, was based.

A core task for ORR has, however, been to set the future charges and charging regime for Railtrack. First John Swift, then Chris Bolt and finally Tom Winsor have had a part to play. The periodic review has many of the features of other utility reviews. The regulator needs to ensure that the business can finance its functions, and thus has sufficient cash in the next period to meet operating and capital costs. These are in part determined by the SRA, whose decisions and views the rail regulator is required to take into account. Next the regulator needs to remunerate shareholders' investments in the company, through the RAB and appropriate cost of capital. Both Chris Bolt and Tom Winsor have used the same general methodology, but not surprisingly they have come up with different numbers for the core financial variables – cost of capital and RAB. There has been a very significant shift in the ORR stance, as Table 2.1 illustrates.

Bolt argued that additional renewal expenditure should not be included in the RAB because these were obligations reflected in the prospectus, and,

Table 2.1   Regulators' estimates of the regulatory asset base and the cost of capital

	Opening RAB	Cost of capital
Bolt, December 1998	No uplift	5–6% (post-tax)
Winsor, December 1999	10% uplift	**7**–7.5% (pre-tax)
Winsor, July 2000	15% uplift	7–**7.5**% (pre-tax)
Winsor, October 2000 (Final determination)	15% uplift	**8**% (pre-tax)

Note: The cost of capital figures in bold are based on the indicative figure chosen by ORR in each of the conclusions documents.

hence, the flotation price, and took a much tougher line on the cost of capital. Winsor allowed a much more generous RAB and significantly raised the cost of capital. (In the latter regard, part of the reason for the higher cost of capital was probably the regulatory risk created by the frequent, very public, criticisms of Railtrack, the increasing frequency of interventions, uncertainty about future action and enforcement.)

At an early stage, ORR took an independent view of the prospects for efficiency, to be reflected in the allowance for operations, maintenance and renewals. Consultants were hired to assess the scope for cost-cutting within Railtrack and, based on their findings, ORR proposed an annual efficiency target of 5 per cent per annum over seven years, subsequently reduced to 3.8 per cent per annum over (probably) five years, and finally to 3.1 per cent over five years. This appears to be broadly in line with the performance of other privatized utilities, but makes little allowance for the impact of volume and the different scale of investment requirements. Whereas electricity and gas are mature networks in which the emphasis is on 'sweating the assets', rail is an investment-driven business. (Water shares this investment characteristic, but against limited volume growth.[4]) There is a question as to whether the public interest is best served by placing tough operating cost reduction targets on a company which should be perhaps more concerned with performance and investment than cutting costs and jobs.

That left the enhancement capital expenditure (CAPEX) to be filled in to determine the outcome. By summer 2000, despite the imminent deadline to complete the periodic review, the position remained unclear. As indicated above, the ten-year plan is a vague general document, and the SPVs are uncertain prospects. The role of the TOCs and the extent of their investments are also largely unknown. Thus, the enhancement assumptions entering into the periodic-review determination are, at best, working assumptions, to be negotiated, adjusted and revised as the contract goes along. Any idea that ORR is setting a *fixed* five-year contract is, at best, naïve. The periodic review is not a fixed-price, fixed-period contract. At best, it is a framework agreement within the envelope of the political price cap (RPI–1). What is delivered for this price cap will depend on the *ex post* continual negotiations between Railtrack, the TOCs, the SRA and the Treasury.

This uncertainty which confronts investors has not, however, blunted the enthusiasm of the regulator to use 'carrots and sticks' on performance (at least up until the Hatfield crash). Railtrack was to have volume incentives, but outputs were to be defined and fixed, and it was to be fined, should it fail to meet them. There was to be much more prominence given to the rail regulator's enforcement regime. This shift to the fines approach is the feature of the regulatory regime which stands out against other utility regulators' conduct, and it has its costs and benefits, which I discuss below.

7. THE CRITIQUE

The regulatory arrangements in the rail industry have not, as yet, proved particularly successful. Nobody would suggest that any other country should adopt them for its railways; and no other regulated industry would want to follow suit. They have created a confusion of roles, functions and incentives; performance has been poor; and the cost of capital high.

The reasons are, contrary to much commentary, not just a function of the personalities – although in a regime which embodies wide discretionary powers on individuals, personalities are bound to count. The main difficulties lie elsewhere – with the institutional structure of the regime and some of the ill-thought-out reforms.

Four main criticisms stand out from the detail:

- the institutional structure;
- the franchise structures and concentration in the industry;
- the periodic review;
- the enforcement regime.

7.1 Institutional Structure

The institutional structure matters because it creates the incentives for regulators; sets the framework for the relationship between politicians, civil servants and regulators; and provides the context within which personalized discretion is exercised. The railways are unique in that the functions of regulation are split three ways – between the Department of Environment,

Transport and the Regions (DETR), the SRA and ORR. Yet, as was shown above, there is an intimate relationship between the government funding, the determination of investment and the TACs. None can be set independently of any of the others. Each institution operates under different rules and different duties. Each has a considerable degree of personalization: it matters that it is Prescott, Morton and Winsor, and not, say, Strang, Salmon and Swift. The words 'I' and 'me' and 'my' litter the decisions of each.

This personalization is not the fault of the individuals (although how it is used is itself a matter of discretion). It is a fault systemic to the institutional structure, and follows the UK administrative tradition of preferring to appoint 'good chaps' rather than subject authorities to the rules of law and judicial procedure. The extent of this personalized discretion problem was recognized by the government in the Green Paper, 'A Fair Deal for Consumers: Modernising the Framework for Utility Regulation', March 1998, and half-corrected in the Utilities Act 2000 through the creation of a board for the new Gas and Electricity Markets Authority. But it was only half, in that the general duties which provide the scope for the exercise of discretion were not constrained in the Utilities Act, but, in practice, were made even more general by introducing a new primary and overarching duty to look after consumers.

The SRA already has a board structure, although the effect has been limited, in that most perceive Morton's views as dominant. ORR does not. There is little reason to allow this weakness to continue, and much to be said for bringing ORR's corporate governance into line with the Utilities Act approach. The Communication White Paper, 'A New Future for Communications', December 2000, takes a similar line.

Constraining personal discretion will not, however, solve the problem of institutional competition between ORR and the SRA, and this problem has, in part, been recognized in the Transport Bill 2000. ORR is to have regard to the SRA's position, which, in turn, comes under departmental guidance. These steps, while introducing some coherence, will not, however, prevent future divergences, since the regulation of Railtrack's performance and TACs bears directly on the SRA's chances of success. The SRA will also be involved in investment itself through the new fund set up under the ten-year plan.

Furthermore, behind the different individuals lie two rather different ideas about the role of Railtrack in infrastructure development. I shall stylize these to illustrate the point. One vision is of a traditional vertical separation between the network and the service providers. The core network provider is regulated and acts in the interests of its users, the TOCs and freight companies. It has a legal guarantee that its regulator ensures that its functions can be financed. Debt is the main instrument, and, *provided* the guarantee binds, it might not be bound by normal historic-cost indicators. It is a bond-generating machine, and its balance sheet is more like a *private* sector borrowing requirement. Its cost of capital should consequently be low. Service providers, by contrast, have few assets, and are primary equity vehicles.

The alternative view is a much messier and pluralistic one. It regards vertical separation as artificial, and investment is determined by a mix of market evolution and franchise 'deals' that can be struck with regulators. Competition is not only unnecessary in service provision, but can limit the scope of 'deals'. A series of vertically integrated monopolies, regulated by the SRA, forms a possible extension of this model. Regulating railways is then about selling monopolies on the basis of 'deals', and then engaging with them in a 'partnership'. Of course, neither of these versions is advocated in pure form by either ORR or the SRA. Yet one can discern a marked difference between them, and it is not hard to see where Morton's and Winsor's preferences lie. (As will be argued below, there is much to recommend the vertical separation model.)

These differences are inevitable when discussing any industry structure. We cannot know what future cost structures will look like. In the railways, however, much is given. Passengers will use stations where trains will stop. Trains will continue to travel on steel tracks for the foreseeable future. The essential public nature of its transportation system will remain: individualization which is facilitated by the car is not a near-term prospect for rail travel. In other words, although signalling, ticketing and coordination may be revolutionized, the basics look likely to be with us for a decade or so at the very least.

It would not matter much that regulators diverged if it were not for the effects on the behaviour of the firms. But regulatory discretion within a multiple institutional structure has two effects: it delays commitment to investment; and it raises the cost of capital. This is reflected not only in Railtrack's cost of capital, but also in that of the TOCs. That Railtrack's investors need an 8 per cent real pre-tax rate of return to invest in the infrastructure,[5] with the regulator having, in effect, a duty to ensure that they can finance their functions, is a reflection of the risks they face, not only in project management, but also from the behaviour of each regulator separately, *and* the interaction between them. Such regulatory risk premia are not, of course, confined to railways: the UK regulatory regime for utilities has generally been associated with costs of capital which are very high by international standards. It is just that it is worse on the railways.

Does it matter? In a mature utility business – such as a gas transmission company or a distribution REC – the answer is probably 'not much'. They undertake little investment. But for water and railways, every 1 per cent on the cost of capital is multiplied through the CAPEX and RAB into the cost base. Higher costs of capital mean higher charges to customers, higher subsidies from government, and a bias in the technique of investment towards more short-term solutions.

Thus, to summarize, the fragmented nature of rail regulation, coupled with the exercise of personal discretion, has led to delays in the process of solving the principal problems of subsidy, TACs and investment requirements, and has put up the cost of capital. The result is detrimental to customers and government. The railways in the next decades will be less good than they could have been. Fortunately, although these institutional problems are of the government's making (this one and the last), they can be remedied. I propose two solutions: a short-term agreement within the scope of the Transport Act; and a longer-term one.

The starting point is to recognize that it was a mistake to set up the SRA while retaining a separate ORR. They should have been merged – and, indeed, the longer-term solution is to legislate to do so, and thereby rectify the fault in the Transport Act 2000. In the shorter term, much more coherence can be achieved within the existing legislation. The Transport Act gives the Secretary of State the power to give guidance to the SRA, and it requires the rail regulator to take account of the SRA. These powers could be exercised in the form of a clear statement by the Secretary of State on how the two bodies are to 'join up' their activities. All sorts of devices could be used: consultations could be joint; comments by each on the other's proposal could be formally published alongside consultation documents; and so on.

Such measures would help. But more significant steps could be taken. The Shadow SRA has managed to act 'as if' it existed legally for some time. OFFER and Ofgas were effectively merged before the Utilities Act 2000 was passed. The existing powers might be retained, but (as in the OFFER/Ofgas case) the same person could be appointed rail regulator and chairman of the SRA. Other options include the Rail Regulator becoming a member of the SRA Board, and SRA Board members sitting in on ORR decision-making processes.

These suggestions are, of course, far from ideal, but point the way to more coherence and consistency. It remains a central difficulty that the rail regulator has powers vested in *him*, rather than in a Board of ORR, while the SRA has a Board. There is, however, nothing to prevent the rail regulator appointing an advisory Board, and acting *as if* the Board made decisions by binding his decisions to those which would normally follow those of his Board. The minutes could be published along with any dissenting comments.

In other words, a single regulatory body could *de facto* be erected now, in advance of a longer-term solution abolishing the rail regulator and ORR. Discretion would not, in consequence, be entirely eliminated, nor indeed should it be. However, the objective of these reforms is to remove the personal part, and have the discretion exercised in a corporately responsible way through a board.

There would remain the question of appeal and the introduction of proper checks and balances. Judicial review has the merit of keeping regulators on their toes, and preventing sloppy arguments and processes being used. In a democracy, it is hard to see why unelected appointed officials should be immune from the normal reach of judicial review. There was *no* case for barring appeals to the Competition Commission, and the Transport Act 2000 rightly remedied this. The recent examples of the Mid Kent and Sutton & East Surrey appeals to the Competition Commission, and the Camelot-instigated judicial review of the Lottery Commission demonstrate how effective such appeals can be. It is hard to argue that either has done anything but good to the conduct of regulation in the UK.

7.2 Franchise Structures: Duration, Vertical Integration and Horizontal Concentration

The second deficiency of the current regulatory regime is the franchising process and, in particular, the way in which franchises are being re-let. As with the regulatory institutions, there are fundamental flaws in the design, but also practical steps that can alleviate some of the consequent problems.

(i) Prices, output or subsidy

The idea of franchising is a very simple one. There are property rights that convey an element of market power. This market power necessitates regulation. Franchising allows competition *for* monopoly. It is used in many areas under a variety of guises – from water concessions to third-generation mobile licences to pizza-house brands.

Typically, the franchising authority fixes the price that can be charged and the general nature of the services to be provided. The competitive bidding process then allocates the franchises to the firms for which they have the highest value. However, it is equally plausible to sell franchises at unconstrained prices, thereby realizing the monopoly rents to government, or to give the franchises away to companies that offer the greatest level of service at lowest prices to customers.

In the railways' case, all three factors have come into play. The government wants to minimize the subsidy, but also to fix prices (RPI–1), and the SRA wants to maximize outputs and investment. Franchising bidding will be less efficient where the trade-offs between subsidy, quality and investment are ill defined, since bidders will not know how to configure their bids to maximize the benefits to the client – in this case, the SRA. Indeed, the absence of clear criteria on which bids will be judged is a major weakness of the current exercise. It may even lead to problems such as those experienced by the Lottery Commission.

(ii)   Optimal length

A second problem with franchising is to design the optimal length. How many years should a franchisee be given? The simplistic answer is that there should be a matching of the investment horizon with the franchise, so that TOCs have incentives to invest, knowing they have a captive market to recoup their expenditure.

It is immediately apparent that this is a nonsense if more than one type of investment is involved. TOCs invest in many aspects of the rail business – from advertising, customer services, new trains, car parks, stations, and so on. Some have long pay-back periods, others do not.

But, even if the franchise period is shorter than the pay-back period, there is not necessarily a problem because many new assets will be needed for the next franchise period, and, hence, can be sold on. As noted above, they are, in economic terms, often fixed, but not always 'sunk'. A quick glance at TOCs' assets indicates that trains are rarely sunk, and, indeed, the ROSCO leasing agreements mean that they may not even be TOC assets at all. It should be well within the capabilities of a franchising office to organize an orderly transfer of such assets. (Again, the lottery provides an example.)

There can then be little defence for the choice of long franchise periods. The real motive appears to have been to offer long monopolies in exchange for more up-front promises of investment. But, as noted above, why should TOCs perform better once the franchise has been let? Once they have the franchise, might they not enjoy what John Hicks once described as 'the quiet life'?

The answer appears to be that the SRA will monitor their behaviour and conduct regular reviews – perhaps every five years. This equates much more closely to the RPI–X-type periodic review, but without the support of a licence. What will the SRA actually do? Will it take franchises away? It is clear that once the franchise has been granted, the TOCs ought really to have an altogether more powerful bargaining position. However, the very real threat of loss of franchise that currently hangs over them gives considerable regulatory leverage.

It has been argued that the short-period franchises give rise to the 'end-of-period problem': that a franchisee will have less incentive to perform towards the end of the period if there is a positive probability that it might not be renewed. However, this is clearly a very weak argument: either the franchisee tries to impress the regulator to continue; or the stick of monitoring and enforcement – which the SRA believes will succeed with very long franchises – will work.

What then should be done? In the long run, it would be better not to grant such long-lived franchises and to consider ways of increasing competition. However, since much of the damage has already been done, the emphasis needs to shift on to the regular reviews. These need to be made formal, and to act as the resetting of the price and outputs in the franchise contract. Long-term franchising will inevitably mean monopoly and the regulation that goes with it. Periodic reviews for TOCs will then look more like those for Railtrack, and this gives a further reason for consolidating regulation in one merged institution.

(iii) Vertical integration: the content of franchises

Much has been made of the desire to encourage franchise bidders to come up with lots of investment ideas. This arose from the SRA's recognition that Railtrack's balance sheet would not stretch far enough to meet the SRA's strategic objectives, and because of a more relaxed attitude towards the infrastructure/service split discussed above. Some elements of vertical integration had already been experimented with – Stagecoach had been allowed to acquire Porterbrook (of which it subsequently disposed), and the West Coast Main Line deal brought Virgin and Railtrack into a closer relationship.

There are three possible reasons for encouraging TOCs to move into infrastructure areas: they might be more efficient capital project managers; they might have more incentives to get the job done since they are the partial beneficiaries; and they may be able to finance projects more cheaply. None is convincing. Most TOCs grew out of bus companies with the associated managerial skills, culture and service-driven focus. They do not have a history of capital project management. Their incentives are no stronger than Railtrack's if infrastructure is rewarded when complete in the RAB. Their cost of capital is higher than Railtrack's.

These project-related issues need to be set in the wider context of the network. An *integrated* network is one where what happens in one part of the system has an effect on others. If train patterns in the Midlands are upgraded so more trains can run to London, then London stations will also need to be adjusted. Incremental investments which maximize returns to regional franchises are not necessarily optimal from the perspective of the network as a whole. That is why a Network Management Statement is needed.

This is not to suggest that TOCs and Railtrack should not cooperate in designing network improvements, nor that TOCs should not, on relevant occasions, be involved in project management. But the vertical move from TOCs to Railtrack's core activities is unlikely to be optimal, and, to the extent that it entrenches further the incumbent franchise, it may limit subsequent competition.

(iv)   Horizontal concentration

The emergence of a small number of dominant bus companies in the franchise market has given rise to speculation that yet more concentration may occur. The bus market concentrated around ninety firms after deregulation to just three major players within a decade, with the need for constant intervention by the Office of Fair Trading.

Even if the franchises are for the same period, it is important to have a number of comparators, to inform informationally poor regulators. In addition, the pool of future bidders will affect the ability to threaten, and, in some cases, carry out, franchise replacement.

7.3   Criticism of the Periodic-review Process

The periodic review has been a long-drawn-out affair that has tried to establish the revenue requirements of Railtrack without a clear idea of what the company is supposed to do for that revenue flow. This problem of incompleteness was discussed above.

However, there are a number of elements of the package that can be established, and, in effect, that is what has been done. The RAB is independent of the outputs, and its determination requires judgements about the first-day premium and the treatment of investment in the first period. The cost of capital applies to two separate elements – the return on the RAB, and the return on new investments. The conventional utility approach is to fix the cost of capital once every five years, and then leave the company to either take the risk, or hedge its position. On the RAB element, there are considerable opportunities to securitize the value, and, hence, to allow the financial markets to provide a fixed cost of capital position. On the financing of forward-looking CAPEX, the position is quite different. The company faces project risk, regulatory risk that CAPEX may not be incorporated in the RAB, and enforcement risk.

Breaking the cost of capital down into its constituent parts, there is a case for allowing some adjustment to the risk-free rate through time. For example, suppose, for the sake of argument, that central bankers took an aggressive policy of raising real interest rates. Would it be sensible to handicap the utility for another x years as a result? Other things being equal, a rise in interest rates would depress the share price, and, hence, its prospects for a rights issue would weaken. There is then a case for taking a more imaginative approach to the forward-looking cost of capital from that taken so far in the periodic review, and providing more flexibility in a mechanistic and predictable way.

Rectifying the cost of capital problem – the fact that it is so high – would require a number of more demanding changes to the regulatory regime. These include some of the institutional measures discussed above to reduce the personalization of the regulatory regime, and to remove the conflicts and inconsistency between regulatory bodies. But, in addition, the concept of a fixed-price contract may also need to be readdressed.

RPI–X as a fixed-price contract regulatory regime is well designed to encourage mature (low-investment) utilities to drive down operating costs. It has worked well in the RECs and in Transco. The placing of risk on companies might raise the cost of capital, but, where there is little investment, it does not much matter. For water and rail, it is quite different. Add to that the uncertainty in rail of the CAPEX contract, and some form of risk-sharing with customers becomes more appropriate. Error-correction mechanisms, as I have argued elsewhere, have considerable attractions in this context.

For the other parts of the periodic review, the regulator has had to make assumptions about operating efficiency and the level of optimal expenditure. On the former, there is considerable uncertainty, and the regulator faces very serious informational asymmetries. The choice of comparators needs to be carefully selected. High enhancement expenditure has ambiguous effects on operating expenditure (OPEX), and, in the next period, the impact of oil prices will need to be considered. Despite detailed consultancy studies, the OPEX targets remain largely 'stabs in the dark'.

Finally, on enhancement investment, there is even greater uncertainty, and the periodic review is best regarded as a negotiation framework to be revised and updated as events – that is, CAPEX – unfold.

7.4 The Enforcement Regime

The area of regulation where the exercise of personal discretion has been greatest since Tom Winsor was appointed has been in the development of an enforcement regime, backed up by fines and model licence conditions. Indeed, the current rail regulator has criticized his predecessors for not choosing to use and develop this aspect of the individual's powers.

The concept that lies behind this approach is that the relationship between the rail regulator and Railtrack should be regarded rather like a commercial legal contract, and enforced in the normal way. Therefore, the argument goes, the way to improve performance is to set targets and then fine Railtrack when it fails to deliver.

The fines-based approach is one which has been heavily researched, and the incentive regime it creates depends on the size of the penalty and the probability that it will be applied, against the constraints – physical and in terms of costs – facing the regulated company. There is no evidence that this research has had any impact on the design of the enforcement regime for rail: about the choice of targets; the practicalities as investment increases; the impact of unanticipated volume growth; and distortions in resource allocation towards short-term objectives. The scale of the fines appears arbitrary.

In addition, there is likely to be a cost of capital effect since in this case the regulatory risk is hard to diversify. Investors, faced with headlines such as '£470m fine to be applied', 'the largest fine in corporate history', and so on, are unlikely to be encouraged to respond positively.

Taking these considerations together, it is hardly surprising that other regulators have not viewed their task in terms so strongly directed towards contract specification and enforcement. The key issue is the design, impact and costs of the regulatory instruments, and there is no evidence either that such a careful assessment has been done by ORR, or that the result is optimal.

8.   CONCLUSIONS

Rail regulation is not a happy story, and showed no signs of settling down even before the Hatfield accident. The fundamental shift of objectives towards the integrated transport strategy necessitated a change in the design of the regulatory regime and in the detail of regulatory conduct. An integrated transport strategy requires an integrated regulatory regime, but this has not been developed.

The poor performance of the rail industry has many causes. In this chapter, the focus has been on regulatory failure, and, in particular, those related to the periodic review and the franchising process. The costs of these failures have been large, and are likely to continue to dog the industry until substantive regulatory reform takes place.

A number of reforms have been proposed. The main one is to merge the SRA and ORR, in order to integrate the periodic review and the regulation of Railtrack with refranchising and franchise regulation. This institutional measure would also facilitate the reduction in personal discretion, thereby reducing regulatory risk and the cost of capital.

Such substantive reform would require legislation. However, much could be achieved in the short run by using the power in the Transport Act 2000 to bring ORR's conduct into line with that of the SRA. With the Secretary of State's guidance, ORR could, in practical terms, be integrated into the SRA, as Ofgas and OFFER worked as a single body in advance of the Utilities Act 2000. If the rail regulator were willing, he could exercise his personal powers by reference to an open, transparent process formally incorporating advice from the SRA and a board of advisers. With clear political intent, the parties could achieve much integration immediately. This institution reform would help to facilitate an evolution to a more coherent form of franchise regulation, and help to provide an integrated approach to network enhancement.

The alternative strategy – to try to make the existing division of powers and the personal agendas work better – is, I have argued, bound to fail. The result will be a continuation of the unhappy story of rail regulation to the detriment of customers, current and future.

NOTES

1. At the party conference, Mr Prescott had to explain to delegates why renationalization would not, in fact, be effected, on the extraordinary argument that this would make fat cats fatter!
2. New Labour Manifesto: *Because Britain Deserves Better*, 1997.
3. Since this could not be coordinated, the TACs have had to be fixed by ORR in the absence of any clear idea of what investment will, in fact, be required. The TACs are therefore bound to be reopened.
4. Note, also, the market reaction to the water periodic review and the Competition Commission reports on Mid Kent Water and Sutton & East Surrey.
5. Because of Railtrack's position, this will be a post-tax return.

CHAIRMAN'S COMMENTS

Tom Winsor

Dieter Helm's central thesis is that the fragmented nature of rail regulation, coupled with the exercise of personal discretion, has led to delays in the process of solving the principal problems of subsidy, track access charges and investment requirements and has put up the cost of capital. He proposes that, until further legislation can be introduced to merge the two organizations, the same person should be appointed as rail regulator and chairman of the Strategic Rail Authority. However, I find his arguments to be quite perverse and I propose to make just a few points in response.

My first point is that the existence of an independent regulator is surely essential if investors are to have the confidence which is required in order to facilitate the investment needed to renew and enhance the network. A situation where the person paying the bill (the SRA) decides how much the goods and services should cost would not be conducive to the efficient financing of investment in the railways. In the longer term, the SRA should therefore be able to achieve more with an independent regulator than without one.

My second point is that there has never been a 'fines culture' at the Office of the Rail Regulator. Neither has there been any fundamental shift in the ORR's stance towards Railtrack. I believe it is clear that urgent action was required shortly after my appointment to ensure that Railtrack addressed certain issues during the first control period. However, the periodic review enabled me to introduce a more robust incentive-based regime which is designed to promote efficient and sustained investment to improve the condition and performance of the network. Although the possibility of enforcement action (including monetary penalties) will remain, greater clarity about what Railtrack is expected to deliver and the implications of under (or over) delivery should greatly reduce the need for such action. This should also reduce perceived regulatory risk.

My third point is that many of the other changes I am introducing should reduce perceived regulatory risk, as well as providing better accountability. The key risks which investors are now concerned about therefore concern the company's ability to deliver (and the inevitable regulatory implications) rather than uncertainty about the regulator's reaction to particular circumstances (regulatory risk *per se*). In particular, the enhancement framework is intended to ensure that the terms upon which Railtrack undertakes enhancements to the network are clearly understood at the outset so that these terms can be adhered to. Similarly, model clauses for track access agreements should provide operators, Railtrack and their respective investors with greater clarity about the risk which they bear under their agreements so that they can manage this risk with their suppliers and customers. Finally, the proposed licence modifications in relation to the annual return, regulatory accounts and independent reporters should improve the quality of information available to the regulator and provide greater transparency for investors and customers.

My final point relates to the reasons why the allowed rate of return is higher than that allowed by other regulators. The first factor is that, compared with other utilities, Railtrack's profitability is a small proportion of overall expenditure or revenues and this means that any given shock will generally have a larger impact on profits, increasing its cost of capital. The second factor is that, given the scale of the programme which Railtrack is expected to finance, I concluded that it was appropriate to set the allowed rate of return towards the top end of the range for the estimated cost of capital. The third factor concerns the need for consistency with the approach adopted by other regulators to the generic elements of the cost of capital calculation. For the reasons given above, it is clear that regulatory risk does not provide any part of the explanation.

It is my genuine hope that following this period of turmoil in the UK railway system we can build on the foundations of the Transport Act 2000 to develop the railway and allow both Railtrack and the train operators to go about their business of meeting customers' needs.

3. Moving to a competitive market in water *

Colin Robinson

---

1. INTRODUCTION

Michael Beesley and Water

In the spring of 1996, when Michael Beesley and I were arranging the Sixth Series of Lectures in Regulation, Michael persuaded me to give a lecture about water, an industry in which he had a considerable interest from his involvement in its privatization and subsequent regulation. I had said to him that regulation of the industry seemed to be diverging from the pro-competitive paths being followed in the other utilities. Moreover, I suggested, most regulatory economists seemed to assume that the industry would be forever regulated following old-fashioned 'public economics' principles, as though its natural form was a group of regional monopolies which had to be tightly regulated (the idea implicit in the privatization scheme). Typically, Michael's response was that, if that was my feeling, I must give the lecture. There seemed no adequate answer, so, like many other people who have lectured in this Series, I ventured into unfamiliar territory on Michael's prompting.

It seemed to me that, in principle, there were just as good reasons for trying to stimulate competitive markets in water as in the other utilities. So, in the lecture,[1] I explained the case for competition and the case against detailed regulation of the whole industry. I also suggested that at least two major obstacles to competition would have to be surmounted: first, ownership of the pipelines by incumbent water suppliers which made entry very difficult; and second, the substantial power wielded by environmental regulators who might well obstruct the evolution of competitive markets.

Water Competition on the Political Agenda?

At the time, there was very little interest in water competition. Even though the Conservative government had issued a (rather weak) consultation paper on the subject, the idea was clearly not on the political agenda. But in the recent past there has been a significant change of attitude towards water competition. In yet another example of how today's 'politically impossible' can rapidly be transformed into tomorrow's consultation paper and the following day's government action (even if the 'following day' has not yet arrived in water), competition in the industry is an idea now taken seriously in the industry and in Whitehall. Moreover, some politicians, impressed by the benefits to gas and electricity consumers from market liberalization, may also see political advantages in moving to a competitive market in water.

The debate now in train, in which the obstacles to competitive markets in water are being emphasized, is a familiar one to those who have followed earlier attempts to liberalize previously nationalized industries. It is reminiscent, for example, of the late 1980s when electricity was being privatized and the incumbent companies went to great lengths to stress the technical obstacles, indeed the dangers to the public, of actions which then appeared radical, such as splitting transmission from generation and giving consumers choice of supplier. The lights would go out, it was said, a warning (false though it was) designed to strike fear into the hearts of politicians, as is the claim now sometimes heard that water competition might compromise public health and safety. To its credit, the government pressed ahead with electricity privatization (albeit with a flawed scheme) in a move which was quite bold in the circumstances.

Differences Among the Major Players

Water competition may now have moved on to the political agenda, if only its outer bounds but, not surprisingly, there appear to be significant differences among the major players in their attitudes towards it. Many water companies seem to regard it as a threat and would prefer to maintain the *status quo*, even though they are not particularly enamoured of the degree of prescriptive regulation to which they are subject. Some of the more enterprising companies, however, can see benefits in lifting the constraints which now prevent them from behaving like innovative companies in a rivalrous market. Some are also thinking about possible structural change, as the 'Kelda proposal' (which I will discuss later) indicates.

Major consumers seem generally to favour more competition, as one would expect, and they have been pressing the regulator and the government to give them the choice they have in other utility markets.[2] Pressure from large consumers was very important in both gas and electricity in helping regulators with pro-competition duties to liberalize the relevant markets. Unlike unorganized small consumers, large companies – acting in their purchasing capacities – can be effective lobbyists for change, so their actions in water are very significant.[3]

The government itself is being extremely cautious. Its consultation paper in May 2000[4] proposed to lower the threshold for inset appointments from 250 to 100 megalitres per year – hardly path-breaking since the regulator had been urging such a change for some time – and to allow insets for co-located premises which, taken together, exceed the threshold. The rest of the consultation paper is mainly devoted to an exercise in which the UK civil service excels – explaining how difficult it is to make any change whatsoever from the existing situation. Other moves may be afoot. Some press reports late in 1999 indicated that the government might change the Director General of Water Services (DGWS)'s pro-competition duty from 'to facilitate' to 'to promote'.[5]

However, the outgoing water regulator, in introducing his 1999–2000 annual report, was much more positive. Sir Ian Byatt said competition in the utilities was 'one of the real achievements of the decade'[6] and continued,

> We have learned that competition can co-exist with monopoly business. For gas and electricity this has come about through competitive use of existing networks, through common carriage. The same principles apply to water.

Furthermore,

> Looking into the future, the focus of Ofwat may shift towards the role of a competition authority. Regulation is now mature. As I see it, the next big challenge to the companies is to develop the competition that can progressively deliver benefits to customers. Ofwat's task will be to encourage and facilitate that process.

If Ian's successor pursues the path set out so clearly in that statement, there will be some very significant changes in the water industry.

Structure of the Chapter

In the rest of this chapter, I want to

- assess, first, the performance of the regulatory regime in water relative to the other utilities, examining some of the characteristics of the present system, such as competition by comparison and the place and impact of quality and environmental regulation;
- consider, second, the pressures for change and what an appropriate reaction might be. In particular, I will look at the extent to which structural change in water and a revised environmental regime might be necessary conditions for a competitive market.

I will concentrate on the water sector, though I think the principles should be equally applicable to sewerage.

2.   PERFORMANCE OF THE REGULATORY SYSTEM

Regulatory Failure

As I shall refer frequently to 'regulatory failure', I should make clear that this does not mean that I am criticizing Ian for his achievements as water regulator. Regulatory failure is the counterpart of government failure in public choice theory[7] and represents the opportunity cost of regulation – the extent to which the regulatory system fails to capture the benefits for producers and consumers which would have been expected in a competitive market.

'Regulatory failure' in water seems to me the consequence of the whole regime laid down at the time of privatization – the vertically integrated regional monopolies, the weak pro-competition duty (to 'facilitate', rather than to 'promote'), the *de facto* prohibition on water-to-water mergers and the general sense of the scheme that prescriptive regulation is the natural way to supervise the water industry. This scheme has been little changed by subsequent legislation and its logical conclusion has been the present state of the water industry in England and Wales where regulation, based on price caps, intrudes into all corners of the industry.

Many economists will say, what is wrong with that? They would argue that regulation will give the protection to consumers which, in other markets, would be provided by competition. What competition can do for consumers, regulation can do just as well. A traditional objective of regulation has, of course, been to simulate the outcome of a competitive market. Indeed, on occasion Ian has set out a similar aim. In *Prospects for Prices*,[8] for example, he said that 'The efficiency targets for companies set by the Director at the Periodic Review would be a proxy for a competitive market.'

But, as I pointed out in the lecture four years ago, such an aim of regulation assumes that the outcome of a competitive market can be observed *ex ante*. If it cannot, it is difficult to see how a regulator can usefully take as an objective an outcome which, by definition, is unobservable. He or she will never know what the target should be and will never be able to check whether it has been achieved.

To illustrate, take the case of efficiency savings which have been such a crucial part of water regulation. In a competitive market, there is no need for regulation to produce efficiency improvements. Companies which are rivals will automatically set standards for each other. Even companies which appear to have strong market positions will behave as though they were in competitive conditions, and have a powerful incentive to be innovative and efficient, provided there is a credible threat of entry. Benchmarks thus automatically appear because of the activities of competitors, actual or potential. Innovations in products, services and management methods emerge naturally as companies seek an edge over their competitors. In such markets, there is a continuing trend to improve quality and reduce costs as part of a competitive process in which firms discover new and improved ways of doing things.

The notion that the outcome of such a competitive process can be simulated defies belief. If one thinks of competition as a state like the long-run equilibrium of perfect competition, it is tempting to believe that a regulator could locate the right price (equal to long-run marginal cost) and impose it: the correct quantity of output would then follow. But, outside such abstract circumstances, if competition is more usefully depicted as the process I have described, its outcome is unknowable. It is not possible to have the outcome without going through the process. Neither a regulator nor any of the participants in the industry knows what costs, quality standards and prices would have emerged in a competitive market.

Another way of putting the same point is, as Hayek argued,[9] to say that knowledge is essentially decentralized and cannot be gathered together at a central point such as a Whitehall department or a regulator's office. It emerges from millions of decentralized decisions. A problem inherent in a regulated industry is therefore not so much information asymmetry as information shortage: the information production process either does not exist or is attenuated. No matter how technically advanced the economic analysis, the information used by a regulator relates to the past and is of questionable relevance to an uncertain future. Of course, the problem of forecasting is essentially insoluble, in competitive or regulated conditions, because uncertainty always exists. It is 'solved' imperfectly in a competitive market because there are competing forecasts and plans which are factors in the success or failure of particular firms. Moreover, entrepreneurial rivalry means that firms continually find new ways of doing things, thus shaping the future rather than just adapting passively to it.

But, in an industry entirely subject to regulation, these processes of information provision and adaptation barely exist. The regulator must take a single, central view of the future and so the difficulties of forecasting are maximized. Indeed, the problems of forecasting and planning which arise are similar to those under central planning. In the debate about the possibility of 'socialist calculation' in the interwar years, both Mises and Hayek explained that, in the absence of prices determined by markets (rather than by planners) it is not possible for socialist planning to place the appropriate weights on competing projects. Hayek stressed the learning process implicit in competitive markets, whereas Mises emphasized the importance of entrepreneurial activity. Between them, they produced a comprehensive refutation of the idea that socialist planning can simulate the outcome of a competitive market system and, in that sense, produce efficient outcomes.[10] And they did so 50 years before socialist planning was discredited in practice. I am not suggesting that the UK's utility regulators are socialist planners but it is important to recognize that, when their efforts are unaided by markets, they face many of the same problems.

To be more specific, there is a case *faute de mieux* for regulation in two sets of circumstances, both of which apply in UK utilities. One is when a market long monopolized by one or more state corporations (a 'pre-competitive' market) is being opened up to competition and regulation concentrates on promoting a competitive process. That form of regulation, which attempts to start the process, rather than guessing what the outcome of the process will be, is quite different from traditional regulation.[11] Moreover, it is, in principle, automatically time-limited, since it should fade away as competitive markets develop. I am not, of course, claiming that in practice it will always fade away.

The other case in which regulation is justified is in the supervision of very strictly defined natural monopolies, such as networks of pipes and wires, shorn of all potentially competitive activities (such as storage, meter provision and meter reading) as they have been in gas and electricity. In the natural monopoly case, there are alternatives to regulation such as periodic franchising which may have advantages because of the danger that regulation will entrench a 'natural monopoly' which would otherwise be undermined by technological and economic change.

But the case I am discussing – water in England and Wales – is one in which a whole industry is being regulated. Any natural monopolies have not been separated from potentially competitive sectors. There is only the feeblest element of competition. In such circumstances, it seems to me inevitable that severe regulatory failure will occur, regardless of who is regulating the industry and what methods are used. I now consider two examples of regulation in water to illustrate regulatory failure. The first is the concentration on comparative competition; the second is environmental regulation.

Competition by Comparison

Competition by comparison is, in my view, inherently inferior to real market competition. It involves static comparisons among companies operating in a non-competitive market where the powerful entrepreneurial incentives to innovate which exist in a genuine competitive market are absent. So, if real competition can be introduced – as I think it could be in water, for reasons I shall explain later – there is no justification for using its inferior substitute.

But let us consider the comparative competition regime in water a little further. Let us assume that, though the prevailing wisdom now accepts that competition in water is a possibility, the powers-that-be were not so persuaded in the early days. So some means of making the best of that bad job was required. Given that assumption, how can one assess the comparative competition regime in water?

A key condition for success in a comparative competition regime is that the only difference among the 'competing' companies should be in their efficiencies.[12] In those circumstances, comparisons can be used to bring down everyone's costs to the lowest in the industry. If each firm's price is set at the average cost of the rest of the firms in the industry, each firm will have an incentive to reduce its costs and costs will eventually be minimized (though that 'minimum' may be above what would have prevailed in a genuinely competitive industry).

But if there are differences among the companies, other than their efficiencies, which affect their costs, useful comparisons become rather difficult. There might, for example, be economies of scale in an industry where companies differ in size; the cost environments of companies might differ; quality of service might vary across companies; and accidents and random events might affect comparisons made at particular points in time. Plainly, such differences are likely to affect comparisons among water companies. As Colin Mayer put it in this Lecture Series seven years ago,

> There are numerous specific factors that influence the minimum-cost base of firms: density of population, age of infrastructure and endowments of natural resources (rivers, reservoirs) are some examples. In practice, it has therefore proved to be formidably difficult to establish 'relevant' determinants of performance in the water industry.[13]

As well as such fundamental differences, there may be differences in accounting conventions among companies which affect comparisons when they are carried out separately for capital and operating expenditures. In principle, it should be possible to standardize these conventions but in practice it is probably quite difficult. Another issue is the likely correlation between capital and operating costs, though Ofwat is well aware of this.

Because of the large number of variables which determine costs in the water industry, a comparative competition regime gravitates naturally towards econometric analyses which attempt to standardize for the numerous 'explanatory' variables in order to estimate efficiency differences. These analyses, as used in water, seem to me to provide a flimsy basis for efficiency assessments. I do not blame Ofwat for trying them, but it seems to me it is time to leave them behind, as appears to be the implication of Ian's remarks about the desirability of stimulating competition in water.

Some early Ofwat research papers, published in 1993 and 1994, are careful investigations of the problem of specifying cost models in the water industry and of estimating company efficiencies.[14] As one of the papers explains,[15] the approach is to formulate a general model based on industry knowledge of the factors likely to influence costs; to simplify that model to the most parsimonious version compatible with the data; and then to evaluate the model using standard econometric procedures for testing the residuals.

Results of the tests were set out both for the water and for the sewerage sectors. However, in the papers for the 1999 Periodic Review, so far as I can see, Ofwat did not give information on what such econometric tests would now show. Apart from the coefficients in the equations, only standard errors and the values of R^2 were shown. The values of R^2 ranged from the incredibly high (0.99) for the water services power model to the surprisingly low for the distribution model.

Values of R^2 are not of much use unless one can see the results of the econometric tests, so there is no basis for judging how much weight can be placed on the econometric results. More generally, anyone who has worked with the kinds of data used in water industry models knows how difficult it is to capture the complexities of the real world in simple models confined to a few 'independent' variables. There is frequently a conflict between using a model which seems comprehensive in theoretical terms and the simplification required for statistical analysis. Often, as in the case of water, trying to use comprehensive explanatory data may reduce the number of degrees of freedom too much for the results to remain significant. In any case, attempts at using large numbers of explanatory variables usually encounter multicollinearity so that intractable problems arise in attempts to estimate the separate effects of the independent variables.

Although, as I have explained, it is hard to judge the models in the absence of details of the econometric test results, a general examination suggests some serious reservations. The water models, in particular, have very few explanatory variables: it seems implausible that they are properly specified given the differences in operating environments of the companies. Use of the models is, of course, laced with 'judgement'. But the water companies may have some grounds for complaint that the process of applying this judgement is rather opaque. Judgement needs to be founded on a more solid basis than is, I suspect, provided by these models. It seems to me a case of interesting research results being asked to bear a weight that is too much for them.

Summing up on the comparative competition regime which has been such an integral feature of water regulation, there are two major problems:

1. Comparative competition has been used when there could have been real competition.
2. The circumstances of the industry are not propitious for using comparative competition and the actual regime is a reflection of the resulting problems.

Another difficulty lies in the unintended and sometimes perverse consequences of the regime. Indeed, for students of unintended consequences there is a real classic. Use of comparative competition produces a fear that there will not be sufficient 'comparators'. In water, this has meant the imposition of a rather absurd ban on water-to-water takeovers.[16] The chain of consequences is fascinating. The absence of product market competition makes entry to the industry or to another regional monopolist's market very difficult. Therefore, the takeover route becomes more attractive than it would otherwise be. But the authorities do not want takeovers of water companies by water companies because of the loss of comparators. Therefore such takeovers are blocked. Hence the perverse result that, in an industry where there is little product market competition, the resulting problems are compounded because the attachment to comparative competition means that the market for corporate control cannot be allowed to function properly either.

Environmental Regulation

Moving away from 'economic' regulation, a characteristic of water is the specific place of the environmental regulators, both home-grown and from Brussels. As is well known, the major factor which resulted in water prices increasing up to the last Periodic Review was the effect of EU environmental directives.[17]

At the 1999 Periodic Review, Ian sought advice on an environmental improvement programme from ministers[18] (who were advised by the Environment Agency[19]). He placed responsibility firmly on the politicians to decide what environmental improvements there should be, within the constraints imposed by EU obligations. Given the regulatory regime, that is clearly where the responsibility should lie.

But how is anyone to determine the proper scale of such improvements, or even what constitutes an 'improvement', when consumers are not making direct choices about the quality of the product they purchase (and indeed where individual choice appears not to be a practical proposition)? Consumer surveys about environmental and quality improvements are obviously unsatisfactory because, in them, consumers are making hypothetical choices, not real choices in which demand is expressed by willingness to pay.

Later I will discuss what a better 'environmental' regime might be, but let me first state why it seems to me that the present system almost certainly results in excessive investment in environmental 'improvement'. It is claimed that environmental regulation is essential in water, as elsewhere, because of the environmental externalities which markets fail to take into account, the general effect of which is to cause excessive environmental degradation. But that view fails to recognize the presence of regulatory failure, one likely result of which is to cause over-expansion of regulation.

A model of regulation which assumes that regulators are wise and disinterested servants of the public good, simply engaged in rectifying 'market failures', is unlikely to lead to useful predictions of their behaviour. Scientific knowledge is not sufficient for anyone to be really wise about environmental issues; regulators are not a breed apart; and the 'public good' is invariably impossible to define. So real-world regulation is unlikely to be conducted by knowledgeable, far-sighted and altruistic individuals but, more likely, by people who respond to the incentives they face much like anyone else.[20]

An unusual feature of a regulator's position is that he or she has the power to coerce – to make others undertake actions which they may find very costly. These costs which are imposed on others, certainly in the environmental field, are typically far larger than any costs borne by the regulator. The costs which fall on the regulatory agency are usually insignificant compared with those imposed on regulated companies (and indirectly on the consumer): in the United States, for example, the costs borne by regulators appear to be only about 2 per cent of compliance costs.[21] So, with the bulk of the costs external to the regulator, regulatory activity is likely to be over-expanded. Thus the common complaints about regulators building empires have some theoretical foundation.

There are other reasons why regulatory activity tends to expand. Politicians favour regulation because it is a low-cost means of appearing to be busy solving problems. Pressure groups will often seek regulation which can, for example, be a useful means for incumbents to keep out competitors, for unions to protect their members from competition or for single-issue interest groups to impose their views on the rest of the community via regulatory action.[22]

In environmental matters, there is never any problem in thinking of actions which could be taken in the name of 'improving' the quality of water or the environment generally. Regulators unconstrained by costs are likely to want to keep on making such 'improvements'. In health and safety matters, in particular, regulators have a strong incentive to show they have done everything technically possible (regardless of cost) so they will appear blameless if accidents occur. In addition, they have the usual technocratic incentive to operate at the frontiers of knowledge: they derive psychic income from being there.

In sum, therefore, I see serious problems with environmental regulation in the water industry. It is not constrained by costs. Nor is it constrained by a duty to promote or even facilitate competition. There is not much to stop its continued burgeoning. Cost–benefit assessments are, in general, not the answer because the relevant costs and benefits of any action lie in the future. They involve so much guesswork that it is not difficult for advocates of regulatory action to show that any measure they wish to implement has an excess of estimated benefits over estimated costs.

3.   PRESSURES FOR CHANGE AND HOW TO RESPOND

Contrasts with Gas and Electricity

The contrast between the water industry and the electricity and gas industries is illuminating. The gas and electricity regulators (now one) have used their pro-competition duties to pare away so-called natural monopolies and have stimulated competition in the rest of their industries. The result is choice for all consumers and substantially lower prices for those who switch supplier (around 20 per cent in gas and 10 per cent in electricity). Many people in the gas and electricity companies who used to be against establishing competitive markets have come to believe that competition has had beneficial effects. The stock market certainly rates the results highly.

In water, the privatization scheme has combined with the regulatory regime implicit in that scheme to produce much less satisfactory results. Water companies and their investors are concerned at how prescriptive regulation has become – with particular concern about regulatory estimates of the cost of capital – and water company shares have been depressed since the last Periodic Review because of the perception that rates of return will remain poor.[23] Water company bonds are poorly rated relative to corporate bonds in general. Yet increasingly detailed regulation is inevitable in an industry which is regulated in its entirety: as the regulatory game is played, companies will try to exploit loopholes which the regulator will then try to close, leading to more and more rules.[24]

It is this contrast between the perceived success of liberalization in gas and electricity and concern about the state of the regulated water industry which seems to be the principal reason why water competition is moving on to the political agenda. As I have explained, it is significant that the pressure from larger consumers to be able to choose supplier has been mounting.

Another issue in water is that political interference has re-emerged, for example in the form of 'water summits' and instructions to cut water leakage. Politicians who observe a regulator taking over many of the key investment and pricing decisions in an industry are bound to become jealous of the regulator's power and want to assume some of it themselves. Most likely, water will become subject to more and more political intervention, until eventually it reverts to a high degree of state control (though not state ownership), unless the regime is changed towards more competition.

Establishing Competitive Markets

Ian has identified the way forward as competitive markets along the lines of gas and electricity. There are signs that the political will, if not there yet, might be just around the corner. How might such markets be established? First, it is helpful to bear in mind the similarities between water and the other network utilities where competition has been successfully introduced. As in gas and electricity, the 'production' end of the industry is potentially competitive and so is the supply. The network of pipes is naturally monopolistic in the same sense as are the networks of pipes (in gas) and wires (in electricity). So there is no reason in principle not to apply the major insight which Michael Beesley and others had about the UK privatized network utilities: that significant competition can be introduced into industries previously considered natural monopolies by separating the network elements and promoting competition in production, supply, storage and any other sectors which are naturally rivalrous markets. The benefits of applying that insight are now clear in both gas and electricity.

One difference from the other utilities, it is claimed, is that there is no national grid in water. Though obviously correct, the argument is an irrelevance when considering competition in water. The existence of a series of regional grids with little interconnection is a symptom of there having been no competition in the past rather than a pointer to the future. If an industry is established as a group of regional monopolists, each of which has customers who are essentially captives, the incentives to connect to other monopolists' systems are minimal. The absence of metering for over 80 per cent of domestic consumers is another problem which has arisen because of the lack of competitive markets in the past.[25] It is hard to imagine that a company competing with others would be unconcerned about how much its household consumers were using and about whether or not they could receive price signals.

Other claimed differences were discussed in my lecture four years ago – for example, public objections to the establishment of new sources of water supply, the problem of mixing different sources in a common network and the division of regulatory functions between 'economic' and 'environmental'. Most of them seem to be versions of problems which have been overcome in the other network utilities. I will come later to the safety and environmental issues which loom so large in water.

Easing Entry

In general, to promote competition in water, it will be necessary to make entry easier to production and supply and to ensure that the owner or owners of the network(s) have no incentive to discriminate among those who wish to use it. To be more specific, the following steps seem necessary.

First, entry to production (including treatment and storage) will have to be made easier if a competitive market at the 'production' stage is to appear. At present, abstraction rights are issued by the Environment Agency, giving protected rights to the licensee: they are not directly tradable so it is difficult for potential entrants to find supplies they can exploit. The government already intends to change this regime, placing time limits on the licences,[26] but more radical action will be required to stimulate a competitive market. It may be possible to use the 1998 Competition Act if incumbents are relying on their protected rights to frustrate entry to the industry.[27] But a change to the licensing system, so licences are more freely available and are tradable, would be better.

Network Separation?

Second, as in all the network utilities, the transportation stage is crucial to the emergence of competition. Ofwat has used the Competition Act to force common carriage on the companies: all of them had published network access codes by end-August 2000.[28] But previous experience in gas and electricity (admittedly not under the new competition legislation) suggests that more is required. It will probably be necessary to separate the water distribution networks from the rest of the industry so that the means of distribution, the natural monopoly element, is in the hands of one or more bodies which have no interest in excluding newcomers. After a transition period, the pipes network would be the only water activity subject to regulation: elsewhere competition would protect consumers.

One of the best analyses of the case for network separation is in the 1993 Monopolies and Mergers Commission report on gas which, in a passage which reads like pure Beesley, said of British Gas that it was

> both a seller of gas and owner of the transportation system which its competitors have no alternative but to use. In our view, this dual role gives rise to an inherent conflict of interest which makes it impossible to provide the necessary conditions for self-sustaining competition.[29]

Separation is required in water, where the companies have the same 'dual role' which the MMC criticized in the case of gas, if entrants to water supply are to have access to potential customers. Accounting separation would be a start, but full structural separation is desirable. The idea of restructuring is beginning to take hold in water, where companies are seeking new forms of corporate organization in response to the pressures they feel.

One result was the interesting proposal made early in 2000, the 'Kelda solution', which would sell the assets of a water company to a customer-owned, not-for-profit debt-financed Registered Community Asset Mutual (RCAM). Operation of the assets would be contracted out. If the proposal were implemented, it could be a means of accomplishing network separation. However, it is different from the separation between networks and other activities which has taken place in other utilities, and not just because it is a proposal to return to mutuality just when mutuality was thought to be dying out, even in financial services where it used to be well established.

To the extent that it is a proposal to replace equity finance by debt finance, many economists will initially react against it. Debt-financing can often appear appealing to an organization which cannot earn an adequate return on its equity capital, but Modigliani and Miller taught us 40 years ago that the value of a company cannot be changed just by altering the method of financing.[30] Purely debt-financed organizations are risky for the debt-holders (in the Kelda case the customers) unless the activity is genuinely ultra low risk. If the activity is risky, moving to debt from a mixture of debt and equity imposes extra risks on the debt-holders: in the event, therefore, the cost of capital will not fall because no one will lend to the organization at a risk-free rate. So whether a 'Kelda solution' would work depends on whether the core which is sold to consumers consists entirely of very low-risk activities, with the rest hived off.

The Kelda proposal, as originally made, now appears dead. Ian's comments on it in July mean that no one is likely to suggest it for another company. He is reported to have said that, though he is not against mutuality in principle, equity ownership in water had worked well and should not be replaced by an untested and more risky structure. He said, as I think most economists would, that it was unclear 'that the proposal would necessarily bring any reduction in risks for the business as a whole'.[31]

But that does not mean that the idea behind the proposal has died also. The Kelda proposal appeared because of concern about the present structure of the water companies which has no real legitimacy: the structure has not evolved in response to market pressures but is a consequence of a particular form of privatization which was itself influenced by earlier forms of 'public' ownership. Shareholders and bondholders appear to be unhappy both with the regulatory regime and with the structure of the industry (which the presence of regulation makes it difficult to alter[32]).

So, whatever the imperfections of the Kelda proposal, it should, I think, be welcomed as evidence that thought is now being given to changing the structure of water companies. These companies do, after all, contain a mix of low-risk and much higher-risk activities which might benefit from separation. Separation, as I have explained, would ease the task of establishing competitive markets and, after an interim period, confine regulation to the natural monopoly network. An incidental consequence would be reduced regulatory risk which would, no doubt, be welcomed by water shareholders and bondholders. It would be very surprising if other water companies and entrepreneurs outside the water industry were not pursuing the idea of restructuring to obtain better value for shareholders and customers. In other privatized utilities, companies have voluntarily (though usually after some prompting by the regulator) separated out operations which were better run as separate businesses. British Gas is the outstanding example of a company which initially resisted change but where supply, pipelines and exploration and production activities either already are or soon will be in flourishing separate companies well regarded by their shareholders.

Constraining Environmental Regulation

A third awkward issue which will have to be tackled if there is to be a competitive water industry is to curb the powers of the environmental regulators. There is an element of denial on this subject: the conventional wisdom is so strongly in favour of more health and safety measures and more environmental protection, apparently regardless of cost, that very few people are willing to suggest that in some cases we might need less. But in an industry where environmental regulators, in the UK and in Brussels, have such an explicit role and can intervene at all stages of the industry with few constraints on their actions (other than Ian's letters to ministers about their preferred environmental programmes), proposals for competitive markets might often be opposed for apparently plausible environmental, health or safety reasons.

Under the present regime, as I have explained, environmental regulators have no incentive to seek such markets. Indeed, their incentives are more likely to favour the continuation of monopolies, which they will expect to control more easily. Because there are so few constraints on the regulations which might be imposed to 'improve' the quality of water and of the environment, I fear the present regime will produce an increasing edifice of regulation with costs which far exceed its benefits. I am not, of course, suggesting that environmental regulators are ill intentioned, but simply that their actions will be congruent with the incentives which they face.

In the long run, the answer to the problem of quality and environmental regulation in water is probably a much more light-handed approach with more emphasis on self-regulation. If there genuinely is a demand from consumers for water of improved quality and for increased environmental protection by water companies, the companies will have every incentive to satisfy that demand: by doing so, they will enhance their reputations and gain competitive advantage, bringing about a 'race to the top'.

Much of the 'regulation' which exists in society is voluntary rule-setting and the establishment of norms of behaviour through the regular interaction of consumers and producers.[33] It has many advantages over rule-setting by government officials and regulators. It arises from preferences revealed in markets and it is adaptive to changing circumstances. Officially set rules, as I have explained, cannot be assumed to be the outcome of a benign process and they often persist long after circumstances have changed: the Sunday trading regulations are an obvious example. As far as commercial behaviour is concerned, voluntary regulation does not exist in a vacuum but is underpinned by the need for consumers to be assured that they can trust their suppliers and for those suppliers to build up reputations which provide that trust relationship.[34]

The idea of voluntary regulation in water may seem startling, but it should be possible to move a long way in that direction to avoid the problems which will otherwise arise as quality and environmental regulation become tighter and tighter. Regulation could become less detailed and less prescriptive, allowing companies to set their own health, safety and environmental standards on which their reputations would then rest. Such a market-based regime would probably in the long run produce faster technological advance, improved safety and greater environmental protection as the standards set become an element of competitive advantage. If purely voluntary regulation in water seems an idea too far for the present, there could be a specific government-set inspection regime to check on the adequacy of company programmes which would be less prescriptive than the present regime. In the case of North Sea oil installations, for example, companies formulate their own safety plans ('safety cases') which have to be verified by an 'independent and competent' person – that is, someone who meets Health and Safety Executive definitions of 'independence' and 'competence'.[35] A similar system could be instituted in water.

In the shorter term, to make progress towards competitive markets some quicker-acting expedient is required. One way would be to place a constraint on environmental regulators by giving them a duty to promote competition so that their actions could be challenged if they were hindering the development of competitive markets.[36] The pro-competition duty is an important part of Britain's utility regulation system, because it acts as a check on regulators who might prefer to continue regulating rather than letting competitive markets develop. Yet it does not at present constrain the environmental regulators.

4.   CONCLUSIONS

My conclusion is that government ministers should now be thinking radical thoughts about a competitive water industry to replace the *de facto* planning regime which has evolved from a flawed privatization scheme. There are practical difficulties to be overcome but so there have been in all the markets that have been liberalized in recent years. *Ex ante*, many doubts were expressed about these liberalization programmes for other utilities, but most of the doubters seem to have been converted by the results of practical experience.

The present regime in water is surely not sustainable. Consumers, shareholders and managers are unhappy with it. In any case, it is unlikely to be maintained for the political reasons I mentioned earlier. But, given the state the industry is in now, a serious effort to consider and overcome the practical difficulties of liberalizing this remaining monopolized utility market should be very productive. By the early years of the twenty-first century there could be a genuine market system of incentives to increase efficiency and improve standards of service in water in place of the present excessive reliance on regulation. Indeed, economic regulation would be confined to the network of pipes and for a time, while there are still pre-competitive markets, to the promotion of competition. Environmental and safety regulation would, over a period, become less prescriptive and more a responsibility of the companies in the industry than of ministers or government-appointed regulators.

One argument used against proposals to liberalize water, as in earlier times against similar proposals for electricity and gas, is that it is too risky. It is claimed that nowhere in the world is there a competitive water market with minimal environmental and quality regulation by government of the kind I have suggested. This idea – that no country can ever make a move unless another country has done it first – is, of course, a recipe for inaction and the freezing of the *status quo* everywhere. There would still be monopolies in all Britain's utilities if the argument had been accepted in the 1980s and 1990s. Britain now has plenty of experience of successful utility liberalization schemes, if not in water. It seems a good time to make another bold move.

NOTES

1. Colin Robinson, 'Introducing Competition into Water', in M.E. Beesley (ed.), *Regulating Utilities: Broadening the Debate*, Readings 46, Institute of Economic Affairs, 1997.
2. For example, 'Water users demand competition', *The Financial Times*, 25 September 1997.
3. Robinson, 'Introducing Competition into Water', pp. 165–66 and Colin Robinson, 'Privatising the British Energy Industries: The Lessons to be Learned', *Metroeconomica*, **43**, 1–2, 1992.
4. Department of Environment, Transport and the Regions, *Competition in the Water Industry: Consultation Paper*, May 2000.

5. For example, 'Road to American dream never runs smooth', *The Financial Times*, 16 December 1999.
6. *Ofwat Press Release* 21/00, 11 May 2000.
7. For an explanation of public choice theory and its applications, see Gordon Tullock, Arthur Seldon and Gordon Brady, *Government: Whose Obedient Servant?*, Readings 51, Institute of Economic Affairs, 2000.
8. Ofwat, *Prospects for Prices: A Consultation Paper on Strategic Issues affecting Future Water Bills*, October 1998, p. 48. This statement does not claim that the traditional aim can be achieved – only that the DGWS is trying to set the efficiency targets which a competitive market would automatically have provided.
9. F.A. Hayek (1945), 'The Use of Knowledge in Society', *American Economic Review*, **35**, September, 519–30.
10. On the socialist side, principal contributions were by Oskar Lange, 'On the Economic Theory of Socialism, Parts I and II', in Benjamin M. Lippincott (ed.), *On the Economic Theory of Socialism*, Minneapolis, University of Minnesota Press, 1938, and Abba P. Lerner, 'A Note on Socialist Economics', *Review of Economic Studies*, October 1936. The views of Hayek and Mises are in Friedrich A. Hayek, *Individualism and Economic Order*, London, Routledge and Kegan Paul, 1949, and Ludwig von Mises, *Human Action*, New Haven, Yale University Press (previously published in German in 1940). For a summary of the debate and a comment on it, see Israel M. Kirzner, *How Markets Work: Disequilibrium, Entrepreneurship and Discovery*, Hobart Paper 133, Institute of Economic Affairs, 1997, pp. 15–16 and 68–71.
11. See, for example, Colin Robinson, 'Britain's Regulatory Regime in Perspective', in G. MacKerron and P. Pearson (eds), *The International Energy Experience*, Imperial College Press, 2000, and 'Utility Regulation in Britain: The State It's In', in G. MacKerron and P. Pearson (eds), *Energy Policy*, Imperial College Press (forthcoming, 2001).
12. A. Schleifer, 'A Theory of Yardstick Competition', *RAND Journal of Economics*, **16**, 3, 1985, and William B. Shew, 'Natural Monopoly and Yardstick Competition', *Economic Affairs*, **20**, 4, December 2000.
13. Colin Mayer, 'The Regulation of the Water Industry: An Interim Assessment', in M.E. Beesley (ed.), *Regulating Utilities: The Way Forward*, Readings 41, Institute of Economic Affairs, 1994.
14. Ofwat, *Research Papers* nos 1 to 4, variously dated from March 1993 to February 1994.
15. Mark Stewart, *Modelling Water Costs*, 1992-93, Technical Annex, p. 1.
16. For example, the separate bids for South West Water in 1996 by Severn Trent and Wessex Water were blocked by the Monopolies and Mergers Commission because a comparator would have been lost.
17. For example, Dieter Helm and Najma Rajah, 'Water Regulation: The Periodic Review', *Fiscal Studies*, **15**, 2, May 1994.
18. Ofwat, *Setting the Quality Framework: an open letter to the Secretary of State for the Environment, Transport and the Regions and the Secretary of State for Wales*, April 1998.
19. Department of the Environment, Transport and the Regions and the Welsh Office, *Raising the Quality*, September 1998.
20. This repeats the point often made by James Buchanan about the error of the 'bifurcated man' assumption. See, for example, James M. Buchanan, 'Summing Up', in *The Economics of Politics*, Institute of Economic Affairs, 1978.
21. For a US study, see Thomas D. Hopkins, *Regulatory Costs in Profile*, Policy Study No. 132, August 1996. Regulatory costs in the US *Centre for the Study of American Business* are surveyed annually in Clyde Wayne Crews Jr, *Ten Thousand Commandments: A Policymaker's Snapshot of the Federal Regulatory State*, Competitive Enterprise Institute, Washington, DC.
22. See John Blundell and Colin Robinson, *Regulation Without the State*, Occasional Paper 109, Institute of Economic Affairs, 1999 and *Regulation Without the State ... The Debate Continues*, Readings 52, Institute of Economic Affairs, 2000.
23. There was some revival after the successful bid by RWE for Thames Water in late September 2000.

24. Colin Mayer, 'Water: the 1999 price review', in *Regulating Utilities: New Issues, New Solutions*, Edward Elgar, 2000.
25. About 87 per cent of consumers other than households have metered supplies. For households, the percentage metered varies from 2 per cent for Portsmouth Water to 45 per cent for Anglian Water. See Ofwat, *Tariff Structure and Charges: 2000-01*, Report, pp. 46-7.
26. *Taking Water Responsibly: Government decisions following consultations on changes to the water abstraction licensing system in England and Wales*, Department of the Environment, Transport and the Regions/Welsh Office, March 1999.
27. *Competition Act 1998: application in the water and sewerage sectors*, paras 3.51 to 3.54.
28. Ibid., paras 3.28 to 3.32 and 'Water Industry in England and Wales Takes a Step Forward Towards Greater Competition', *Ofwat Press Release* PN43/00, 7 September 2000.
29. Monopolies and Mergers Commission, *Gas and British Gas plc*, 1993, Vol. 1, para. 1.6.
30. M.H. Miller and F. Modigliani, 'Dividend Policy, Growth and the Valuation of Shares', *Journal of Business*, **34**, 1961.
31. 'Kelda abandons plans to sell assets to new mutual company', *The Financial Times*, 26 July 2000.
32. Corporate governance structures tend to evolve over the years but, in companies which are owned by national or local governments or heavily regulated, evolution is seriously restricted. See, for example, Martin Ricketts, 'Competitive Processes and the Evolution of Governance Structures', *Wincott Discussion Papers 01/00*, University of Buckingham School of Business.
33. Blundell and Robinson, *Regulation Without the State*.
34. Daniel B. Klein, *Reputation: Studies in the Voluntary Elicitation of Good Conduct*, University of Michigan Press, 1997 and Klein, 'Reputation, Assurance and Trust in a Great Society', *Foundation for Economic Education*, 2000.
35. Blundell and Robinson, *Regulation Without the State*, pp. 35-6.
36. Ibid., pp. 28-30.

CHAIRMAN'S COMMENTS

Sir Ian Byatt

I begin with a delayed tribute to Michael Beesley. We first met at LSE, when he was Reader in Transport Economics. I learned much from him about how to do cost–benefit analysis. We were later joint members of a government group on urban roads, where Michael straightened out the criteria for evaluation. Later, when I was in the Treasury, his work on the liberalization of telecommunications and his work with Stephen Littlechild on the identification of competitive and monopolistic elements in nationalized industries guided us in how the government might approach its developing privatization programme.

When I became a regulator, Michael gave me some very good advice, in particular the idea that water industry stock should be an income stock, rather than a growth stock. This was quite contrary to the standard City view at the time, but guided me through many cost-of-capital debates.

I also found the lecture series, which he founded and which continues in full vigour after his death, immensely valuable in exchanging ideas and explaining what we are doing in an atmosphere which was tough and challenging, but dealt with the real issues rather than the battle for the public ear. Michael would have enjoyed Colin's chapter, with its vision, its clarity of thought and its powerful arguments. As a regulator – or as a former regulator – I found it both powerful and timely. Like Colin, I think the time is ripe for achieving greater competition in the water industry and, like him, I believe that this is the right way ahead.

I say this despite – or perhaps because of – the fact that I disagree with one important sentence in which he says, 'The present regime in water is surely not sustainable'. It is perhaps only too sustainable, not necessarily in its exact form at the moment, but as an evolutionary strategy, that is developing in a sustainable way. There are various elements in it, however, which I find unattractive – in particular the degree of detailed regulation driven by politicians and environmental regulators.

Competition presents an alternative strategy, which I think is equally sustainable. But the development of the existing approach could be inimical to the further development of competition. A variety of factors are driving the existing arrangements into ever more detailed involvement with governments (in Brussels as well as in London) and with quality and environmental regulators. This is not only undesirable in its own right but damaging to the longer-term interests of customers. I believe that there is an urgent need to re-establish the position and the power of the customer.

The best way to do that is to strengthen competition. But how? It will have to be done carefully and not rushed.

There appears to be limited appetite in the government for action. Its consultation paper early in 2000 duly canvassed the competitive possibilities – and the disadvantages. Since then, silence. We have not yet been told what legislation there might be to strengthen competition, and some of us now wonder whether there will be any legislation on water in the next session of Parliament (2000/2001). I even wonder whether, if there were to be such a Bill, it would strengthen competition or constrain it. I am glad to note that the government has legislated to bring down the threshold for inset appointments from 250 to 100 Ml/year. But it took four years to persuade it to take this modest step and I believe that there is now a case – based on experience – for going further.

The charging system for water and the disposal of wastewater involves a large number of sensitive cross-subsidies. Such cross-subsidies are unlikely to be sustainable as competition is intensified. Removing them will be painful, especially if it happens quickly.

As Colin argues, large users welcome the prospect of competition. They believe that they are being over-charged. Some household customers would also welcome competition. But as can be seen from the statements of the National Consumer Council, there is a significant number of household consumers who fear the effects of more competition.

So fast action is difficult. But that does not rule out progress. I think there is a whole range of things to be done.

First, faster progress could be made in reducing the threshold for inset appointments. Do we need a threshold at all? The administrative arrangements for insets have been much improved, so that it would, I believe, be possible in quick succession to reduce the threshold until it was eliminated.

Second, the arrangements which are developing for common carriage could be accelerated if the Drinking Water Inspectorate were to accept responsibility for the testing of all water supplied through a public supply network. The water companies have argued persuasively for this and it should be straightforward to achieve.

Third, the granting of abstraction licences should involve a competitive bidding process; that is, there should be a market in abstraction licences. This is a matter for the Environment Agency and currently there are some constraints on its charging powers. These constraints could be simply removed – to the benefit of the Agency's income. There is scope for some action without any legislation. There are many sources of water not being used and better treatment of wastewater is making more water available.

Fourth, faster progress on incentive charging arrangements could increase the scope for competition through self-treatment of industrial water and wastewater discharges by industry. There is a steady stream of complaints about the provision of unsuitable water for industrial processes and a good deal of evidence that more self-treatment of wastewater would be environmentally and economically desirable.

Fifth, there are signs, as Colin notes, of a greater emphasis on the contracting out of competitive services by water companies. This appears to be a response to a tough price settlement. I refer not to the financial engineering which characterized the Kelda approach in summer 2000, but the results of patient examination, from the perspective of the operator, of exactly what processes can be outsourced. This will depend on who is there to take up the contracts, as well as considerations of what can be managed through the marketplace and what has to be within immediate management control. It also depends on practical matters such as the exact design of contracts.

Finally, I would like to speculate on the issue of industry structure. Much has already been achieved by competition. The market for corporate control has been restrained by the desirability of maintaining a sufficient number of comparators in a situation where entry was difficult. But that did not, of course, inhibit owners from demanding good returns from management, and there has been a significant degree of management change resulting from those competitive processes.

The regulator has been able to develop competitive ways of setting price limits, which has put additional pressure on poorly performing companies, such as Hyder, to the point where companies are obliged to sell out to someone who can make better use of the assets.

Should entry become easier through insets, but particularly through common carriage, it would seem sensible to relax the restrictions on informal industry mergers which reduce the number of comparators. This need not involve legislation. The criteria to be used by the Competition Commission in judging the public interest in the case of water–water mergers already allows the Commission to take account of the scale of the detriment to the water regulator resulting from
mergers and of the benefits deriving from any other matters arising from the merger.

4.   The new gas trading arrangements

George Yarrow

1.   INTRODUCTION

The new gas trading arrangements (NGTA) is the name given to a package of reforms in the gas industry, the first elements of which were introduced in October 1999.

The NGTA were and are part of an evolutionary process of development in the industry, with origins stretching back several years. The reforms have been more incremental than in electricity, where the abolition of the Pool and the introduction of the new electricity trading arrangements (NETA), analysed by David Currie in Chapter 1, mark a larger step change. Nevertheless, the pace of change in gas has sometimes been quite rapid, as many readers will know all too well, and the introduction of NETA, coupled with the strengthening interactions between gas and electricity markets, now increases the priority that needs to be given to outstanding issues.

An occasion such as this provides an opportunity to stand back and look at the general direction of market and policy developments, and that is what I propose to do. The emphasis is therefore on general issues, rather than on the detail of latest proposals. I hope that this will make the material of more interest to the general reader, whilst not disappointing those at the coal-face (or is it the well-head?) of the NGTA programme.

2.   THE NATURE OF THE ISSUES

Gas is a network industry, by virtue of the economic significance of the dedicated facilities required to transport the commodity from point of production to point of use.

In the most general terms, a network is simply a set of interconnected nodes. Visually, the transportation structure can be thought of as a set of points (nodes), with lines joining some of those points to one other (connectors).

Network industries differ according to the characteristics of the facilities required at nodes and to connect nodes, and gas has its own particular set of characteristics. In air transport, for example, nodes are populated by airports and associated facilities, such as parking and maintenance areas. Airplanes provide the physical means of connecting nodes, but there are no direct 'physical' connections, only a set of 'routes'. In gas, the nodes are physically connected by means of pipes, but there is no equivalent of airplanes.

A general feature of network industries is that what goes on in one section of the network can have significant economic implications for what goes on in another section. When a network is run as a fully integrated operation, this economic interdependence is not transparent to outside parties – the trade-offs are internalized within the integrated utility. There has, however, been a trend toward separation/unbundling of network activities, which brings the interdependence issues to the fore.

I will not discuss the various drivers of this trend here, but simply make three points about the trend:

- It has clearly been given a substantial boost by developments in information and transactions technologies.
- The fact that the UK is a world leader in these developments in the energy sector means that, in pushing forward, there is frequently (though by no means always) a lack of directly applicable international experience to draw on.
- With the visual picture of a network in mind, there is obviously considerable scope for unbundling of the various elements of the network structure, right down to the individual facility level (whether the facility be a particular pipeline connection or assets at a particular node, such as a compressor or storage facility). There are, however, trade-offs in the unbundling process, which are influenced by factors such as transactions costs, information conditions and market power. Unbundling issues therefore raise one of the most fundamental questions in industrial organization (the Coase question): what is the most effective division of activities between markets and firms?

Given at least some unbundling, such that network users can choose which particular combinations of services they wish to purchase, a 'textbook' solution might say that prices of network components should be set to reflect the costs imposed by particular patterns of use. Thus, if one activity affects what can go on in other parts of the network, these effects should be reflected in the charges for the first activity.

Such an outcome can be achieved to at least some degree of approximation via market processes governed by appropriate rules, but not exactly (at least with current transactions technologies). If it could be achieved, the necessary coordination required for system balancing in gas could be handled by the prices determined in markets. As in electricity, however, a difficulty emerges in that there can be high costs of system imbalance, so that the degree of approximation required for efficient outcomes is beyond current capabilities. In such circumstances, the role of system operator emerges as a distinct, unbundled activity (in a fully integrated network, system operation is bundled with all other activities).

The role of the system operator is to deal with those coordination problems not dealt with via the market mechanism, or, put another way, to improve the market approximation to a level required to prevent inefficient imbalance. Yet another way of putting this is to say that the system operator corrects for economic externalities in the networks (that is, effects on other parties not reflected in prices/charges).

It can be seen, therefore, that the scope of the role of the system operator depends upon the effectiveness of markets: the better are network effects reflected in market prices, the smaller the system operator role will be.

Given these points, developments in the gas industry can be seen as part of a general shift from internal organization to markets as mechanisms for allocating economic resources and coordinating behaviour. Unbundling/network disaggregation is one aspect of this process; developing trading arrangements that more effectively promote value discovery and coordinate the activities of network users is another. The first directly increases the scope of markets; the second is aimed at making markets function more effectively.

I need hardly add that the second of these tasks is not easy. Integrated network operation has, historically, been a favoured option precisely because the complex economic interactions that take place within networks can be difficult to capture in trading arrangements. It can also be noted that inappropriate trading arrangements can sometimes cause more problems than they solve – they can increase, rather than reduce, network externalities, so some care is required in evaluating new sets of rules.[1] Nevertheless, whilst challenging problems lie ahead, significant progress has been made, and there is no indication that the (current) limit of the general trend from internal organization to markets has yet been reached.

Before leaving general issues, I would like to add a few words about market power. As noted above, this is one of the potential limiting factors on the extent to which resource allocation and coordination can be effectively handled by markets. Network disaggregation/unbundling may lead to a situation in which significant market power can be exercised by parties controlling services provided in parts of the network, or controlling rights to use parts of the network. Exploitation of such market power is itself a source of economic externalities, and it is therefore potentially dysfunctional in terms of overall network performance (as well as being more directly damaging to consumers). In relation to traded markets, market power issues also surface in relation to questions of liquidity and depth, about which more will be said later.

The general point that I would make is an obvious one: the extent to which such power limits market developments depends in part on the availability of mechanisms to mitigate its exploitation. The greater the mitigation, the greater will be the scope for markets. There is, however, an obvious tension here: network disaggregation can enhance the role played by the price mechanism, but it may also create new sources of market power. Dealing with market power issues in network industries is one of the principal challenges facing regulatory policy today, and policy performance in this area will be a major determinant of the effectiveness of developing trading arrangements.

3. CAPACITY, ENERGY AND SPATIAL DIFFERENTIATION

In Nirvana Economics, strong competition could be imagined for all network components. The result would be a set of spatially differentiated prices for gas (energy), varying from moment to moment as inputs, offtakes and the *state of the system* changed. Every possible location would have its gas price, although it is easier to think only of prices either side of the network nodes (entry and exit points, compressors, storage facilities, pipeline junctions, and so on). The difference between gas prices at two locations would be the price for transporting gas from one location to another. As should be obvious, in these circumstances the price for transportation from A to B is equal and opposite to the price for transportation from B to A.

I have stressed the relevance of the *state of the system* in price determination because of its practical importance for what follows. It includes factors such as temporarily reduced capacity along connectors and at nodal facilities (due to failures and planned maintenance, say), and also pressures within pipelines. Much more than in electricity,[2] the storage capacity of network components provides a buffer between inputs and offtakes, so it is not necessary to maintain an instantaneous (flow) balance between the two. Prices through the network can, therefore, vary substantially for any given input and offtake flows, depending upon whether the system is relatively full (pressures are near upper limits) or relatively empty (pressures are near lower limits).

The UK gas system is not, and probably never will be, close to Nirvana. The issues before us are to do with lower-order incarnations. By the mid-1990s the position reached in relation to the national transmission system (NTS) could be summarized as follows:

- Administered transportation charges were based upon capacity and commodity elements.
- Spatial differentiation occurred via locationally differentiated entry and exit capacity charges, in that different charges were set for different entry points and exit zones.
- Energy could be traded at the national balancing point (NBP), as well as at particular locations (beach terminals).
- Transco, in its role as system operator (SO), could buy and sell gas through the flexibility mechanism, a trading arrangement in which the SO was always one of the two contracting parties.

These arrangements have an interesting structure. The NBP can be viewed as a 'virtual hub' in that its physical location is not specified. One interpretation is that it is anywhere inside the Transco system. Another is that it is everywhere inside the Transco system, in that the values of gas are, in effect, equalized within the system for trading purposes. Such equalization has the effect of increasing liquidity in trading, at the cost of losing some spatial signals (it is one of the 'approximations' judged to be acceptable).

It can be noted in passing that this approach depends upon the fact that the NTS is not itself disaggregated into separate pipeline companies. In jurisdictions where there are several pipeline companies (for example the USA), the natural tendency is for energy trading to emerge at geographically defined hubs, such as where major pipeline systems connect with one another. That is, disaggregation of transmission forces greater spatial segmentation in energy markets.

Given these points, the NTS entry and exit charges can be interpreted respectively as charges to transport capacity from beach terminals to the NBP and from the NBP to NTS offtake points. This yields a conceptual hub-and-spoke pattern: the movement of gas from, say, the St Fergus terminal to inner London can be decomposed into a move from St Fergus to the NBP plus a move from the NBP to inner London. And, implicitly, spatial differentiation is confined to the defined entry points and exit zones.

If there are n entry points and m exit zones, the arrangements potentially lead to $n + m + 1$ energy prices (the +1 is the price at the NBP). Liquidity is concentrated at the NBP, since, on the hub-and-spoke analogy, all gas has to pass through the NBP. At some entry points, however, there may be a much smaller number of players on the selling side of the energy market, and at exit points the number of buyers of gas may be restricted.

4. PROBLEMS ARISING

Two major sets of issues can be identified in relation to the above arrangements:

- A general lack of liquidity in energy trading, notwithstanding the pro-liquidity effects of the NBP concept.
- Inefficient pricing signals in the transportation charging regime.

I will focus on the second of these in this section, which is most readily discussed by restricting attention to entry charges (an area where reforms have subsequently been implemented).

The release of primary entry capacity at prices based upon estimates of long-run costs clearly does not necessarily provide efficient signals of system costs in the shorter term (a problem exacerbated by the lack of temporal differentiation in the charges – there were no summer/winter variations, for example). The spatial pricing structure is thereby distorted, and this will potentially lead to inappropriate decisions concerning use of the network.

Secondary markets can potentially improve the (relatively poor) first approximation. If, say, there is excess entry capacity at a particular terminal in a particular period, prices in the secondary market may be much lower, providing incentives for greater use of the network. Such incentives can be reinforced by use-it-or-lose-it provisions to prevent capacity hoarding, and by short-term sales of available capacity by Transco (for example on a day-ahead basis).

This does not, however, resolve the problem of more persistent excess capacity, since primary acquisition of capacity has to occur at the regulated price. There is also a more difficult problem that arises when there is excess demand for entry capacity at a particular location in a particular period. Under the old arrangements, Transco was required to offer as much capacity as network users wished to buy at the regulated price (an arrangement motivated by a desire to facilitate new entry by preventing capacity hoarding). Secondary markets cannot deal with this issue since no one would want to purchase at a price higher than the equivalent regulated price. That is, the secondary market price is effectively constrained by the regulated price.[3]

In the face of excess demand, therefore, network users have an incentive to purchase extra capacity from Transco, and Transco is then faced with the problem of rationing available capacity among holders of entry rights. This was the issue that emerged at the St Fergus terminal, in the period before the introduction of the first tranche of the NGTA, as a result of lack of capacity availability for a period.

5.   THE NGTA

One of the major issues addressed by the NGTA was a set of problems surrounding the flexibility mechanism, which was seen as leading to high costs of maintaining system balance. A new on-the-day commodity market (OCM) was introduced in October 1999, providing opportunities for shipper-to-shipper as well as shipper-to-Transco trading. This encompassed both NBP and locational trades, and provided enhanced capabilities (supplementing over-the-counter trading) for shippers to more closely balance their own input and offtake positions. The OCM is a screen-based, cleared market, operating on a near 24-hour basis.

A second major reform was the introduction of auctions for primary entry capacity, in monthly blocks and initially for six months ahead. These are sold as firm rights so that if, in the event, that Transco is unable to meet its contractual obligations, it is required to buy back capacity from the holders of rights to capacity. On the other hand, if Transco can, in any period, make more capacity available than has been sold in the primary auctions, it makes that extra capacity available to the market on a short-term basis, via incremental sales. As with energy balancing (see below), Transco is incentivized to some extent in relation to these day-ahead and on-the-day buy and sell actions.

These arrangements not only increase the scope for value discovery at the stage of primary release of capacity (although elements of the administered arrangements continue to exist in that levels of reserve prices in the auctions are high, at least in relation to short-run marginal costs at unconstrained terminals) but, perhaps more importantly, eliminate restrictions on secondary trading.

Whilst there has been much discussion of the design of the Transco auctions, the most substantive issues raised by the new entry capacity arrangements concern the duration of the rights offered at any one time and the amount of capacity that is made available. As the gas storage auctions indicated, there is clearly scope for making some capacity available on a longer-term basis, although the implications of market-clearing prices for Transco's controlled revenue are an added complicating factor that is not present in storage. No major conceptual issues are involved in such a development, and the prime regulatory requirement is only that, whatever the form of the contracts, there is no discrimination among different categories of network users.

In relation to the quantity of capacity offered for sale, difficulties arise because the capacity available varies over time: as noted in section 2, what can be done in one section of the network depends on what is happening in other parts of the network. Thus, at any time, the capacity available at a particular terminal will depend not only upon the physical dimensions of relevant network assets, but also upon the pattern of inputs and offtakes throughout the system, and on the state of the system itself (for example, in the very short term, the pressure or linepack position). The solution adopted in the NGTA was to profile capacity offered to patterns of seasonal normal demand (SND).

In some circumstances, the amount of capacity offered in primary auctions does not matter very much: the more important consideration is that, in any relevant period, all the capacity that can be made available is offered to the market. Thus if, in the primary auctions, Transco systematically made available less (more) capacity than was found subsequently to be available, the difference could be made good by short-term sales (buy-backs).

The issue acquires significance largely because of perceived failures in these short-term capacity markets and/or inappropriate Transco incentives. Entry capacity markets are locationally specific, and are therefore vulnerable to problems of liquidity and market power. This means that outcomes will not be neutral as to the division of capacity sales between the longer-term and shorter-term mechanisms. In addition, there can be concerns that Transco incentives are insufficiently strong to counteract the general tendency, not completely eliminated by the overall price control, to favour higher capacity prices (and therefore to be conservative in releasing capacity to the market).

For the future, it will be necessary to consider more closely the interactions between Transco SO incentive schemes and the incentives provided by the overall price control, which are of great significance for longer-term investment decisions. One possible resolution is to incorporate, into the price control process, forward commitments by Transco to offer certain levels of capacity by way of primary auctions. Such capacity could be offered on contracts for a variety of durations, and could potentially be sold forward in advance of physical capabilities. Adjustments in capacity availability, again of varying durations, around these forward commitments could then be handled via an enhanced SO incentive scheme, with Transco relying on a variety of contractual instruments, including capacity options as well as spot purchases and sales.

6. SYSTEM BALANCING

As explained in section 2, increased reliance on markets implies a diminished role for the system operator. One aspect of developments in gas has been to encourage greater self-balancing by shippers, leaving fewer problems to be resolved by the system operator. However, while the general intent of policy in this area is clear, balancing arrangements in gas have proved particularly problematic.

The intent is that shippers should be confronted with the costs that their imbalances (differences between inputs and offtakes) impose. To date, such costs have been approximated by a cash-out regime that is intended to pass back costs incurred by Transco to shippers in imbalance.

The targeting of (SO) imbalance costs has, however, been poor. Shippers have been granted tolerance bands for imbalances, within which the imbalances are cashed out at the system or market average price. Only when imbalances fall outside the tolerance band do cash-out prices reflect the incremental actions taken by Transco when the system is short or long.

Cash-out also only occurs at the end of the gas day (that is, every 24 hours). It is therefore incapable of reflecting the costs imposed by within-day imbalances, which raises mounting problems in relation to interactions between the gas and electricity markets (where imbalances are cashed out every half hour). To date, within-day problems have been addressed only via rules concerning within-day profiling of flows, which leave something to be desired in terms of effectiveness.

The first phase of the NGTA reforms has made some contribution to the improvement of the balancing regime by:

- establishing the OCM, which allows shippers more easily to adjust their balance positions through the day;
- enhancing incentives for shippers to balance their own positions through a reduction in tolerances.

The second of these measures does, however, have limitations. Like end-of-day balancing, questions can be raised about whether such reforms are even working within the right conceptual framework. For example, as indicated earlier, it is not in general efficient for inputs and offtakes to be exactly balanced at every moment through the day, and even less is it necessarily efficient for the cumulative inputs and offtakes to be matched at the end of every 24-hour period. Within certain bounds, which themselves vary with inputs and offtakes, the inventory of gas within the Transco system can be run up or down. A more fully cost-reflective set of arrangements would signal this through to shippers, and would incentivize them to take account of the state of the system when adjusting their own positions.

A set of trading arrangements that might better fit with the general objectives of moving to more market-based arrangements is as follows:

- Shippers acquire linepack or inventory rights from Transco.
- Inputs and offtakes are monitored on an hourly basis.
- Differences between inputs and offtakes in each hour either add to or subtract from inventory holdings.
- If inventory holdings move outside the acquired limits, shippers are

exposed to charges reflecting balancing costs imposed on the system operator.

- Shippers can manage their positions by some combination of sales/purchases of gas and of inventory rights.

In addition to a requirement for this 'missing market' (in linepack or very short-term storage) to be developed, a further set of issues arises in connection with interactions between gas and electricity markets/networks. We already have two interrelated networks, such that what is done in one part of one affects what can be done in some parts of the other, but the interactions will probably grow stronger over time. For example, changing within-day patterns of electricity generation from CCGT (Confined Cycle Gas Turbine) plant could have important implications for the operation of the gas network.

There is not room to discuss these further issues here, but it is clear that there will be a strong requirement for coordination and harmonization of balancing arrangements for gas and electricity. The advent of NETA will probably mean that any initial burden of adjustment will fall mostly on the gas sector, but it will not always be a one-way street. The initial NETA framework is by no means the last word, and adjustments can be expected over time.

7. ASSESSMENT

I am conscious of having touched upon only a few of the outstanding issues now being addressed in the gas sector, and then only at a broad-brush level. I think, however, that it is useful to frame the issues in terms of a shift from internal organization to markets, because this broad perspective draws immediate attention to major factors that can be expected to influence where, in any given state of the art, the most appropriate boundary between the two mechanisms is likely, very roughly, to lie. Such factors include transactions costs in general, information conditions in particular, and market power. Each of these can be expected to play a major role in determining the detail of the next incarnation of gas trading arrangements.

The other general point that is worth emphasizing is the degree of linkage between different aspects of the trading arrangements. Commercial conduct can be expected to be determined by many interacting factors, and progress in one direction may be impeded by lack of progress in others.

The development of the OCM illustrates both points. In its July 2000 review of the NGTA, Ofgem concluded that the OCM had experienced periods of low liquidity since its launch in the previous October. One of the factors influencing this outcome was identified to be the charging structure (transactions costs). This could be potentially addressed by, among other things, increasing the scope of the screen-based trading offered to encompass trading in such things as entry capacity and storage, thereby spreading fixed costs of the platform and reducing unit transactions costs.

Other relevant factors that were identified in the review, and that are more directly related to other aspects of the trading arrangements and therefore more amenable to influence through the NGTA process, included shippers' use of imbalance tolerances and Transco's approach to trading in the market. In effect, the arguments here are that an individual shipper's imbalances are being cross-subsidized under the existing cash-out regime – reducing incentives to trade so as to balance the position – and that Transco has insufficient incentives (or, for some reason, is failing to respond to existing incentives). Reform of other relevant aspects of the gas regime could, therefore, have beneficial effects on the OCM.

Whether such developments (increasing the coverage of the trading platform, reforming cash-out, changing Transco conduct) would themselves be sufficient to address all major issues of liquidity is a more open question. Lurking in the background is the issue of market power. On this I am moderately optimistic. The NBP concept helps concentrate liquidity in energy trading and, despite the high headline level of concentration in the wholesale market, competition in gas supply has developed reasonably well, not least because of interactions, at the retail level, with electricity. There are also other policy instruments at hand that are targeted on market power problems.

I am less optimistic about liquidity (and market power effects more generally) in capacity markets. Although there is some scope for substitution among entry and exit flows, locational specificity is a much more significant issue. Market trading is characterized by smaller numbers of players, and recent evidence on prices paid by Transco in buying back capacity at St Fergus (during a period in which capacity was reduced by levels of flow in other parts of the system) provides no reassurance that markets are functioning in a fully competitive way. More generally, liquidity in secondary trading of capacity has been low.

Here, I think, we can begin to see some of the existing limits on how far market trading can be taken in certain areas. There are steps that can be taken to improve the position. The exploitation of market power can be monitored for compliance with competition law and licence obligations, Transco could be more active in its use of forward contracting, use-it-or-lose-it provisions can help prevent capacity hoarding, and so on. It is also relevant that markets do not have to be fully competitive to make a useful contribution to improving economic performance. Even where limited, they can provide extra options and flexibility for network users. It might, however, be too much to hope that secondary markets in entry capacity will become deep and liquid at every entry terminal (to say nothing of trading at exit points, which the NGTA process has not yet touched).

The limitations of secondary capacity markets imply that a greater degree of importance should be attached to the way in which primary rights are sold by Transco. With effectively functioning secondary markets, the primary allocation process would not matter very much from the perspective of economic efficiency – although there would still be issues to do with discrimination, including possible impacts on retail supply competition – since shippers' positions could readily be adjusted through secondary trading. Illiquid secondary markets, however, mean that it is more important for network users that they secure a better approximation to their final requirements at the primary allocation stage.

The design of the existing Transco auctions is relatively simple, and leaves scope for development. In my view, however, the bigger issues are to do with the questions of what is being sold (should rights of longer duration be offered?) and with shippers' skills in purchasing their requirements. The auction outcomes to date indicate that, while there was considerable price dispersion at the outset, significant learning has since taken place. This can be expected to continue as participants gain experience and as successive auctions increase the information that is available to bidders.

There are obviously some distortions to auction outcomes arising from the existence of the overall Transco price control, since over-recovery (or under-recovery) of allowable revenues leads to adjustments in commodity charges for gas transportation, the effects of which can, to some extent, be anticipated by bidders. Close analysis indicates that the effects are not likely to be large, however: a bidder considering whether or not to raise an offer price will only benefit from revenue recycling on the amount by which the (raised) price exceeds the price offered for any quantity that is displaced by the higher bid; and whilst bigger players have an incentive to bid a bit more, they have counteracting incentives to bid less in order to exploit monopsony power. In the round, therefore, the primary auctions would not appear to be fatally flawed on account of price control effects.

The big issues for the future probably lie in those areas that have not yet been fully addressed by the NGTA – long-term investment incentives and the exit capacity regime (including interruption) – and in the balancing regime. The balancing mechanism is not well founded conceptually, and its weaknesses are being increasingly exposed by developments such as the emergence of substantial interconnector flows and interactions with the electricity market. Its reform will inevitably, therefore, be a high priority in the next stage of the NGTA process.

Key to such reform will be a more appropriate treatment of gas inventories within the Transco system (linepack), since only if all storage options are available, through markets, to network users is it likely that efficient self-balancing incentives can be established. Other desirable developments would be a shift to a shorter-term balancing period, together with other measures to ensure effective coordination between gas and electricity trading arrange-ments, and with improved incentive arrangements for Transco in its role as system operator. Among other things, Transco should be encouraged to rely on a wider mix of contractual instruments, subject always to the overarching requirements that it trades in a non-discriminatory manner and in a way that, where relevant, complies with the financial services regime.

Finally, there is the issue of market power. Short-term demand and supply inelasticities are a less acute problem than in electricity, and the incidence of market power problems can be expected to be more weighted towards locational issues. Nevertheless, pricing anomalies in the wholesale gas market in summer 2000 indicate that not all is well. How the combination of the Competition Act, the existing licensing regime (including obligations in regard to system balancing) and reformed balancing arrangements will cope with the potential problems remains to be seen. All I would say, by way of conclusion is: get this one wrong and the likely outcome will be a more administered, less market-based set of arrangements than is currently hoped for.

NOTES

1. The sensitivities here can be high – a poorly constructed rule can have substantial adverse effects, and deficiencies in rules may be hard to spot.
2. Inertia in electricity also provides some buffer between inputs and offtakes, but the timescales involved are much shorter.
3. Note that the restriction of secondary markets is not necessarily the same as a price cap at the regulated price, on a daily equivalent basis. If primary capacity is only available on an annual basis, a market participant seeking additional capacity for a period of a month may be willing to pay much more than the daily equivalent (regulated) price.

CHAIRMAN'S COMMENTS

Eileen Marshall

As the person within Ofgem with key responsibilities for the development of the gas (and electricity) trading arrangements, I found George Yarrow's chapter, in which he takes a strategic look at the general direction of market and policy developments, insightful and thought-provoking.

For gas to be transported safely through Transco's integrated pipeline system, shippers must be able to ship gas through an entry point and make arrangements for the exit of that gas elsewhere, and these gas inputs and offtakes must be in balance within certain tolerances. Improvements to these access and balancing arrangements are what we have described as the new gas trading arrangements (NGTA), and a closely related issue is that of developing better signals and incentives for Transco to invest efficiently in expanding the capacity of its gas infrastructure.

Inefficient trading arrangements can cause operational difficulties for Transco in ensuring safety and security are not jeopardized; can raise the direct costs of shipping gas; have a knock-on effect on spot and forward gas prices in certain circumstances; and harm competition in retail gas supply. That is why Ofgem has placed a high priority on developing more efficient arrangements under the guise of NGTA.

The previous trading arrangements were introduced in March 1996 and incorporated in Transco's network code, a contract between Transco and shippers. The objective of the code was to allow open and equal access to the Transco pipeline network for all licensed shippers. It was the first standard contract in Europe between a pipeline operator and shippers for regulated third-party access to its system. Some of its key principles, such as the daily balancing by shippers of their inputs and offtakes and the creation of the flexibility mechanism – a method for shippers to enable Transco to keep an overall system balance by supplying extra gas to, or removing gas from, the network – were without precedent. These trading arrangements allowed domestic supply competition to be introduced, whilst maintaining a safe system balancing and transportation regime.

However, changes in the gas market in Great Britain, such as the greatly increased demand for gas and hence for gas transportation, have put increasing pressures on both the existing Transco gas network system and on the contractual arrangements that surround its operation and use. Fundamental inefficiencies, some of which were acknowledged when the network code was put in place and others that were exposed after three years or so of operation, had to be tackled. These inefficiencies have been accurately and succinctly described by George.

Moreover, the costs associated with these inefficiencies can be expected to rise over time. Patterns of supply and demand continue to change and develop, in particular in relation to interconnector flows with continental Europe and with Ireland, and increased interactions with the electricity market. With regard to the latter, gas-fired plant is more and more important in the plant mix, and the new within-day electricity trading arrangements (NETA) emphasize the economic importance of flexible plant. Thus the greatest benefits of reform of the gas trading arrangements can be expected to lie in the avoidance of cost escalation and operational difficulties through timely action.

George has identified a necessary role for a system operator, to ensure an economic overall balance (in gas inputs and offtakes and to overcome network constraints). But he has also pointed out that the scale of the system operator's role depends on the extent to which previously integrated network services are unbundled, and more generally the scope given to market mechanisms. He describes development in the gas industry as part of a general shift from internal organization to markets as mechanisms for allocating economic resources and coordinating behaviour.

It is certainly true that Ofgem has consistently argued the case for participants (including the monopoly system operator and transportation asset owner) to be exposed to the economic costs of their actions and that such costs are best determined through markets. This approach was behind the introduction, as part of NGTA, of an independently operated on-the-day commodity market (to replace the flexibility mechanism) which both shippers and Transco can use to trade gas to keep in balance; it was behind the establishment of firm-tradable entry capacity rights via price auctions to replace the previous administered arrangements; and it is central to our proposals for improving longer-term signals and incentives on Transco to expand the capacity of the national transmission system in an efficient way, by using longer-term capacity markets to signal the locational value of capacity and setting firm capacity output measures for Transco to meet. (The same principle of better targeting market-determined costs lies behind NETA.)

George points to the degree of linkage between different aspects of the trading arrangements and tends to infer that a 'big bang' approach might be more efficient than piecemeal reform. I accept this might be preferable, and even necessary in certain circumstances (Offer concluded that it was not feasible to reform the Pool-based electricity trading arrangements effectively by piecemeal change). But it is not always possible to achieve, for various reasons, including regulatory and industry resource constraints. Some prioritization necessarily occurs, within the application of a consistent economic framework. For example, a concerted and prolonged effort to unbundle gas storage and introduce price auctions for various durations was particularly important to the development of effective competition in retail supply (given winter peaks in domestic demand for gas). The reform of the transmission network entry capacity arrangements, by contrast, was thrust upon the regulator and the industry, as the previous way of allocating capacity proved unworkable in the face of system constraints.

George rightly highlights the issue of market power as likely to be something of a persistent problem in capacity markets. It may also be an issue in 'close-to-real-time' gas trading markets, although because of the storability of gas in the pipeline itself, it is less of an issue than it is in electricity. What have now become accepted ways of mitigating the exercise of market power are, however, in use in the on-shore gas market. The imposition of use-it-or-lose-it provisions for network capacity is one example and all shippers are also subject to a licence condition prohibiting them from jeopardizing the efficient balancing of the transmission system, whilst Transco now has commercial incentives, previously lacking, to balance the system efficiently and to ensure all transportation capacity is available for use on the day. Along with still sharper commercial incentives, we wish in the future to allow Transco greater freedom to contract ahead for its gas balancing and capacity needs. This can increase the efficient operation of the system as well as being a well-tried and tested way of ameliorating the short-term market power of other participants. To the extent that on-shore market power is a problem, I am hopeful that continuing market-based reforms, together with powers under the Competition Act and the Gas Act, can deal effectively with the issue.

George has provided a valuable insight into the new gas trading arrangements by stepping back and analysing them from first principles. This is particularly useful because, as he points out, we are still travelling down the road of reform. Far-reaching changes are on the horizon, including the separate sale of storage in the pipes (linepack), which will mark the conclusion of the storage reforms and, perhaps most important of all, the alignment of the gas and electricity balancing regimes.

5. A review of privatization and regulation experience in the UK

Irwin M. Stelzer

I should like to begin this chapter by declaring an interest, a practice that I understand is at times followed by some members of your Parliament. In addition to my work at the Hudson Institute, and at *The Sunday Times*, I serve as a consultant to News International, BSkyB, and several energy companies that have a presence in the UK.

That the topics of privatization and regulation should be linked is proof that monopoly power cannot be entrusted to private, profit-maximizing corporations.[1] (It must be placed under the control of the state, either through direct ownership, or by regulating its exercise. In this chapter I shall argue that regulation is a more efficient means of controlling monopoly power than is state ownership, that introducing competition is superior to both, but that merely chanting, in the manner of the Chicago school, that all monopoly power is transitory, is to elevate hope over experience, or at a minimum to give a very generous definition to the number of years that can be included in the word 'transitory'.

But what I am about to say should not be taken as a failure to recognize that privatization involves social costs, most notably those associated with the elimination of overmanning,[2] or naïve belief that regulation is a perfect process. As Alfred Kahn has pointed out in his magisterial work on the economics and institutions of regulation,

> Regulated monopoly is a very imperfect instrument for doing the world's work ... Regulation is ill-equipped to treat the more important aspects of performance – efficiency, service innovation, risk taking, and probing the elasticity of demand. Herein lies the great attraction of competition: it supplies the direct spur and the market test of performance.[3]

The quality of regulation is limited not only by the intrinsic difficulty of substituting administrative processes for the marvellous self-regulatory tool we call the competitive market. It is limited as well by:

- the resource advantage that regulated companies generally have over the agencies charged with regulating them;
- the information asymmetry that gives the regulated an advantage over the regulator;
- the ever-present dangers of regulatory capture or, at the other extreme, the hostility that regulatory staffs often have for the companies they regulate;
- the abilities of the men and women chosen for the arduous task of substituting their judgements for that of the absent competitive market; and
- the abilities and interests of the legislators who create the framework within which regulators must operate.

This last point is especially important: the legal instruments handed to regulators by legislators often constitute a poisoned chalice, containing a brew that includes often-contradictory economic and equity potions, a dash of economic policy, a bit of social policy (subsidize this or that favoured group), and a large portion of political self-seeking (keep prices low and service quality high).

And the regulators themselves are of varying quality. I have known regulators who cannot distinguish a demand curve from a supply curve, and who think that marginal cost is the sum written in the margin of some accounting statement. I have dealt with others who are quite comfortable dealing with the intricacies of econometric models (the best know just how many pinches of salt to take with their regression equations), and with various sophisticated techniques for measuring the cost of capital. I have dealt with regulators who engage with intellectual integrity in the difficult search for answers that maximize efficiency and fairly balance the interests of consumers and investors, and with others who search only for the answers that will require more staff and prolong their tenure in office. This experience inclines me to agree with one leading scholar that 'Individual persons ... have mattered a great deal in regulatory history'.[4] I know that the constitutionalists among you like to think that your government – and mine – is a government of laws, not men. Even a brief descent from an ivory tower will convince you that both matter, and in the case of regulation it may be men that matter more.

Regulation, in short, is not a perfect instrument for controlling private monopoly power. But it seems to serve the public interest better than does state ownership. To reach that conclusion, of course, requires two judgements – one ideological, the other economic.

On the ideological side there is the usual room for differences of opinion. If one has a general bias in favour of limiting the role of the state, it will not take elaborate comparative efficiency studies to persuade you to come down on the side of private as opposed to public ownership. If one generally favours stronger rather than weaker trade unions, one will inevitably favour a greater role for public ownership, since the politicians who ultimately control publicly owned enterprises are more likely to bow to the wishes of trade unions than are the managers who control the affairs of private sector enterprises, presumably (although not certainly or always) in the interests of the shareholder–owners of the enterprise. To the extent that one believes that businesses should pursue non-economic, social goals, one will favour public as opposed to private ownership. And to the extent that one is certain that regulation of privately owned monopolies is doomed to failure, perhaps because 'regulatory capture' is inevitable, one will prefer that monopoly enterprises remain in state hands, that being less evil than unconstrained private power.

That considerations such as these, rather than a pure drive for greater economic efficiency, was a – some might well say 'the' – driving force behind the UK's privatization wave few can doubt. One clear goal was to reduce the role of government in the economy and therefore in the lives of UK subjects. That goal was achieved. Between 1979 and 1992 the portion of total employment accounted for by state-owned enterprises fell from 8 per cent to 3 per cent, the portion of output from 10 per cent to 3 per cent, and the portion of total gross domestic fixed capital formation from 16 per cent to 5 per cent.[5] All in all, state assets totalling some £45 billion were sold off.[6]

Another goal was to create a political force to offset the trade unions. Prime Minister Thatcher, as she then was, made no secret of her desire to alter the balance of political power by creating a 'share-owning democracy',[7] with more shareholders than there were trade union members.[8] This goal, too, was achieved. When the privatization programme began, there were 3 million shareholders and 13 million trade union members in the UK. Today, there are almost 13 million direct shareholders and fewer than 8 million trade union members. Needless to say, the achievement of the Thatcherite objective of creating a new shareholding class did not ensure permanent Tory tenure at 10 Downing Street. But it may be one reason for the 'New' in New Labour – the people may well be closer to controlling the commanding heights of the economy than they were when the several 'barons' ran the nationalized coal and other industries.

It was the pursuit of the goal of creating a shareholder class that led to the underpricing of the shares of to-be-privatized companies. The theory was quite simple: underprice the shares of such enterprises as British Telecom and British Gas so that the small shareholders (the so-called 'Sids') to whom shares were allocated at the time of privatization – allocation being necessary because the underpricing resulted in over-subscriptions – would immediately see the value of their shares rise. This would persuade them to become active capitalists in the future, and to support the free-market, low-tax and other policies of the Conservative Party. The fact that huge values had been transferred from taxpayers to shareholders[9] was not deemed troublesome, and was anyhow remarked upon only by economists/quibblers whose voices were drowned out by the clanging of tills in the offices of investment bankers and the cheers of new shareholders. Not to mention the applause of the managers of the newly privatized enterprises, men (almost no women) who suddenly realized just how valuable they were, and proceeded to adjust their compensation accordingly, this being a time before shareholders became somewhat more aggressive in attempting – so far with only indifferent success – to relate compensation to performance.

To the ideologue – and I include myself in the group of those who think that taking away from government those things that can be done by the private sector is intrinsically a good thing – privatization, then, was a success. It pushed back the frontiers of the state; it reduced the power of ministers over many industries; and it created a new class of shareholders.

To the economist, too, privatization was a success, although it must be noted that the evidence concerning the economic differences between the efficiency of various industries when in state ownership, compared with performance after privatization, does not point unambiguously in one direction.

That evidence is in any event not easy to appraise. For one thing, it is somewhere between difficult and impossible to separate the effects of privatization from the effects of such things as trends in the economy. For another, measuring productivity remains more art than science, as those now engaged in the debate over whether we have a 'new economy' or merely the same old one in the midst of a productivity-enhancing cyclical upturn are finding out.[10] Most important, 'It can be argued that the degree of product market competition and the effectiveness of regulatory policy typically have rather larger effects on performance than ownership *per se*.'[11] So, simple before-and-after analyses of labour or total factor productivity cannot be considered dispositive.

This is why a survey of the literature throws up some evidence that challenges the proposition that privatization resulted in important improvements in efficiency. David Parker, reviewing several studies that compare the performance of public and private sector companies, reports, 'It is difficult to see what general conclusion can be drawn from this record.'[12] Michael Pollitt, comparing the pre- and post-privatization performance of several firms, concludes, 'Privatization itself does not seem to be associated with an acceleration of productivity growth or profitability.'[13] The key word here is 'itself'. It seems that it is the introduction of competition where that is attainable, and efficient regulation where elements of natural monopoly remain, that account for the improvements in efficiency that followed the entry of several firms into the private sector.

But it must be remembered that the liberalization of many of the markets occurred precisely because the government no longer had a stake in preserving the monopoly positions of the one-time nationalized firms once they were no longer state-owned. So, although competition or regulation produced the efficiency gains, the privatization of the enterprises was a necessary predicate to the introduction of competition where feasible, and regulation where necessary. In fact, it might be well to think of the history of these firms in three phases.

1. As state-owned enterprises: the firms looked to the government to protect them from competition and to subsidize them when they couldn't cover their costs.
2. As firms operating during the period immediately preceding privatization: the government was seeking to maximize the value of the enterprises' shares, to the extent that was consistent with its desire for widespread share ownership. It therefore had a continued stake in preserving some of the monopoly protections enjoyed by the firms – the grant of so many Heathrow slots to BA is one example, the preservation of British Gas's vertically integrated structure is another, the preservation of BAA's monopoly of airports serving London yet another – and in promising that regulation would be merely 'light-handed'.
3. As firms operating after privatization: the government generally came to realize that if consumers ('voters' in the politicians' jargon) were to get some semblance of value for money, and something approximating a quality service, competition or effective regulation was required.

And it does seem to be the case that once competition and/or effective regulation was introduced, performance improved markedly. Real operating costs declined at a compound annual rate of 3.7 per cent in the water industry, 4.1 per cent in the sewerage industry, 6.5 per cent in the transmission of electricity, 6.8 per cent in electricity distribution, and 9.1 per cent in gas transportation.[14]

But I hasten to emphasize again that the literature is not unanimous. Indeed, the very report that I have cited includes data that show that the rate of increase in total factor productivity of several privatized companies declined after privatization.[15] My own conclusions after a meander through the literature, and first-hand observation of some industries, are as follows:

1. Privatization was the first step on a long road to improving the efficiency of the nationalized industries.

2. In many cases the road was made rockier by the government's failure to consider the form of privatization that would most likely maximize competition and minimize the burdens placed on regulators.[16]
3. When competition or effective regulation was introduced, many dimensions of performance improved. These gains included better financial performance,[17] a reduction in overmanning and an increased responsiveness to customer demands, either because competition induced it, regulators mandated it, or government ministers changed from industry protectors into industry critics.
4. Important aspects of privatization have been the conversion of managers from agents acting for their government departments to agents acting for their shareholders; the substitution of options and bonuses for honours as a motivating force; and the substitution of capital markets for ministerial largesse as a source of capital. An electric supply industry beholden to the government for funds was certainly more likely to make a deal to sustain inefficient coal producers than one subject to the discipline of capital markets, although vestiges of the old pressure to protect mining jobs certainly remains, at a high cost to the environment and the efficiency of the supply industry. A telecoms CEO who has to please investors is likely to behave differently and to hone different skills than one whose goal is to please ministers, although the increase in efficiency, profitability and quality of service may be some time in coming.

Perhaps the best current example of the difference between private and public sector operation is provided by the media industries. The BBC, admittedly woefully inefficient and steadily losing market share, is rewarded by government with an increased flow of funds confiscated from taxpayers, despite its clear dilution of its public service broadcasting obligations, and a drive to expand in areas where no market failure can be found to justify such expansion. Efficiency is unnecessary; clear corporate goals are unnecessary; satisfying viewers is unnecessary. Indeed, even cocking a snook at the responsible minister proves no impediment to unlimited funding.

Contrast that with a private sector broadcaster. A performance such as that of the BBC would result in reduced access to funds, another way of saying that funds would gravitate from the company that failed to satisfy viewer needs and wants to those that succeed in doing so. Economists call this the more efficient allocation of capital.

As I have already pointed out, privatization was a necessary but not sufficient condition for the attainment of these gains. True, as a matter of theory some of the advantages of privatization – reliance on capital markets, creation of incentives for managerial and worker efficiency – might be obtained within the nationalized structure. But history suggests that these advantages were not often achievable in practice, although where competition was introduced nationalized companies did respond by becoming more efficient.[18] And the history of these companies since they entered the private sector encourages the belief that privatization was indeed a key factor, if for no other reason than it set the stage for a more competitive or more effectively regulated industrial environment.

This brings me to the next stage of this chapter. I would like now briefly to appraise the way in which regulation and competition have developed in the industries that were once state-owned. This appraisal starts with a bias, and proceeds to a set of impressions – no claim is made for the systematic or scientific nature of what follows.

The bias is this: competition does a better job than regulation in producing a variety of goods and services, at prices that are most closely related to costs that are themselves minimized by competitive pressures. All of you are familiar with the virtues of competition as set forth in the various economic textbooks to which those of you fortunate enough to have studied the dismal science were exposed in your formative years; I need not repeat them here in any detail. Competition in product markets forces firms to give consumers what they want at acceptable prices; it allocates capital and other resources to their best use; within any given distribution of income, it maximizes welfare; and it creates a fairer and more stable society, one in which opportunities to exploit one's talents are not foreclosed by monopoly power.

That is why attempts to regulate industries in which effective competition is possible – either because of the notion that competition would threaten product quality, or safety, or produce unacceptable discrimination among customer classes, or prevent the subsidization of groups favoured by politicians – have generally produced disastrous results. As Alfred Kahn put it in his discussion of 'the deregulation revolution' that has swept through America's airline, trucking and bus industries, its stock exchange, and to some lesser extent its cable industry,

> About most of these a consensus was already emerging in the early 1970s among disinterested students that regulation had suppressed innovation, sheltered inefficiency, encouraged a wage/price spiral, promoted severe misallocation of resources by throwing prices out of alignment with marginal costs, encouraged competition in wasteful, cost-inflating ways, and denied the public the variety of price and quality choices that a competitive market would have provided.[19]

The appropriate public policy for these industries is relatively easy to arrive at – deregulate and rely on markets, preserved in their competitive state by a vigorous antitrust policy when necessary. It is when we have to deal with industries in which some mixture of regulation and competition is required – industries in which producers are not yet pure price-takers, or industries in which one horizontal level has natural monopoly elements – that the problems arise.

In such industries, complex judgements concerning when to intervene and when to leave things alone must be made. Regulators must decide:

- when a price run-up constitutes the manipulation and the exercise of market power and when it merely reflects supply and demand conditions and the responses to them of competing sellers;
- when vertical integration will reduce transactions costs and generate savings that will be passed on to consumers, and when it will create distortions at other horizontal levels of the industry;
- when intervention in response to short-run problems such as price 'spikes' is appropriate, and when such action will create long-run disincentives to new entry; and
- when mandating access to bottleneck facilities will increase the rate of innovation and the pace of new entry, and when it will discourage investment in such facilities.

In these instances in which the regulator must balance his desire and the pressure upon him to intervene against that small, inner voice that attempts to remind him what he has learned about the superiority of market forces, the temptation to intervene can become irresistible. Not for most regulators Ronald Reagan's advice: 'Don't just do something, stand there.' As Kahn has put it, 'In making complex judgments like these, the anticompetitive bias of the regulatory mentality has ample opportunity to manifest itself.'[20] After all, if the regulator decides in favour of a monopoly structure as opposed to a competitive one, he has in effect created a chosen instrument to which he guarantees freedom from competition in return for obedience to his views on prices, the desired quality of service, and the social functions it should accept as part of the 'deal' with the regulator.

It is the importance of what Kahn calls the regulator's 'mentality' that lends weight to my view that the quality of regulation is often a function of the quality of the regulator, and of the legislative tools given to him by the politicians. If the regulator has a bias in favour of competitive solutions, and if the legislative structure within which he must work permits him to exercise that bias, regulation is likely to work better than if these two conditions are not met. So I want to spend a moment examining, first, the tools available to the UK's regulators, and then the way in which the regulators have used these tools.

The Tools

It must be remembered that when it launched the programme of privatizing firms that were to retain substantial monopoly power, the UK had no significant experience with economic regulation or regulatory agencies on the scale that privatization would necessarily engender. All talk was of 'light-handed regulation', of tiny regulatory bodies with small budgets and few staff, and of avoiding 'American-style adversarial litigation'. Such was the stuff that Tory dreams were made of.

In the event, the government was heading down a path that would involve the creation of an entire new branch of government, agencies with enormous power over the fate of key industries and over the prices that consumers would pay for necessities such as water, electricity and natural gas. Given the importance of the regulators' missions, and what Sir Bryan Carsberg has called the 'conflicting vested interests' that are inevitably involved,[21] it was somewhere between foolishness and wild optimism for the government to imagine that regulation is a process that can be performed by a few folks applying uncontroversial techniques to determine prices that will be fair to consumers and at the same time yield returns adequate, but no more than adequate, to attract capital in sufficient quantities to maintain service at acceptable levels.

The resources and tools bequeathed by the government to the regulators proved woefully inadequate, especially since the government paid little attention to the need to restructure the privatized companies so as to maximize the possibility of competition.[22] The problem was compounded – and I say this with all respect to our chairman – when antipathy towards 'American-style cost-plus' regulation, as it was mistakenly called here, led to reliance on the RPI–X formula. I have elsewhere commented on the failings of that formula, and will repeat here only two points. No one knew how to measure and to forecast 'X', the anticipated cost-savings due to greater efficiency. And no one anticipated the political consequences of a formula that placed no effective and visible constraints on the profits that a monopoly utility might be permitted to earn.

When the newly privatized companies proved capable of wringing cost-savings far in excess of anything contained in the 'X-files', profits soared, in some industries at the expense of service quality. So regulators found themselves in the difficult business of trying to force prices down so as to contain profitability, and of developing efficiency standards, a chore carried out with a wonderfully optimistic view of the power of regression equations, and to its highest level of detail by the water[23] and electricity regulators of those distribution networks.

This is not to criticize the individual regulators. In part, the evolution of the regulatory regime to something closer to the American model was predictable, and not a function of any failure on the regulators' part to implement the unrealistic expectations that regulation could be kept to a minor chore. The regulators had been given flawed tools. They had to overcome a huge information asymmetry problem, most notably in the early days of the regulation of the vertically integrated gas monopoly that the government of the day had seen fit to unloose on an unsuspecting public and on under-resourced regulators; and they had to overcome the residual arrogance of the 'barons' who ran the state-owned companies and, backed by the trade unions, were accustomed to having their way with mere ministers and parliamentarians, not to mention regulators. Which brings me to my final subject: the regulators.

The Regulators

The amazing thing to this long-time observer of the regulatory process in the UK and the USA is that the entire system did not collapse. The agencies responsible for regulating these key industries did not have adequate resources; the companies they were asked to regulate were not in a cooperative mood and proved unwilling to share data or concede that regulators had a legitimate role to play; the formula on which regulation was to be based was flawed.

Yet here we are, in the twenty-first century, with regulated utilities that are somehow continuing to function, and regulatory agencies that have grown in expertise. This is in large measure because, as I mentioned earlier, the people who get these jobs matter, and the UK has been fortunate in its selection of regulators. They have been truculent when necessary, attempted to maximize the scope of competition,[24] and wrestled with difficult conceptual problems with some success. It would be out of character for me to heap undiluted praise on regulators, so I must add that their performance has not been without its flaws: the water industry may be suffering from overly constrained revenues; the electric industry is at the mercy of a regulator who believes he can separate good behaviour from bad; the telecoms industry has not opened up to competition as rapidly and completely as some would like. But all in all, given the difficulty of the task of creating what is indeed an entirely new branch of government, it is fair to say that the UK's regulators should be given good marks.

Oddly, this seems to be truer of those regulators charged with overseeing the monopoly utilities – electric, gas and water distribution – than of those responsible for industries in which competition is more feasible. In the 'wire industries' – cable and telephony – regulators have been reluctant to mandate the open access that is necessary to break the competitive 'bottlenecks' that incumbents have set up. I recognize that the advantages of open access have to be weighed against the possible disincentive such access creates to investment in new facilities.[25] And that there is not unlimited capacity in the buildings of incumbent telephone providers to accommodate new entrants. But a re-examination of the balance being drawn between the desirability of lowering entry barriers and treating incumbents fairly might just produce a greater tilt in favour of more rapid market opening.

In the highly competitive broadcasting industry, where competition is distorted by the amazing ability of the BBC to extract ever-larger sums from taxpayers in pursuit of an ever-expanding role, and by generous spectrum grants to chosen instruments to the disadvantage of potential entrants, and where cultural considerations inevitably affect regulatory decisions, regulators nevertheless have greater freedom than they have chosen to exercise in promoting competition. Instead, we see a web of regulations stupefying in their complexity, often based on economically illiterate definitions of relevant markets, and aimed at favouring this or that competitor. Perhaps the White Paper that is due will take a scissors to all of this red tape and nonsense, and remove impediments to the rapid development of the new technologies that hold such promise. And perhaps some guidelines will be established to limit the BBC to specified areas, and thereby prevent that organization from continuing to use the hoary anti-competitive tactic of pre-announcing services to discourage potential entrants.

I want to conclude with a thought on where the regulatory regime might go from here. First, all regulators should concentrate on getting the incentives right: you cannot create an incentive for punctuality by fining operators for late arrivals of trains, and hope that they will not respond by elevating punctuality over safety. You cannot induce efficient overall performance by creating incentives to lower one set of costs, and hope that the regulated companies will not meet that goal by incurring higher costs in other areas of their operations.

Second, where competition exists or is possible, the regulatory burden should be reduced. Note: the long arm of the regulator remains necessary where the invisible hand does not operate.[26] But in other places, every effort should be made to substitute competition for regulation, including in the so-called 'network industries', in which natural monopoly elements are of 'diminished significance' and in which 'encouraging competition generally leads to greater dynamism and welfare gains'.[27] After all, since the UK began creating regulatory bodies, two things have changed: many of the regulated companies now face at least some competition, and the UK has a new and more potent competition policy. The need for sectoral regulation has certainly diminished, although by just how much can only be determined by sector-by-sector study of the effectiveness of competition. Such studies must be undertaken in full awareness of what public choice theory teaches us – that regulators have a strong disinclination to declare victory and return to the academic, business or government careers from whence they came.

Third, regulatory procedures must be improved. In many instances they lack sufficient transparency; regulators do not adequately explain the basis for their rulings; and there is no adequate appeals process that provides regulated companies with an alternative to the often-hostile staffs of the regulatory agencies.

Finally, in the telecoms/media area overlapping, multi-forum regulation must be rationalized. As Professor Ian Hargreaves has pointed out, 'A system that currently involves ... 14 separate regulatory bodies, overseen by two government departments, must be unified. A regime sown with the risk of double jeopardy needs to be simplified, both in the interests of consumers and in the interests of business...'.[28]

But that is a topic for another occasion, after we have seen the government's White Paper.

NOTES

1. Not all state enterprises need be monopolies; liberalization, that is, competition, is possible without privatization; competitively structured industries are sometimes regulated. But this chapter deals primarily with the privatization of enterprises that are monopolies at the time they pass from state ownership.

2. For a discussion of these costs see Peter Self, *Rolling Back The Market: Economic Dogma & Political Choice*, London, Macmillan, 2000.

3. Alfred E. Kahn, *The Economics of Regulation: Principles and Institutions*, New York, John Wiley & Sons, 1970 (Vol. I) and 1971 (Vol. II), pp. 325–6 (Vol. II). Reprinted in a single volume by The MIT Press, Cambridge, in 1988.

4. Thomas K. McCraw, *Prophets of Regulation*, Cambridge, MA, The Belknap Press of Harvard University Press, 1984, p. 303.

5. Michael G. Pollitt, 'A Survey of the Liberalisation of Public Enterprises in the UK Since 1979', University of Cambridge, Department of Applied Economics working paper, January 1999, p. 1. The most notable remaining public enterprises are the Post Office and the London Underground.

6. David Parker and Stephen Martin, 'The Impact of UK Privatization on Labour and Total Factor Productivity', Working Papers in Commerce, The University of Birmingham, 24 November 1993, p. 2.

7. Seth Thomas, 'The Privatization of the Electricity Supply Industry', in John Surrey (ed.), *The British Electricity Experiment. Privatization: The Record, The Issues, The Lessons*, London, Earthscan Publications Limited, 1996, p. 41.

8. 'The encouragement of share ownership, especially by company employees, was another major goal of the program...'. John Vickers and George Yarrow, *Privatization: An Economic Analysis*, Cambridge, MA, The MIT Press, 1988, p. 159.

9. Discounts, the difference between the price at which the government sold the shares of 'the major natural monopoly privatizations' and the prices at which they were initially quoted ranged from 20 per cent in the case of power generators to 86 per cent in the case of BT. Mike Wright and Steve Thompson, 'Divestiture of Public Sector Assets', in Peter M. Jackson and Catherine M. Price (eds), *Privatization and Regulation: A Review of the Issues*, London and New York, Longman Group Limited, 1994, p. 55.

10. In this connection, see my 'Crash or Boom? On the Future of the New Economy', *Commentary*, October 2000, pp. 23-7, and several recent studies by Goldman Sachs.
11. Vickers and Yarrow, *Privatization*, p. 3.
12. David Parker, 'Nationalisation, Privatisation, and Agency Status Within Government: Testing for the Importance of Ownership', in Jackson and Price, *Privatisation and Regulation*, p. 150.
13. Ibid., p. 23.
14. European Economics, 'Review of Railtrack Efficiency', 9 December 1999, p. 15.
15. Ibid., p. 18. That may, of course, have been the consequence of a pre-privatization spurt in efforts to spruce up these firms' performances in order to increase their market values. Parker and Martin found that 'in most cases a performance improvement occurred in the run-up to privatization, suggesting rationalisation by management in anticipation of having to survive in the private sector.' 'The Impact of UK Privatization', p. 19.
16. In this connection see, for example, Colin Robinson, 'Privatising the Energy Industries: The Lessons to be Learned', *Metroeconomica*, **XLIII**, 1-2, February–June 1992; and Robinson's 'Profit, Discovery and the Role of Entry: The Case of Electricity', in M.E. Beesley (ed.), *Regulating Utilities: A Time For Change?*, London, Institute of Economic Affairs, 1996. 'In electricity, as in other privatisations, a good idea has been imperfectly executed' (p. 109).
17. Pollitt, 'Survey', p. 23.
18. For example, the Post Office seems to have become more efficient as competition became more intense. 'We found that when the competitive environment became tougher, *tfp* [total factor productivity] increased significantly. Strikingly, this was as true of those firms which have remained in public ownership, notably the Post Office, as for those that have been privatised.' Matthew Bishop and Mike Green, 'Privatisation and Recession – The Miracle Tested', Discussion Paper 10. London, Centre for the Study of Regulated Industries, 1995, p. 33.
19. Introduction and Postscript to the 1988 reissue of *The Economics of Regulation*, p. xvi.
20. Ibid., Vol. II, p. 114.
21. Bryan Carsberg, 'Injecting Competition Into Telecommunications', in Cento Veljanovski (ed.), *Privatisation & Competition: A Market Prospectus*, London, Institute of Economic Affairs, 1989, p. 81.
22. 'It would have been possible, for instance, to have split British Telecom into a number of separate enterprises or ... to have sold the UK's two major international airports separately rather than privatising the British Airports Authority intact.' Michael Fleming and Kenneth Button, 'Regulatory Reform in the UK', in Kenneth Button and Dennis Swan (eds), *The Age of Regulatory Reform*, Oxford, Oxford University Press, 1989, p. 92. And there was no need to sell off British Gas as a vertically integrated monopoly, sowing the seeds for future regulatory problems.
23. The water industry provides a good example of the problems, as a reading of Ofwat's 1999 Periodic Review shows. First, the underestimation of potential efficiency gains: 'Since the 1994 price review, the companies have significantly outperformed the Director's expectations about how efficient they could become' (p. 27). Then profits hit unexpectedly high levels: 'The rates of return on capital have been high...' (p. 31). Then the inevitable overreaction, driving profitability down to the point where several companies are attempting to extract their remaining equity capital from the industry.
24. Many of the UK's leading regulators have been devoted to competitive solutions. 'Whenever I become aware of a problem ... I ask first whether the problem can be alleviated by bringing about more competition or better competition.' Carsberg, 'Injecting Competition', p. 82. 'Competition, whether existing or merely potential, is a vital protection for consumers against ... higher prices, lower quality of service and reluctance of service and reluctance to innovate.' S.C. Littlechild, 'Ten Steps To Denationalisation', in Veljanovski, *Privatisation Competition*, p. 18.
25. For a concise discussion of the question of access, especially in the context of vertical integration, see Lars Bergman et al., *Europe's Network Industries: Conflicting Priorities*, London, Centre for Economic Policy Research, 1998, pp. 24–7.

26. 'I would love to go down in History as the last energy regulator but I believe the gas and electricity markets will continue to need some regulation...'. Callum McCarthy, Director General, Ofgem, quoted in Keith Boyfield, *The Politics of Regulation*, London, European Policy Forum, 2000, p. 36.
27. Bergman et al., *Europe's Network Industries*, p. 39.
28. *Financial Times,* 25 May, 2000.

CHAIRMAN'S COMMENTS

Stephen Littlechild

I agree with much of Stelzer's chapter, and appreciate the kind remarks about the UK being fortunate in its choice of regulators. But it would be out of character for me, as chairman, to heap undiluted praise on any contributor. So I shall attempt to seek out some issues where we might provoke further discussion.

The comments on communications policy are particularly stimulating. When choice is increasingly available, it is indeed not clear what justification there is for the government to run more than one TV or radio station, and to finance this by what is in effect a poll tax. Does it even need to run one station when it could alternatively buy time for programmes on other stations? Such issues are much debated elsewhere.[1] I suspect that most of our discussion here will be on the regulated and privatized utilities.

The author makes a strong case that private ownership is preferable to state ownership. The defects of regulation are set out, as indeed they should be. We have gone beyond the stage where identifying a 'market failure' automatically justified state intervention to cure it. 'Government failure' is equally plausible and pervasive. Indeed, one recent text[2] does not mention regulation without appending the epithet 'inefficient'. But it would seem only fair to set out the defects of state ownership as well as of regulation, and the merits of each form of ownership or control, in order to come to an informed conclusion.

Whether private ownership is more efficient than public ownership is much debated, as the author indicates. It seems to me that the case for private ownership is stronger than he and some others generally allow. He rightly acknowledges that competition and effective regulation are only possible when an industry is privatized, and hence the benefits associated with these latter factors should be attributed, at least in part, to the change in ownership. One might note, in addition, that the benefits of competition in the capital markets, and of further industry restructuring via mergers and acquisitions, are only possible in the private sector. At a more rudimentary level, anyone familiar with the operation of public utilities in developing countries, where there is often widespread operation at enormous and continuing losses, will acknowledge that this gross inefficiency could not continue if the firms concerned were in the private sector.

The author claims that competition is better than regulation. Where competition is possible I agree strongly. But does anyone now disagree? The real issue is what to do where competition is not obviously possible. And here I wonder whether the author's message might be clarified.

Where competition does not now exist, but could exist if the conditions were right, there is a case for regulation to help bring about these conditions. The author perhaps gives insufficient credit to the UK regulatory framework, with its duty to promote or facilitate competition. This has led, *inter alia*, to greater competition in the energy sector than in most other countries.

Where there is likely to be a continuing monopoly, and competition is not likely to be possible, at least in the foreseeable future, the issue is not competition versus regulation, but what kind of regulation is best. The author makes a number of criticisms of RPI–X regulation, but how convincing are these? He says that 'the resources and tools bequeathed by the government to the regulators proved woefully inadequate'. It is of course true that over time they have increased their staffs and access to consultants. But I am not aware that any of them have complained about being deprived of necessary resources.

He says that 'No one knew how to measure and to forecast "X", the anticipated cost-savings due to greater efficiency.' But when this type of regulation was first proposed, in the context of privatizing BT, it was not suggested that X should measure cost-savings alone, nor has that generally been the practice of the utility regulators. The level of X, and any associated cuts into (the initial price), reflect a wide variety of considerations. In any case, the emphasis on incentives means that it is not necessary to 'get it right' with respect to forecasting efficiency improvements in any particular period, since companies are encouraged to beat the efficiency target, in the knowledge that customers will also share the benefits in due course. In this context, perhaps the author gives insufficient credit to the RPI–X formula, and the general UK regulatory approach, in securing the very significant efficiency gains that he applauds earlier in the chapter.

The ultimate question is not whether UK regulation and RPI–X have deficiencies, since they undoubtedly do. The question is, what system of regulation would be better? Can it really be what the author says is mistakenly described as 'American-style cost-plus' regulation? The author is silent on this point.

The author concludes on a constructive note. Where should the regulatory regime go from here? First, he says, regulators should get the incentives right. This is an important point. Ofgem, for example, recognizes this in its Information and Incentives Project, with respect to setting penalties and rewards for quality of supply. But if the author thinks 'the electricity industry is at the mercy of a regulator who believes he can separate good behaviour from bad', is this not what he is asking the same regulator to do in the context of network performance?

The next recommendation is to substitute competition for regulation wherever possible. Agreed, and great strides have been made in both the wholesale and retail markets for electricity and gas. Serious attempts have also been made to reduce the scope of the network monopoly, for example by encouraging competition for connections and in metering and meter reading, and in transmission storage and capacity availability in the gas network. But it is not easy, and the scope may be limited.

Finally, he suggests that regulatory procedures must be improved. I wonder if this is a somewhat out-dated point. In recent years, transparency has been much increased, and explanations are now as full as can be expected. There are also in effect two appeals processes, one via the Competition Commission and the other via the courts, both of which have been readily used.

Perhaps I have taken issue too much with Dr Stelzer's chapter, since I agree with so much of what he says. Really, my only qualification is that I believe that there is a little more to be said for UK regulation than he allows.

NOTES

1. For example, Sir Alan Peacock, 'Market failure and government failure in broadcasting' and other contributions in the special issue on The Future of Broadcasting, *Economic Affairs*, **20**, 4, December 2000.
2. David M. Newbery, *Privatization, Restructuring, and Regulation of Network Utilities*, Cambridge, MA and London, MIT Press, 2000.

6. Converging communications: implications for regulation[*]

Mark Armstrong

1. COMMUNICATIONS MARKETS IN THE UK

This chapter is about the current and future market for electronic communications and how it should be regulated. The word 'convergence' refers to the observation that the same communications services can now be supplied over a variety of transmission infrastructures, such as telephone lines, mobile networks, satellite and over-the-air broadcasting. One can now watch TV and make voice telephone calls via a PC, and one can use email via a TV (together with a telephone line). See Figures 6.1 and 6.2 for a schematic description of the old and the new order in electronic communications. Given that different regulatory bodies and regulatory regimes are typically associated with these different infrastructures, there is then the danger of asymmetries and inefficiencies emerging. Many of the existing structures are a legacy of the old era when there was a one-to-one correspondence between services and delivery systems: delivery systems could not carry a variety of services, and services could not be carried over a variety of delivery systems. (See Figure 6.1.) This made separate regulation based on delivery systems, while not necessary, at least fairly harmless.

Important recent (and future) dates in the UK's experience of convergence include:

- January 1996: government paper *Regulation of Conditional Access Services for Digital Television* gives Oftel the role of regulating conditional access markets (in cooperation with the ITC).
- April 1998: government publishes *Broadband Britain: A Fresh Look at the Broadcast Entertainment Restrictions*, which, among other measures, relaxes the ban on BT regarding the conveyance and provision of entertainment services (from 2001).
- July 1998: Green Paper *Regulating Convergence: Approaching*

* I am grateful to Mark Schankerman for helpful comments. All views and errors are my own.

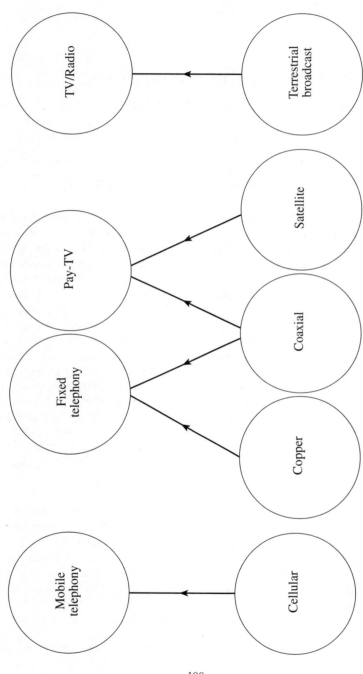

Figure 6.1   The old order

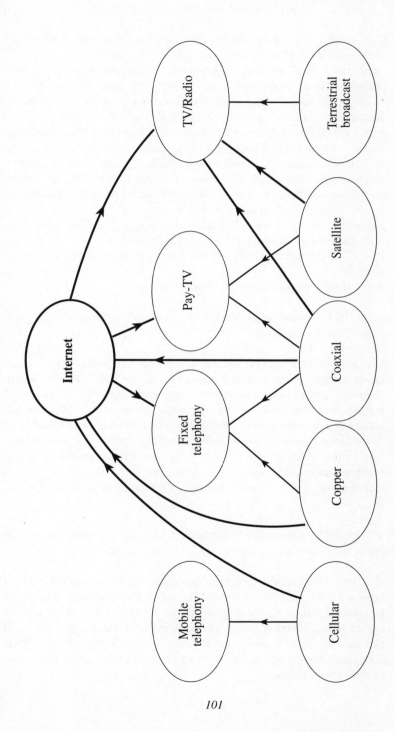

Figure 6.2 A converged communications industry

Convergence in the Information Age announces the government's plans to reform the regulation of the communications sector.

- June 1999: DTI publishes *Regulating Communications: The Way Ahead*, which summarizes the results of consultation on the convergence Green Paper, and invites further industry advice in the preparation of the White Paper, planned for the end of 2000.
- July 1999: Davies Report on *The Future Funding of the BBC*, published by the Department of Culture, Media and Sport, suggests that a 'digital licence fee' be introduced to help fund the BBC's entry into new digital markets, and that the BBC's commercial arm, BBC Worldwide, be partially privatized. The March 2000 government paper *The Funding of the BBC* rejects both of these proposals.
- Summer 2000: Oftel and BT embroiled in controversy over unbundling BT's local loop for use by rival broadband networks.
- End of 2000: White Paper on the future of communications to be published.
- 2006: BBC's Royal Charter to be renewed.

The current UK system of regulation for the communications markets is, with great simplification, as follows:

- telecoms: Oftel, now with some concurrent powers with OFT;
- broadcasting: charter and self-regulation for the BBC (and the Welsh channel, S4C); ITC and Radio Authority (RA) for commercial broadcasters; the Broadcasting Standards Commission (BSC) handles complaints on content from all broadcasters; Oftel handles regulation of the broadcast transmission network, as well as conditional access issues (for instance, access by content providers to the set-top box and electronic programme guides for digital TV);
- non-defence spectrum management: Radiocommunications Agency, ITC.

Perhaps especially within the broadcasting market, asymmetries in the treatment of the different participants are immense. Thus:

- The BBC's core services, including its digital channels, are funded by a licence fee mechanism, so that viewers of all TV companies must pay a licence fee, all of which is given to the BBC (once government has taken off its collection costs). Thus anyone who watches any TV at all can view the BBC's core output for an incremental price of zero. Other companies must compete against this free service while at the same time covering their own costs.

- The BBC cannot show advertisements (except for its own services). The commercial terrestrial broadcasters are funded by advertising revenue and sponsorship, although the quantity of advertising per hour is controlled by the ITC.
- The cable and satellite suppliers are funded by a mixture of subscription and advertising, and are not regulated as to the amount of advertising they show.
- The 'quality' of the BBC's output is not explicitly controlled, except perhaps by its governors. The quality – amount of news, drama, documentaries, religious programmes, and so on, as well as a few important scheduling issues – of the commercial terrestrial broadcasters is monitored by the ITC, and for the ITV companies this formed part of the franchise contract when these were awarded in 1990. Cable and satellite firms are exempt from quality control (save for taste and decency provisions).[1]

Recent estimated market share data for TV broadcasting (unweighted viewing hours) for the 12 months up to September 2000 are: ITV 29.6 per cent, BBC1 27.6 per cent, BBC2 10.7 per cent, Channel 4 10.1 per cent and Channel 5 5.7 per cent, with the rest taking about 15 per cent.[2] Thus, despite its great funding advantage, the BBC only just holds its own in terms of market share with its comparable commercial rivals. According to their respective web sites, in the financial year 1999/2000 the BBC spent £823m on the BBC1 channel (together with £207m on regional programming), whereas the ITV collection of regional companies spent £627m on networked programming for the ITV channel (together with £200m on regional programming).

2. TV AND TELECOMS: PARALLELS AND CONTRASTS

In this section we discuss three groups of issues that are, to a greater or lesser extent, common ground across the two communications sectors.

2.1 Universal Service and Public Service Obligations

There is a strong parallel between the universal service obligation (USO) placed on BT in the telecoms sector and the public service obligation (PSO) placed on the BBC (and to a lesser extent on the commercial terrestrial broadcasters) in the television sector. This is true both of the advantages offered to consumers of the services, and in the likely inefficiencies caused by their funding arrangements. In both sectors, the key questions are:

(a)   At what level (if any) above *laissez-faire* levels should universal service or public service obligations be set?
(b)   How should these services be funded?
(c)   Who should provide these services (and how are these providers chosen)?

In very broad terms, the policies followed in two sectors in the UK have given the following answers to these questions. For (a), there is a belief that services need to be provided at a level or price at which the market will not deliver. For (c), the answer is that it is the 'incumbents' (respectively, BT and the BBC) who will perform this task. It is concerning (b) that the two sectors differ substantially: for telecoms, BT has to finance these services out of its own funds, whereas for TV it is viewers of all broadcasters who contribute to public service content via the licence fee.

2.1.1 The USO in telecoms

The USO means that BT has a duty to provide basic services to any subscriber, regardless of location and almost regardless of cost. Roughly speaking, BT is required to cross-subsidize loss-making subscribers (for instance, in rural areas) from profits generated elsewhere. This arrangement has the following three implications for the telecoms market:

1.   There is a danger of cream-skimming entry into BT's artificially profitable markets, and entry can be profitable even if the entrant has higher costs than BT.
2.   There may be inefficient lack of entry into the subsidized sectors, in the sense that a potential entrant could have lower costs than BT for serving the loss-making subscribers, yet still cannot compete against BT's artificially low tariff. (For instance, it could be that mobile networks could have had more of an impact in rural areas if fixed line tariffs had been more closely related to the underlying costs.)
3.   If widespread cream-skimming does occur, then profits in the erstwhile profitable sectors will be eroded and BT will have difficulties in funding its loss-making services.

One solution to these three problems would be to rebalance BT's tariff better to reflect its costs. However, this may be politically unacceptable in the short term. In any event, Oftel is itself unwilling to rebalance BT's tariff in this way, and has recently stated:[3]

> As part of the last Price Control Review Oftel set out the principle that those basic elements of telecoms service would be provided at geographically averaged prices so that they are available to all consumers at the same price throughout the country.

... It has the benefit of ensuring that the benefits of competition in areas of the country where BT faces strong competition are extended throughout the country.

A second 'solution' is to ban or discourage entry (as in letter post). This is clearly an unimaginative and inefficient policy.

Another solution is to require BT to finance its loss-making services out of its own funds (while these funds remain available). This is Oftel's current position, although the situation is under review. This policy can be applied so long as problem (3) above is not important, but it does nothing to counter problems (1) and (2). In this sense, then, this policy runs counter to Oftel's stated aims for the USO:[4]

> Social and consumer policy objectives will not necessarily be achieved through the operation of a well-functioning market, for example universal service. To the extent that an economic regulator is also charged with the implementation of these objectives they should be required to ensure that such rules are enforced in an efficient and cost effective way, that their effect is competitively neutral and they do not inhibit competition and choice.

Another solution is to 'de-link' the loss-making from the profitable markets. The latter could be freed from control, and competition could drive prices down to cost. The loss-making markets could be funded out of some kind of industry fund or from public funds. Alternatively, the right to offer services in the loss-making markets could be auctioned off (as for parts of the rail industry), a mechanism that will more likely pick an efficient operator. Such schemes will mean that geographically uniform pricing will cease, however.

If the uniform tariff arrangement is to be maintained, each of these three undesirable features could be eliminated provided a carefully designed USO fund were to be implemented, where all relevant telecoms firms contributed to the fund in profitable markets, and where all relevant firms could serve the loss-making sectors by drawing on subsidies from the USO fund. Such a system generates a level playing field, and potential inefficiencies are thereby mitigated.

Finally, some have suggested extending BT's USO to include broadband services. Given the above problems caused by USOs, I would suggest that this be treated with caution, at least if no well-designed USO fund (or funding from direct taxation, as favoured by the EU Commission for any possible enhanced USO) is first put into place.[5]

2.1.2 The PSO in broadcasting

The BBC's Royal Charter requires it to 'educate, inform and entertain'. More specifically, in 1998 the Secretary of State for Culture, Media and Sport set out five principles for what he thinks a public service broadcaster such as the BBC should do:[6]

- the BBC should act as a benchmark for quality, driving up standards across the board;
- it should provide something for everybody, making the good popular and the popular good;
- it should inform, educate and entertain, expanding people's horizons with new and innovative programming;
- it should operate efficiently and effectively and provide value for money for licence fee payers;
- it should stimulate, support and reflect the diversity of cultural activity in the United Kingdom, acting as a cultural voice for the nation.

These considerations apply to the content of the programmes themselves. A second, and perhaps equally important, aspect of the PSO, at least as applied to the BBC, is the required lack of advertising.[7] Finally, as with the USO in telecoms, it is important that the great majority of the population are able to gain access to the programming, in terms of both availability and affordability.

The big question is how the achievement of these objectives is funded. The current mechanism – the licence fee, due to be used at least until the Charter renewal in 2006 – clearly works as a source of funds, but has some dramatic implications for the efficient operation of the TV market.

Before going on to discuss the more negative aspects of this funding arrangement, it is worth mentioning one of the classic justifications for the licence fee approach: given that the marginal cost of broadcasting programmes to additional citizens is zero, the economically efficient charge for consuming these services is zero. Obviously this is true, but it applies much more widely than to the BBC's services. For instance, it applies with equal force to BSkyB's content. Marginal cost pricing is probably rather rare in 'information goods' markets, and for some good reasons. Thus, even an old-fashioned – and competitive – communications market like book publishing will price its output significantly above the marginal cost of printing a book. While it is true that, given that the book has been written, it is socially optimal to price it at, say, £2 instead of £8.99 – for otherwise some readers would be excluded from the market despite being willing to pay the marginal production cost – no one is suggesting moving to some kind of marginal cost pricing regime for this industry. It seems likely that the positive effects of an above-cost pricing policy, in terms of the incentives it gives to find, commission or otherwise produce desirable content that people want to consume, outweigh the *ex post* welfare gains caused by marginal cost pricing. Similar effects would seem to apply to the desirability of the licence fee funding mechanism.

A quite separate issue is that the entirety of the 'PSO fund', that is, the proceeds from the licence fee, is paid to a single entity, the BBC, and there is no mechanism to allocate funds to other companies (who may also be able to offer good PSO-type programmes). Therefore, there is no way to ensure that the most efficient firm – 'efficient' in the general sense of providing quality programmes at reasonable cost – undertakes PSO-type programming.

Of course, other TV companies can gain access to listeners and viewers via their own channels and platforms, but in that case they face a terrific disadvantage: the BBC can afford to provide its services without the need for subscription or advertising, whereas everyone else cannot. To take a perhaps small example, people sometimes complain that Classic FM is inferior to Radio 3 because it broadcasts short pieces of music interrupted by advertisements. However, it has no choice! It is simply not known how enjoyable its service would be if it had access to the same external funds as does Radio 3. Similarly, for a commercial terrestrial broadcaster to make a programme as attractive to viewers as a similar programme on the BBC, it must make a superior product ('superior' in the sense of being more attractive to viewers rather than in terms of being more 'educative or informative') in order to compensate for the intrusion of its advertisements.

Therefore, as with the USO in telecoms, there is a danger of inefficiency, in the sense that a rival to the BBC may be capable of making or funding superior programmes, and yet it still cannot compete against the BBC's subsidized service. Much discussion has rightly centred on the danger of the BBC using its licence fee income to subsidize its entry into new areas.[8] There are doubtless several problems to be tackled here, such as the need to enhance the transparency of the BBC's annual accounts to check exactly how the licence fee is being spent. However, these problems seem of secondary importance compared to those caused by the subsidy awarded to the BBC, in the form of the licence fee, in the core broadcast television markets.

Given this great asymmetry in treatment between the BBC and other broadcasters, it is natural to ask whether there are better ways to organize the market. One policy might be to relax or eliminate the PSO over time, so that programme provision was determined more by market forces (that is, viewer preferences). This is perhaps analogous to the radical 'rebalancing' policy mentioned above in the telecoms context. Again, though, this may be politically unacceptable in the short term.[9] It is also less obviously a good thing, even from a pure efficiency point of view. For instance, it is hard from a technological viewpoint to restrict access to broadcast radio, and yet it may be efficient to have some radio stations advertising-free. The only solution is somehow to finance these stations with external funds.

Given that some form of PSO will be required in the medium term, it is natural to ask in what ways it can be implemented with minimal inefficiency. What seems important is that there be some kind of process to select the broadcaster which is best at providing the designated service actually to do so. At the moment there is no such process. As has been said, 'It is a leap of logic to go from the premise that there is a role for public service broadcasting to the view that the BBC as we have it is the sole instrument for achieving it.'[10] Natural procedures to consider might be where broadcasters can bid for funds from the licence fee revenue. Thus, for instance, Classic FM could at periodic intervals bid for the 'advertising-free classical music franchise', and the associated funding, against the BBC's Radio 3. Alternatively, an 'Arts Council'-style body whose aim is to subsidize worthy artistic ventures could award funds for particular programmes that would not otherwise be made.[11] As has recently been suggested:[12]

> The new Communications Act should include provisions for a new 'public services fund'. This would ensure that, if market failure were clearly identified, public resources aimed at remedying it would go to the best provider in a competitive bid. ... Even if the BBC were ultimately deemed to be the best provider, it would be likely to provide a more focused and cost effective proposal by facing competition in this way.

What seems almost inevitable, however, is that the public's willingness to pay the present BBC licence fee at current (and increasing) levels will gradually evaporate. Somewhat like the fact that extensive competition will erode the profits that allow BT to fund loss-making services out of its own pocket, a gradual loss of market share by the BBC will erode public support for the licence fee. As chapter 5 of the Davies Report puts it, 'the digital age will increasingly be one in which many or most consumers of television pay for packages closely tailored to their needs. As they become more accustomed to choice, to subscription and to pay-per-view, it could be that the licence fee will come to seem an anachronism.'

2.2   Gateways and Bottlenecks

The previous discussion highlighted the similarities between the effects of social obligations in telecoms and in broadcasting. Here we discuss another superficially powerful similarity between the two markets: essential facilities in telecoms and the conditional access (and other) gateways in pay-TV. However, we will argue that the parallels here are somewhat misleading.

2.2.1   Call termination in telecoms

In telecoms there is a variety of 'bottlenecks', that is, facilities that are controlled by a firm and which are needed by rival firms if they are to be able to offer a complete service. The most clear-cut example is call termination: when a subscriber joins a given network, that network then controls communications (of the relevant type) to that subscriber.

This is obviously the case when there is only one network of the relevant type in place (say, an incumbent's fixed network). More subtly, this is also a problem when there is competition for subscribers. To take a simple example, consider a hypothetical competitive mobile market. Mobile networks may compete with great energy – with 'free' handsets and other offers – with the result that profits are driven down to normal levels in the market. However, if networks are free to set termination charges, which are the charges that other networks must pay to have their calls delivered by mobile networks, then there is little competitive pressure to keep these charges low. Once a subscriber has been induced to join a mobile network, callers to that subscriber have to pay the termination charge of the mobile network (at least if they wish to use mobile rather than fixed technology). Therefore, even if mobile networks compete hard for subscribers, they retain significant market power when providing calls made to their subscribers.

How important this effect is depends on how substitutable are other ways of contacting the subscriber. If the subscriber is likely to be at home or at a fixed place of work, then a caller could just as well use the fixed network to make the call, and the market power over mobile call termination is smaller. However, if different means of contact are not closely substitutable, then market power is important, and so there is a need to control the termination charge (even in competitive markets).[13]

2.2.2   Call origination in telecoms

Call origination in telecoms raises different issues, since whether or not this service needs to be regulated depends upon the strength of competition for subscribers. (We argued above that with call termination, competition for subscribers did little to overcome the need for regulation.) To take a related example to that used for call termination, consider the market for calls from the fixed networks to the mobile networks. To the extent that BT has significant market power in the market for subscribers, these charges should be brought under its retail price controls. Just like any other call service, if subscribers have little choice but to use BT for making their fixed network calls, then left to itself BT has an incentive to raise its call charges above efficient levels.[14] However, as competition in the market for fixed subscribers gathers strength, the need for the control of this, or any other outbound call service, falls away. Even if the service makes up a small part of the total bill for the typical subscriber, we would expect that potential subscribers will look at a broad basket of call charges when they decide on their network, and so BT then has an incentive to keep down its charges for calls to mobiles.

2.2.3   Premium content and the role of exclusivity in broadcasting

The most clear-cut example of monopoly power in the TV market is its most 'upstream' sector, the originators of premium content: film rights, sports rights and so on. Almost paradoxically, this problem has become more important as competition in the TV market has strengthened. (In the old days, the terrestrial broadcasters seemed to agree to rotate sports rights such as football, and very low payments were made to, say, sports bodies.) In June 2000, the Premier League sold its TV rights for live coverage for the three years from 2001 for £1.11 billion, with Sky being the main recipient of these rights.[15] Direct control of the market power of the providers of premium content lies outside the remit of the existing broadcasting regulations, as well as any likely future regulations.

It is true that, currently, this upstream market power is extended downstream when sports bodies and the like allocate TV rights exclusively to a TV retailer. On the surface, this is a strange way to maximize revenues from selling the rights: why deal only with a retailer who has access to a fraction of the available viewers, when by allocating rights non-exclusively one might generate revenues from the entire viewer base? However, granting exclusive rights can be a revenue-maximizing strategy because of the effect it has on the loser's ability to attract subscribers – a TV retailer will pay a great deal to avoid having to offer an inferior contents package. This effect is illustrated by a simple abstract example (Table 6.1):

Table 6.1   Profits of two broadcasters with rights to content

	A's profit	B's profit
Neither firm has rights	£100m	£100m
Both firms have rights	£110m	£110m
A has exclusive rights	£200m	£50m
B has exclusive rights	£50m	£200m

Here a holder of rights such as the Premier League is considering how to allocate the rights to screen its live matches to two symmetrically placed broadcasters, denoted by A and B. The fallback position if neither gets the rights is that both generate profits of £100m. If both can screen matches, then profits increase modestly for both firms. (Perhaps the whole pay-TV market expands because of superior content.) By contrast, if only one broadcaster has the rights, it increases its relative attractiveness to potential subscribers, with the result that market share and profits fall for the rival broadcaster. By selling rights exclusively to one firm, the sports body can obtain £150m.[16] (For instance, if it auctions off the exclusive rights to the highest bidder, each is prepared to pay the difference between the profits it obtains with exclusive rights, £200m, and what profits it gets if its rival gets the exclusive rights, which is £50m.) On the other hand, if it offers the rights on a non-exclusive basis, it can only generate £120m. (For instance, suppose that firm B has already obtained the rights. Then A is prepared to pay the difference between its profits when both firms have the rights, £110m, and its profits if its rival alone has the rights, which is again £50m. Since this difference is £60m, the sports body can get only £120m from the two firms by using this method.)

Thus we see that rights holders can have an incentive to deal exclusively with downstream broadcasters. This is unlikely to be a desirable outcome from the point of view of society as a whole (except perhaps if all potential subscribers end up joining the winner's network), since the loyal subscribers to the losing network will not be able to view all the programmes they would like to. However, it seems unlikely that such exclusionary incentives will continue to exist if pay-per-view becomes the dominant method of viewing. For instance, suppose that all boxing fans would pay £10 to watch a given match live, and that the technology is in place on all pay-TV delivery platforms to extract this payment in exchange for viewing (say, at a cost of £1 per viewer). Would the boxing promoter wish to deal exclusively with one platform (say, BSkyB)? Unless the platform had a particularly dominant market share, the likely answer seems to be 'No'. For the boxing promoter can extract all available surplus by simply selling the match directly to viewers on all platforms, that is, for a fee of £10 per viewer (while paying £1 for delivery per viewer to each platform).[17]

In a similar way, if a TV retailer produces its own channels (that is to say, there is vertical integration between retailing and content production), then it will most likely be prepared to offer these channels to rival retailers, at least if the payment for the channels was made on a per-subscriber basis. (It is surely in BSkyB's interest to supply its channels to the cable retailers, as otherwise it will miss out on a significant number of potential viewers for its own content.)

In sum, a potential problem is the market power of the originating premium content providers (Hollywood studios, Premier League, and so on). However, it is misleading to state that the TV retailer that has been granted exclusive rights to such content then has market power in providing premium content. After all, presumably it is the seller of rights that sets the terms of the sale and decides whether the exclusive access route generates higher revenue. And, to a first approximation, auctions for rights start from a level playing field: the highest bidder will generally win. Obviously there are factors that perhaps favour previous winners of similar rights – an entrant needs to win several auctions before it has enough viewing hours to fill a whole new subscription channel; an incumbent may have a large existing subscriber base to which it can readily market its new rights – but the scale of the revenues generated by the recent Premier League settlement indicates that the market for such rights is likely to be reasonably competitive.

2.2.4   The set-top box 'gateway'

The allegation is often made that the set-top box used for digital television is a kind of 'bottleneck', and that there is therefore a need to control the terms of access by content providers to this gateway. As the convergence Green Paper puts it:[18]

> The operator of a gateway can exert significant influence on the markets for services provided to the consumer. This is of particular concern when the gateway operator also has interests in those other markets. A gateway technology which is first to the market will tend to become a de-facto standard. However, the critical influence of gateway control can often be exerted before an abuse of dominant position occurs; as in the case of conditional access, all the key contracts and relationships will have to be drawn up before the market for digital services is in operation.

Or as the earlier government paper puts it:[19]

> While it is possible that there will be fully competing conditional access systems operating, it may well be that conditional access for terrestrial broadcasting will develop with only one or two providers. Equally, there may be only a single provider of comprehensive satellite direct-to-home conditional access services, at least in respect of each significant satellite market. The owners of such conditional access systems could be in a position to exert considerable power in the market, without facing the constraint of competitive pressures. This is because it will quickly become difficult for new conditional access providers to enter the market, as the emergence of a large population of set top boxes using one conditional access system, combined with consumers' reasonable and almost inevitable reluctance to invest in a second box or dish, will create a real barrier to market entry.

Focusing more on the possible distortions in the market for content, the BBC has recently written:[20]

> There is a distinct advantage to dominant vertically-integrated companies in keeping other companies' content off their networks, or erecting de facto barriers to it, such as an unfavourable position on the operators' electronic programme guide. By doing so they can build a stronger market position for their own content and premium rights, and use this position to leverage their dominance into new markets and new technologies.

These worries sometimes seem to be exaggerated, or at least no worse than possible worries about foreclosure that exist in many other, unregulated markets. In the above quotes there seem to be three distinct concerns. First there is the worry that BSkyB was first in the market for delivering programmes, and therefore somehow will get to dominate that market via its 'first-mover advantage'. The second worry is that, since a gateway operator has a monopoly over providing programmes to its subscribers, it will use this power to set high prices for access to the gateway. The third is that a vertically integrated TV firm could use its market power in the market for delivering services to subscribers to distort the upstream market for content provision. We discuss these three points in turn.

First-mover advantages: The idea that a first mover in a market obtains an advantage has several facets. While it is obvious that in a durable goods market (perhaps such as set-top boxes) the customers of the first firm will not usually buy a rival product subsequently, this on its own is surely just part of the normal competitive process. (It would apply equally to, say, digital cameras.) What is needed for this argument to have some force is for there to be some kind of 'bandwagon' effect at work, so that unattached potential subscribers would, all else being equal, prefer to join the network with the largest existing base of subscribers. For instance, an example of such a market is for PC operating systems (such as Microsoft Windows). Here, if many people use a given operating system then there will tend to be a greater variety of compatible software available, which in turn makes the operating system more attractive for new customers. These bandwagon effects can imply that this is almost a 'winner takes all' market.

There is clearly the potential for such effects to be at work in the market for conditional access systems. For instance, if having a high subscriber base meant that a conditional access operator then offered a greater variety of programming exclusively available via that platform, this could create momentum for the network with the most subscribers. However, BSkyB provides the bulk of its channels for viewing on the other platforms, which must mitigate this bandwagon effect. In addition, the discussion in the previous section argued that content providers may not always have an incentive to offer their services exclusively to any particular platform, especially as pay-per-view gains favour. In any case, events have shown that the barriers to entry are not insurmountable: in October 2000 the new entrant ONdigital had around 900 000 subscribers after two years of operation, compared with BSkyB's 3.6 million digital subscribers in June 2000.[21]

High charges for access to gateways: To distinguish this possible danger from the one below, suppose that the gateway operator has no interests in related content markets (that is, it is not vertically integrated). To be concrete, suppose charging arrangements are such that the gateway operator sets a carriage fee (possibly differing according to the content provider), and that content providers set the terms at which subscribers to the gateway can view their content. Thus, a channel like FilmFour sets the price at which ONdigital's customers can subscribe to its channel, and the channel in turn pays an agreed sum to ONdigital for carriage. The gateway operator also charges a monthly fee to its subscribers, for instance for the use of its set-top box and for the other services provided via the box.

Superficially, this market is a bit like the call termination market for telecoms as described above, in that once a person has joined a particular network, that gateway operator controls access by content providers to that person. (As with call termination, this is so even if there is strong competition among gateway operators for subscribers.) However, the analogy is not close: if a gateway operator sets high access charges this will feed through into high viewing charges for its subscribers, and this will drive subscribers onto other networks. Thus the major difference between call termination and access charges for gateways is that in the latter case, the subscribers themselves bear the cost of high charges.[22] (If mobile subscribers paid for their incoming calls, as in the United States, then the analogy would be more exact.) Rather, the better analogy is between call *origination* and access charges for gateways: if an operator sets a high access charge for one or more content providers, this means that its potential subscribers will pay more for these services, and this will surely affect their choice of gateway operator. Thus if one gateway operator in a moderately competitive market threatens to charge the BBC excessively for carrying its digital channels, the operator is in a very weak negotiating position, as the broadcaster can get its content shown on another platform, which will then disadvantage the operator with high access charges.

However, just as with call origination, if the gateway operator does have significant market power then it of course has the ability to overcharge, and this should be controlled by one means or another.

Incentives for a gateway operator to favour its own content: We turn next to the effect on the upstream sector of content provision, which is perhaps the most complex of the three dangers. While it may seem quite intuitive that a vertically integrated network will favour its own content over that of rival content providers, after some thought it is less obvious that such a motive exists. For instance, if the rival has better content than it does itself, the gateway operator could make more profits by allowing access to the superior channel – and then charging its subscribers more for the combined package of services – than it could by denying access to the rival content provider. This is basically what is known as the 'Chicago critique' of foreclosure, which states that (under certain restrictive conditions) vertically integrated gateway operators will deny access only to inferior rivals.

To see this, consider a simple example. There is a monopoly gateway operator so that market conditions in this sector are at the most concentrated level – which produces its own, say, 24-hour news channel, giving its subscribers (incremental) utility of say £50 and which costs it £30 per subscriber to make. (The number of its subscribers is fixed in this example.) There is a potential rival producer who can make another news channel which generates utility £U per subscriber and costs £C per subscriber once the fixed production cost is spread over the subscriber base. Clearly it is socially desirable to have the rival news channel instead of the network's own channel whenever $U - C > 20 = 50 - 30$. If the network forecloses the rival, it can make a profit of £20 from each subscriber by providing its own news channel. If it decides to offer access to the rival channel instead, it can obtain the content by paying the rival its costs £C per subscriber, and it can charge its subscribers their incremental utility £U, that is, it can obtain profits of £(U − C) per subscriber. Therefore, if it chooses the most profitable strategy, it will allow access to the rival's channel whenever the rival has a superior service, and the market for content is not distorted by vertical integration.[23]

Obviously this example is too stylized to offer a firm basis for policy – for instance, what if viewers differ in their tastes for the two channels? – but rather suggests that it is by no means obvious that favouring its own content is a profitable strategy for a vertically integrated gateway operator. And there is no hard evidence that content providers are running into difficulties in getting their content delivered via gateways linked to rival content providers, at least in the case of BSkyB which is the operator with probably the greatest market power.[24] For instance, Oftel has the role of determining access terms to BSkyB's gateway in the event that the two parties cannot agree terms, and yet I am not aware that it has had to perform this task so far.

In some ways the delivery market in pay-TV behaves like the supermarket sector. The latter, if it had significant market power, could distort prices (both for consumers and for wholesalers). But when there is no significant market power this is not possible, even allowing for the fact that consumers tend to use one shop exclusively (as with digital TV gateways). Similarly, while they may have the ability to favour their own brands of, say, cereal over rival brands, there is little evidence that this is going on.[25] Like the supermarket sector, there is certainly the potential for abuse of dominance, and investigations should be carried out when evidence comes to light of such behaviour, but there is perhaps not a need for continued sector-specific regulation of access to gateways in digital TV markets.[26]

2.3 The Internet as a Means with which to Bypass Effective Regulation

Another parallel between telecoms and TV is a possible future in which both industries use the Internet – that is to say, IP networks – as an alternative transmission network.

Telecoms: It is now possible to use the Internet for two-way telephone communication. The call quality (and other aspects of the service) are patchy at present, but will surely improve. If it becomes a reasonable substitute for the standard dedicated channel (or 'switched circuit') telephony, then there will be scope for arbitrage between using the two kinds of services. There are then two outcomes: Internet telephony will dominate the current signalling technology for telephony (perhaps dedicated channels are just too costly compared to the IP technology), or the tariffs for the two services will have to be brought closely into line. While the former is surely a long-run possibility, the latter could be important for the medium term. If so, then careful thought has to go into the structure of, say, BT's network charges offered to Internet service providers as compared to its own retail tariffs. If the former is charged for on a different basis to the latter (say, per call versus per minute), then this may not be sustainable without causing major inefficiencies.[27]

Broadcasting: It is also possible to view moving images over the Internet, albeit often of a low quality. As bandwidth rises, pictures of broadcast TV quality will be possible, which implies that we will be able to watch TV on our PCs. This could either be of live broadcasts, or we could download specific programmes to watch as required. Radio gives an indication of things to come, as it is now quite possible to listen to a large number of live radio broadcasts from around the world by logging on to the relevant web site. If this trend becomes established, the acceptability of the licence fee could be undermined. (It seems unlikely that there could be any consensus for levying the licence fee on PCs as well as regular TV sets.) Obviously, if Internet service provider charges are low enough, then many people will bypass the TV set with its associated licence fee, and choose to watch live TV over the Internet. However, just as with IP telephony, the Internet is an opportunity as well as an issue for regulatory concern: high bandwidth Internet is the ideal platform for delivering a vast range of films and TV programmes to be viewed as and when convenient.

3.   DESIGN OF REGULATORY INSTITUTIONS

As has already been said,[28]

> Excessive attention has been devoted to questions of institutional design in UK policy debates. At worst this may be indicative of one of the general dangers for future policy making in communications, namely the intrusion of bureaucratic agendas that can have chilling effects on entrepreneurship and innovation. What matters is that the UK develops a clear and effective regulatory strategy (a non-trivial exercise) – not that it produces busy-looking organisational charts for the public sector.

Be that as it may, we here turn to questions of the structure of communications regulation in Britain.

3.1 General Issues

What can we say at a general level about institutional design?[29]

Single vs multiple regulators? If regulators were sure to be well informed and benevolent, it would not really matter how regulatory duties were allocated: the different regulators would cooperate to carry out the ideal set of policies. It is more realistic, however, to suppose that regulators act as other people do, and need incentives to (i) find out the market information needed to carry out effective regulation, and (ii) act in the interests of society as a whole rather than the narrow industry interests.

The obvious argument against multiple regulators is that their decisions and policies may not be well coordinated. Even if there is a well-defined role for each regulator, so that there are no overlapping functions, major inefficiencies could result from uncoordinated decision-making. The classic example is the separate regulation of the economic and the environmental aspects of, say, the water industry. For instance, if the environmental agency were to require an increase in a certain water quality standard, this would inevitably have an economic impact as well, and policy would usually be improved if the environmental and economic impacts of the decision were considered simultaneously. Of course, just because policy needs to be coordinated does not imply that a single regulator is essential. And conversely, just because there is a single regulator, this does not ensure that policy is coordinated.

Another set of issues arises when regulators have overlapping jurisdictions. Thus, if convergence has brought us to a world where several regulatory bodies potentially have jurisdiction over the same set of policies, then inefficiencies will result. As Oftel has recently put it:[30]

> The argument for such a single sectoral regulator dealing with all elements of the communications markets is powerful. There are currently too many bodies involved in the regulation of the communications markets. ... The risk of double jeopardy and 'forum shopping' must be removed.

At the very least, overlapping regulatory jurisdictions will increase uncertainty about future decision-making, something that is especially damaging in a fast developing sector like communications.

Another possible advantage of having a single super-regulator is that, if it becomes apparent that regulation is no longer needed for some sector, the regulatory body may find it easier to give up its responsibilities in that area. A very focused regulator may be reluctant to take deregulatory decisions that could do it out of a job.

Finally, it may be harder for big players in the industry to put pressure on a single super-regulator than a series of focused regulators. A regulatory body that constantly works closely with its industry may come to alter its objectives to fit more closely with those of the industry. (But see the opposing point below.)

Nevertheless, there are also some positive features of multiple regulators. Roughly speaking, these involve the operation of a system of checks and balances, much like the ones implemented in the separation of powers proposed for government under the American constitution. Put simply, a super-regulator may have too much power concentrated in a single body, and also may be better able to conceal poor performance. Thus:

- Having multiple regulators could allow for some kind of implicit 'yardstick competition' between the regulators. If one regulatory body were seen to be doing a much better job, then steps could be taken to improve practice in the others. For instance, there are benefits to having separate national regulators for telecoms in the EU, as performance across countries can be compared and future policies chosen according to current best practice.
- One regulator may be well placed to detect and expose undesirable behaviour such as having unduly sympathetic or even corrupt attitudes to firms in its sector by a separate regulator in another related market.
- Public (and private) sector organizations often perform better if they have highly focused missions.
- Finally, for reasons that are not always well understood, large organizations do not always work well. In the private sector, it seems intuitive that two firms merging to a single entity cannot do worse (in terms of profits, say) than the two firms did separately. (After all, the merged firm could pursue the same policies that the two separate firms would have done, and usually it should be able to do better than this.) However, we do see voluntary de-mergers taking place, which indicates that mergers are not always beneficial. The same issues of control and inefficiencies within large organizations could apply also to a super-regulator.

Finally, it is worth saying that the distinction between a single and multiple regulators is not clear-cut: separate regulators that cooperate effectively (as perhaps Oftel, the OFT and the ITC have done recently) may implement more coherent policies than a single entity that perhaps contains semi-autonomous sector-specific divisions within it.

Competition policy vs regulation? Another important set of choices is the balance between competition policy and (sector-specific) regulation as the instrument to achieve desirable outcomes. For instance, in New Zealand the telecoms regulator was disbanded, leaving regulation to competition policy alone. Like the distinctions between single and multiple regulators, it is not always easy to distinguish cleanly between the two kinds of control. In fact, a competition authority like the Office of Fair Trading is really a kind of super-regulator in the sense of the previous discussion, and so many of the trade-offs there apply here as well. In addition to this point, the main lines of demarcation between the two as conventionally practised are:

- Competition policy does not normally aim at redistributive policies (across consumers or across regions), whereas regulation does often include such aims. For instance, it is hard to imagine that competition policy would maintain and enforce a policy of geographically uniform tariffs as Oftel currently does.
- Regulatory bodies are usually more powerful than competition agencies. The former (subject to various appeal procedures) can set prices and line-of-business restrictions, whereas the latter typically assess the lawfulness of conduct. In addition, the former are less bound by legal precedent and other consistency requirements.
- Regulatory bodies often act *ex ante,* setting a dominant firm's prices for future years and so on, where competition bodies often act *ex post* (with the exception of mergers). In a fast-moving industry like communications there may be advantages for firms to 'know the rules in advance', although this effect is mitigated by the fact that the regulatory policy might change in an unpredictable way over time (see above point). In addition, legal precedence is a powerful instrument for policy inertia.
- Regulatory bodies tend to be more knowledgeable about their industries. This is because they are industry specific, they have long-term interactions with firms in the industry, and they may have greater staff resources.

3.2   Implications for UK Communications Regulation

From the above discussion it is clear that how to divide up regulatory and competition policy responsibilities in the communications sector is far from straightforward. However, we attempt to make a few points, under the following headings:

Coherence within the TV sector: It is clear that convergence does have implications for regulatory institutions in the overall communications sector.

But it seems even more obvious that there should be a 'convergence' of regulatory institutions just within the broadcasting sphere. It is hard to think of any reason, except for history, why one broadcaster, the BBC, should be allowed to operate under a more lax regulatory regime than others. Indeed, because of the unique (and privileged) way it is funded, one might think that it should have a narrower remit and a tighter regulatory regime than other broadcasters. Therefore, self-regulation of the BBC should cease as soon as is practical, and be brought under the same regime as that of the other broadcasters.[31] In addition, the direct link between the funds from the licence fee (assuming this fee is maintained) and the BBC should be broken, and other broadcasters should be able to compete for finance for desirable programmes from this fund. A substantial consultative process should be instigated into the relative merits of the licence fee funding mechanism and its alternatives (such as subscription), prior to the Charter renewal in 2006.

Within the pay-TV sector, the marked asymmetries between the treatment of BSkyB and the cable companies needs to be either better justified or abandoned. Why should BSkyB be forced to operate an 'open' platform, whereas the cable companies continue to operate under no such obligation?[32] Why should BSkyB be required to offer most of its (non-interactive) channels to rival platforms, yet, say, ONdigital/ITV has no such obligation? Clearly there may be justifications for these policies, but at the least they need to be better explained. Moreover, at present different bodies handle these two, somewhat similar issues, and this should cease. (Oftel handles issues broadly to do with access to platforms, whereas, roughly speaking, the ITC handles issues to do with making content available on other platforms.)

This is also a good time to think hard about how much regulatory attention should be paid to content. In particular, requirements to have a certain minimum quota on domestically produced (or European) content seem to be a kind of hidden protectionism that would not be tolerated in other markets. (This is not to deny that broadcasters will choose to offer content that is well tailored to its local audience.) In addition, current requirements about impartiality, minimum quotas on religious programming, and so on, now seem a bit outdated. The newspaper, magazine and book market seems to work well enough without such controls, and given the diversity of channels now available we are surely moving towards the 'publishing' model of communications (even if we are not quite there yet). Moreover, the remaining content requirements should be explicitly decided (and explained) by government rather than being left to regulators (whose task should be to monitor compliance).[33]

Radio spectrum: At present Oftel has little formal role in deciding how the radio spectrum related to telecoms is allocated. (Rather, this is done by the

Radiocommunications Agency.) This contrasts with the important role that the ITC has in allocating spectrum for broadcast TV. It makes more sense for Oftel (or its successor) to play an active role in this process. The apparent success of the recent mobile licence auctions suggests that there are better ways to allocate precious spectrum resources than regulatory dictat, and that both auctions and a secondary market for spectrum will become the normal way to assign spectrum rights. An agency such as Oftel, with greater experience of the competitive process, seems better suited to handling these issues than the Radiocommunications Agency.

Links between telecoms and broadcasting: It seems clear enough that the economic regulation of electronic transmission networks should be done within a single regulatory body, 'Ofcom', say, as is largely the case now. However, this is not to say that detailed *ex ante* rules are needed for all parts of this. For instance, it is not clear that the gateways in the digital TV market need the same level of detailed regulation as do, say, many network interconnection services in telecoms, given the present market structure in the two sectors. One possible model would be for Ofcom to gather information on conduct in this sector, and to recommend that a formal inquiry be carried out periodically by the Office of Fair Trading as the evidence demands. If one were starting from scratch this would perhaps be a good model. On the other hand, given that Oftel has now built up some experience and expertise in this area, a practical solution might be to give Ofcom the role of investigating conduct in this area.

It is not obvious that content regulation – however major or minor a government decides this activity should be – should or should not be brought under the Ofcom umbrella. Given that the Utility Review White Paper, *A Fair Deal for Consumers, Modernising the Framework for Utility Regulation*, already imposes a duty on regulators to give collective consideration to matters of common interest, it is hard to think of a powerful argument for or against having both content and economic functions within one organization.

POSTSCRIPT: DECEMBER 2000

Since this chapter was written, the White Paper *A New Future for Communications* has been published, jointly by the DTI and the Department for Culture, Media and Sport. The outline proposals that are relevant to the preceding discussion include:

- A new unified regulator (Ofcom) responsible for the communications sector, including telecommunications, broadcasting issues including programme quality, the management of the relevant radio spectrum, and the monitoring of advertisements for offensiveness and honesty. Roughly speaking, this new body will combine the relevant duties of Oftel, the ITC, the Broadcasting Standards Commission, the Radio Authority and the Radiocommunications Agency. It will be led by a group of people rather than an individual.

- No plans to relax the geographic uniformity of BT's tariff for basic services, nor to set up a universal service fund.
- No plans to change the BBC's role or remit (with the exception of a plan for Ofcom to have power to determine the BBC's amount of regional programming).
- Current requirements for impartiality, religious programming, and so on, to remain in place (although there is a suggestion that Channel 5 may have its public service obligations relaxed in the future).
- Somewhat vague plans for sector-specific rules for access to gateways for operators with significant market power.

NOTES

1. There is an excellent recent example of this asymmetric treatment of the BBC and ITV regarding content. During the summer of 2000, ITV tried to move its late evening news programme from 10pm to 11pm, something that it achieved with enormous difficulty after negotiations with the ITC. Once it did this, however, the BBC was able very rapidly to change its own news from 9pm to 10pm, with no need to ask any outside body for permission.
2. Source: *ITC Press Release*, 31 October 2000.
3. See paragraph 3.27 of Oftel's *Universal Telecommunications Services: A Consultative Document*, 1999.
4. See paragraph 23 of *Oftel's Response to the UK Green Paper – Regulating Communications: Approaching Convergence in the Information Age*, January 1999.
5. See Oftel's *Review of Universal Telecommunication Services* (September 2000) for more details on their current thinking on this topic, which is *not* to use the USO as a tool (in addition to their other regulatory activities) to encourage the take-up of broadband access.
6. Speech to the Royal Television Society, 14 October 1998.
7. The commercial terrestrial broadcasters, ITV, Channel 4, Channel 5 and the Welsh channel S4C, also have public service requirements: (i) they must offer a certain mix of new drama, news and documentary programmes, and so on; and (ii) the amount of advertising is strictly controlled (with so many minutes per hour, depending on the time of day). Save for certain geographical coverage requirements, the pay-TV companies have no public service obligations.
8. For instance, chapter 3 of the Davies Report on *The Future Funding of the BBC*, Department of Culture, Media and Sport, July 1999, analyses this issue at length.
9. However, it is important to recognize that what constitutes 'public service broadcasting' can change over time. For instance, in 1985 Thames Television (an ITV company) secured the rights to *Dallas* instead of the BBC, which had previously been broadcasting this drama. The then regulator, the Independent Broadcasting Authority, declared it was 'impossible to over-emphasise the seriousness of what has been done'. The end result was that Thames was forced to hand back *Dallas* to the BBC, together with substantial financial reparations. For an account of this crisis, together with an interesting discussion of the philosophy of public

sector broadcasting, see the speech by Michael Jackson to the Royal Television Society on 10 May 2000.

10. Chapter 5 of the Davies Report.

11. In contrast to the UK's system, in Germany the funds from the licence fee are paid to more than one broadcaster. Also, in New Zealand public money is given to commercial operators to provide public service content.

12. Presentation to the Royal Television Society, 31 October 2000, by Ray Gallagher (Director of Public Affairs, BSkyB).

13. See the Monopolies and Mergers Commission Report on *Cellnet and Vodafone*, December 1998, for more detailed discussion of these points. Obviously, if a subscriber cares about the welfare of the people who call him – for instance, if it is only close family members who call – then the subscriber will not be attracted to a network which charges excessively for call termination.

14. For more details see the Monopolies and Mergers Commission Report on *British Telecommunications plc*, December 1998.

15. Ultimately, these high payments end up being paid to individual players: the football clubs themselves are often rather unprofitable.

16. Notice that both broadcasters are made worse off by the introduction of the exclusive sports rights. (The broadcaster without rights gets profits of £50m, whereas the 'winner' generates gross profits of £200m, but pays £150m of this to the sports body.)

17. To take the argument to an extreme point, Sony pictures has no incentive to allow, say, the Blockbuster video rental chain to be the exclusive rental outlet for its video releases. For more formal discussions along these lines, see section 3 of Armstrong, 'Competition in the Pay-TV Market', *Journal of the Japanese and International Economies*, 1999, pp. 257–80.

18. *Regulating Communications: Approaching Convergence in the Information Age*, DTI, 1998, para. 4.7.

19. *The Regulation of Conditional Access Services for Digital Television*, DTI, January 1996, para. 14.

20. Page 5 of its *Initial Submission to the Government's Communications Review*, July 2000.

21. Figures taken from respective web sites. Note that a new and significant digital platform is likely to be introduced shortly, which is the fixed telecoms network upgraded – either by BT itself, or by rivals using BT's unbundled local loops – to broadband capability (for instance, by ADSL technology).

22. The analogy with call termination is closer for those entertainment services that rely on generating revenues by selling advertising space (rather than subscription). For instance, if an internet site were free to web users but made money by offering advertising space on the site, then it is possible that a gateway operator could extract the profits from the web site by setting high gateway charges for access to web users. It seems quite farfetched, however, that the bulk of core content will be provided by this kind of funding mechanism.

23. However, the rival content provider here obtains no profit, and so this outcome will not be popular with this company. This feature may well have an undesirable impact on the rival's incentives to provide high-quality programming.

24. The BBC has claimed that it has had difficulties in getting some of its digital channels shown on the cable networks – see its *Initial Submission to the Government's Communications Review*, July 2000.

25. See the Competition Commission, *Report on Supermarkets*, October 2000.

26. This contrasts with the view expressed by the (then) Director General of Telecommunications, in the Foreword to Oftel's *The Pricing of Conditional Access Services for Digital Television* (October 1997), where he states: 'Oftel has spent twelve years overseeing the framework for regulating interconnection prices in the telecoms market. ... I am in no doubt as to the central importance of those rules on interconnection in the development of competition in the telephony market. ... I am equally convinced of the importance of the framework for conditional access in the development of a dynamic market in television and interactive services.'

27. One example of this might be seen in the United States. There, telephone calls made over the Internet do not pay the access fees used to fund universal service. This could end up

making it hard to fund universal service. In the UK, there has been little regulatory action on this topic, save for worries about safety features of IP telephony (such as call traceability for emergency calls). However, the recent Oftel consultative document *Price Control Review*, October 2000, considers the effects on BT's profitability of future migration of traffic to IP networks.

28. George Yarrow, 'Regulating for competition', Regulatory Policy Institute, Oxford.
29. This section is partly based on section 7.2 of Laffont and Tirole, *Competition in Telecommunications*, MIT Press, 2000.
30. Paragraph 64 of Oftel, *Communications Regulation in the UK*, July 2000.
31. As one would expect, the BBC disagrees, and on page 23 of its July 2000 *Initial Submission to the Government's Communications Review* it writes that 'Although there are common strands between the BBC's role and remit and the public service elements within the obligations placed on commercial broadcasters, they are essentially different in nature, and arguably diverging. It is difficult to see how they could be combined within the oversight of a single regulatory body without compromising those characteristics which ensure that the BBC serves the public interest in a unique way.'
32. The number of subscribers connected to cable companies and the number connected to BSkyB are not so dramatically different that we may be confident that one is 'dominant' in the market for delivery while the other is not.
33. This is also suggested in paragraph 74 of Oftel's *Communications Regulation in the UK* (July 2000).

CHAIRMAN'S COMMENTS

David Edmonds

First I want to thank Mark Armstrong for his interesting and wide-ranging chapter. Second, I would like to make just a couple of points.

A word that Mark did not use very often is 'consumer'. The job that I perceive to be of key importance for the regulator is to ensure that consumers get the best deal in terms of quality, choice and value for money. This is a simple goal; it is at the heart of what Oftel does; and I think it should be at the heart of what a new regulatory agency does. Despite its simplicity, it is a goal that is incredibly difficult to secure in the complex world that he described. I think the development of the new technologies offers extraordinary potential. But predicting where the new technologies are going to end up is virtually impossible. As far as the consumer is concerned, he or she does not care whether they get their television picture through ADSL, through satellite, through digital television, through terrestrial television; the fact that it is there, the fact that it comes into the home is what matters; and in the UK I think the expansion of that choice, based on convergence of the technologies, is going dramatically to increase.

Third-generation telephones are certainly going to be capable of downloading into a PC huge quantities of data. So I see my job, in the context of telecommunications regulation, as providing an environment in which competition flourishes. It is about setting the appropriate conditions. I also feel that, to a very large degree, the market should be left to decide who succeeds and who fails. To take an example, why should any regulator care whether the News is at 9pm or at 10pm, providing that somewhere within the obligation on the company it is provided to an adequate quality at some stage in the daily schedules? It is a very interesting question as to whether that is a regulatory issue or an issue for ministers and Parliament; and quite clearly Parliament can ultimately decide to do what it wishes. The extent to which regulators get sucked into those issues is debatable.

Undoubtedly the foreseeable future development of competition will need the support of the sectoral regulator. Many of the principles that we have developed in Oftel are applicable across this converging world. I am quite certain of that because – and again Mark touched on this in regard to call terminations – direct access to the home or workplace will remain limited, either for technical reasons or because of capacity. Network operators with market power have the ability and the incentive to foreclose markets to service providers. Also, despite what Mark said about gateways, there are some serious regulatory issues there which we have to address; and that is where the focus of regulation should lie.

Oftel has set out some principles about regulation of networks to guide intervention; for example, firms should have market power, the benefit of intervention should outweigh the costs and any action should be proportionate to the concern.

In my view the two present separate legislative frameworks – telecoms and broadcasting – are not sustainable. What we need is a regulatory regime for a new sector which can be defined in the phrase I used in my submission in July on the future regulatory regime; the European Commission also calls it 'Electronic Communications Networks and Services'. I profoundly believe that we need a harmonized framework to encourage competition and to deliver the services that consumers want. We should promote effective competition by enabling competitors to have access to the networks and gateways of operators with market power, which explains why at this stage we have not mandated access to the networks of the cable operators; in some cases we need to safeguard the quality of service and content which the market will not deliver. I believe it can be done in part through making maximum use of co-regulation, and self-regulation. Backed by some legal powers we can create a regime that will see the UK through into an extraordinary expansion of those services in the next ten years. And we must not forget Brussels. At this lecture last year, the speaker was worrying whether or not the European documentation on the new framework for regulation would be published.

It is now published and it sets out a very comprehensive legal framework that we in the UK must adapt to. I am not sure that all parts of the communication sector have yet understood how powerful that framework will be. I disagree with Mark's view that it is appropriate to have separate regulators for economics and content. I subscribe to the law that Aaron Wildavsky enunciated, to do with why decisions taken in Washington DC could never actually be implemented on the ground in Oakland, California. It is a very powerful principle which says that if one agency wants to secure something and nobody is against it, it has an 80 per cent chance of success; if two agencies both want to secure the same thing, the chance is 40 per cent. With three agencies – the ITC, the Broadcasting Standards Council and Oftel – the chance of success even if they wanted to secure the same thing is down to 20 per cent and with four agencies 10 per cent, and so on. It is a very powerful law and though I quoted it to you somewhat facetiously, I have enough evidence of trying to get organizations to work together to know that the problems that actually arise through trying to deliver a policy on, for example, access are difficult, notwithstanding the fact that both parties share the same goal.

So I am a committed advocate of a single regulatory agency for electronic communication networks and services. I believe that that regulatory body should be constructed on the basis that there is no takeover, there is no federal structure, there is no creation of an alliance of ITC, Oftel, BSC, some of the Governors of the BBC, bits of the RA or all of the RA. I believe that we need to start again, looking at some fundamental principles. What are we trying to regulate? What are we trying to deliver? I do not want cohabitation, I do not want living together. I want to start again with a blank sheet of paper on which people can map the process. Then I want the government to design a structure based on clearly defined functions. I want the classic architectural principle of form following function to apply to the new agency. Whether or not that will actually be delivered in the White Paper I have no idea, but I certainly have advocated that and I will continue to do so until the White Paper is published.

Those are my responses to what Mark has said. A final interesting question is: 'Who would want to be a regulator in the world that I have described?' It is tricky enough regulating telecommunications. In a single week I was asked to resign by *The Economist*, *The Financial Times* and *The Times*. My friend and colleague at the ITC has taken a little bit of flak lately. Philip Fletcher at Ofwat is being kicked round the park, Callum McCarthy is having rather a hard time with his electricity trading arrangements. My colleague, who used to run Oflot, no longer does so.

It is a pretty complex world that this new agency is going to be asked to address, 'if new agency there be'. As an afterthought, there are some very interesting questions about the nature of regulation in the UK, the role that governments and politicians are asking regulators to take on; and I hope that this White Paper and the creation of a new agency will allow us to stand back a little bit.

I suppose the fundamental dichotomy I see is perhaps best encapsulated by the two hours I spent in front of the House of Commons Select Committee on Trade and Industry where I argued Oftel's case for 'local loop' bundling, I thought rather successfully, for about an hour and a quarter, and was then ambushed at the end by the Committee, who demanded to know why I was not doing much more to secure lower prices for payphones around the UK. Arguing that this would lead to forcing the company in unfamiliar directions was of no avail. Equally they argued that I should be setting out the telephone tariffs of mobile phone companies. That level of intervention on the one hand with, on the other, the pressure to move towards a regulatory regime that simply supports competition and is based on economic principles is a complex issue which we in the UK must address in the next couple of years. In the context of communications I think the White Paper offers a very good opportunity to do so.

7. Opening European electricity and gas markets

Graham Shuttleworth

1. INTRODUCTION

In this chapter, I take a look at market opening in European electricity and gas markets from an economic point of view, which means from three separate angles:

1. I consider whether the move towards competition is being driven simply by the economics of the sector, without the need for specific interventions by governments and regulators.
2. Since I will answer this first question in the negative, I will look at the measures that governments and regulators need to introduce, if they are serious about introducing competition.
3. I will list some outstanding issues, that is, problems that legal and regulatory institutions in European markets have yet to deal with, but which are crucial to achieving the benefits of efficient competition.

Note that the last point refers to 'institutions', rather than just to governments and regulators. There is only so much that one can expect of the government agencies responsible for energy sector regulation. As we shall see, some of the outstanding problems may not be solved without the attention of legislatures and/or the judiciary.

1.1 Promoting Competition, Not Competitors

Before embarking on a discussion of competition, I need to stress that the promotion of competition should be synonymous with promoting efficiency and not (for example) with promoting the existence of (potentially inefficient) competitors. In fact, I would go further. *Unless a reform creates an environment that promotes more efficient choices, it cannot be said to promote competition.*

Competition is only beneficial if it improves economic efficiency, which means that a competitive environment should allow the producer with the lowest incremental costs to capture the customer. A producer with sunk costs may start with an advantage over new entrants, if as a result that producer has lower incremental costs – but this advantage should be exploited, not handicapped. This view contradicts a number of oft-stated, but impractical views of competition:

- that more competitors in the market means more competition;
- that all new entry is beneficial; and
- that incumbents must be obliged to sell their produce as if they were a 'stand-alone business', incurring the full costs of a new entrant.

In the UK, discussion of competition has moved beyond the mere counting of competitors. However, in the UK, and in Europe generally, there is still a need to distinguish between reforms that promote efficient competition and reforms that 'merely' promote competitors or lower prices. Neither is good for the economy as a whole.

Many appraisals of 'competition' focus primarily on whether or not prices fall. However, it would be only right and proper to ask whether the price cuts reflect real falls in costs, or whether they reflect transfers to customers from the owners of production facilities. Transfers of wealth come from eliminating monopoly profits, or from denying the recovery of costs (usually sunk costs). Neither will provide a compelling case for retail competition in countries where prices are determined by regulation. On the one hand, if there are monopoly profits, the regulator should eliminate them anyway. On the other hand, if it is beneficial to consumers to deny recovery of sunk costs, the regulatory regime should disallow them anyway.

The real rationale for introducing competition, where previously there was regulation, is therefore not to eliminate monopoly profits, or to prevent recovery of certain costs. The purpose of introducing competition is to achieve the real reductions in cost (or improvements in service quality) that count as improvements in economic efficiency. Anything that diminishes efficiency is not promoting competition, but something else. Accept no substitutes!

1.2 A Basic History Lesson for Novices

The electricity and gas sectors have had a history of development based on integrated monopolies. Monopolies have been more strongly entrenched in the electricity sector than in the gas sector (which competes with oil and electricity for some customers). Trade between consenting monopolies has been possible for many years. However, both sectors now have to deal with demands for access by 'third parties', that is, they must allow independent generators and traders access to the network, so that they can serve the monopolies' existing customers. These demands create interesting conflicts and challenges.

Individual Member States (MSs) have taken their own initiatives to promote competition, with the UK being a leader within the European Union (and Norway being a leader just outside it). However, the major impetus now comes from European institutions. Following adoption of the Single European Market principle in 1985, the European Commission began to consider the possibility of creating a single internal market for energy. In 1990, a European directive required Member States to facilitate the 'transit' of power, that is, the transmission of power from one Member State to another, over the network of a third.[1] Then, in 1992, the Commission forwarded proposals to the Council of Ministers advocating common rules for electricity and natural gas markets across Member States. After much discussion of different proposals (to which NERA made a small, but timely contribution[2]), the European Commission issued directives for the creation of internal markets in electricity and gas.

The European electricity directive (96/92/EC) entered into force on 19 February 1997 and was to be implemented by most Member States within two years. (Belgium and Ireland received an additional year for implementation, and Greece two years.) The directive required MSs to allow third-party access (TPA) to national transmission and distribution networks or to set up arrangements for a 'single buyer' that would have the same effect as TPA. (MSs immediately abandoned attempts to define such a single buyer.)

The European gas directive (98/30/EC), requiring TPA on gas pipeline networks, entered into force on 10 August 1998 and was to be implemented by 10 August 2000. The majority of Member States have implemented the requirements of the directive, but Portugal and Greece were granted some derogations as 'emerging markets'.

Details of the electricity and gas directives are set out in sections 2 and 3.

1.3   A Brief Progress Report

The benefits identified by the Commission in creating liberal energy markets had already been recognized by several Member States. The UK, Spain, Sweden, Finland and (outside the EU) Norway all liberalized earlier. The reforms undertaken in these countries were often more extensive than those proposed by the Commission and in these states the subsequent directives had little impact.

The directives prompted a new round of liberalization measures and several more states have gone further than the directive requires. The German electricity sector, in particular, moved overnight from a system of protected monopolies and cartels to full retail competition, in which all customers are (in law at least) eligible to choose their supplier. However, liberalization has not been without its problems:

- *Liberalization is still delayed in some Member States.* For example, the Commission has sent formal notices to Germany, France, Portugal and Luxembourg over their failure to implement the gas directive. The Commission also started legal proceedings against France for its failure to properly implement the electricity directive.
- *Liberalization has not produced noticeable benefits in all countries.* Some classes of industrial consumers in the Netherlands, Greece and Spain have experienced increases in electricity prices over the last two years, as have some domestic consumers in the Netherlands, Ireland and Denmark.[3] Moreover, small traders often voice a belief that the provisions of the directives are inadequate to secure competition.[4]

The state of competition in gas and electricity markets contrasts sharply with the situation in telecoms. Consumers readily switch between telecoms suppliers and there is competition developing between competing networks (that is, copper and cable, fixed and mobile). Developments in technology and economic pressures are driving telecoms markets away from natural monopoly and into the competitive arena.

These developments give rise to two questions that this chapter addresses:

1. Will similar economic pressures produce competition in electricity and gas? (Section 4).

And (since the answer to this question is 'No'):

2. What challenges will European regulators face if they try to enhance competitive pressure?

The answer to this second question comes in two parts. First, the economics of energy networks mean that European regulators will have to take some deliberate measures to promote competition in energy markets, specifically various forms of unbundling (section 5), real-time balancing markets (section 6) and the treatment of cross-border trade (section 7). In addition, however, European regulatory regimes will have to rediscover some principles of economic regulation that have lain dormant for many years, to avoid descending into 'regulatory opportunism' (sections 8 and 9). General lessons are summarized in section 10.

To begin at the beginning, however, I describe the two key directives for electricity and gas in sections 2 and 3, respectively.

2.   FEATURES OF THE EUROPEAN ELECTRICITY DIRECTIVE

The objective of the European electricity directive is to establish a set of common rules for the generation, transmission and distribution of electricity that leads to a single, common market for the commodity. The following subsection presents a selection of key elements in the directive.

2.1   Conditions of Network Access

The conditions of access to transmission and distribution networks are vital in ensuring that the benefits of liberalization are realized. Articles 17 and 18 of the electricity directive offer Member States three alternative approaches to providing access: single-buyer procedure, regulated third-party access (rTPA) or negotiated third-party access (nTPA).

The single-buyer procedure requires the single buyer to purchase electricity contracted by eligible customers at a price equivalent to its published retail tariff (for the customer concerned) *minus* the tariff for use of the network. This condition effectively renders the single-buyer model equivalent to rTPA, since the single buyer retains only the published tariff for use of the network. *No Member State has chosen to implement the directive using the single-buyer model.*

Several Member States announced their intention to adopt nTPA. However, Germany is the only country that actually adopted nTPA rather than rTPA. Germany's choice reflects a tradition of letting industry and its customers develop sector-specific rules within a pro-competitive framework rather than establishing sector-specific regulators.[5] Every other MS has opted for a regime of regulated access that would be broadly familiar to a UK audience.

2.2   Eligible Consumers

The potential for competition depends on which eligible customers are free to choose between different suppliers. Article 19 of the directive establishes a timetable for the minimum requirements for market opening defined by annual consumption levels, as shown in Table 7.1.

The requirements for extending the number of eligible customers are minimum requirements only. Member States are required to open up 33 per cent of their national markets to competition from 2003, but may go further. The majority of Member States have pursued quicker and more extensive liberalization timetables than established in the directive.[6] As already noted in the introduction, the extent to which this has succeeded in promoting effective competition remains open to question in some Member States.

Table 7.1   Electricity directive's timetable for liberalization

	Market opened to consumers with annual electricity consumption over:	Market share open to competition (%)
Stage 1: 19/2/99	40 GWh	26.5
Stage 2: 19/2/00	20 GWh	28
Stage 3: 19/2/03	9 GWh	33

2.3   Unbundling of Accounts

The directive does not require the structural unbundling of generation, transmission and distribution. Vertically integrated electricity operations can be designated by Member States as the transmission system operator (TSO) and distribution system operator (DSO), with no need for independence. The only prescription on unbundling requires the production of separate accounts for generation, transmission, distribution and any other non-electricity activities.

2.4   Tendering and Authorization of Power Stations

The directive envisages that new power stations will be constructed either by holding competitive tenders, or by setting up a non-discriminatory system of 'authorizations' (equivalent to the UK system of licences and consents). The idea of competitive tenders makes most sense when there is a single buyer, whilst authorizations would most probably be needed under TPA. However, the directive did not explicitly link the form of network access to the method of introducing new power stations.

2.5   Reciprocity

The directive envisages a form of mutual reinforcement of liberalization by Member States. If Member State A fails to declare a type of customer as 'eligible', other Member States may block sales to their own customers of the same type by traders from Member State A. This provision is intended to encourage 'reciprocity', that is, parallel market opening. In practice, the existence of wholesale markets provides an outlet for traders to which access cannot be restricted, which renders the reciprocity sanctions ineffective. The degree and form of liberalization is, subject to the minimal requirements of the directive, whatever each Member State chooses it to be.

3.   FEATURES OF THE EUROPEAN GAS DIRECTIVE

As part of the framework for a single energy market, the European gas directive was intended to establish, through a set of common rules, the internal market in natural gas.

The gas directive provides Member States with two systems for access to gas pipeline networks: nTPA and rTPA. Only Austria, Germany, Denmark and Belgium have chosen nTPA as the basis for access to gas pipeline networks, whilst the Netherlands has a hybrid system.[7] Under nTPA, incumbent gas suppliers are required to publish the main commercial conditions for access but are not required to provide full explanations of tariff structures (although in Belgium, indicative tariffs are subject to the approval of the regulator). This has led to the accusation that nTPA suffers from a lack of transparency that could hide discrimination against new entrants.[8]

As with the electricity directive, the gas directive sets a timetable for the minimum level of market opening. The criteria for eligible customers are based on the annual consumption level of final consumers but, in addition, Member States have to ensure that specified shares of the market are open to competition; see Table 7.2.

Table 7.2   Gas directive's timetable for liberalization

	Market opened to consumers with annual gas consumption over:	Minimum market share to be open to competition (%)
Stage 1	25 million m³	20
Stage 2: 2003	15 million m³	28
Stage 3: 2008	5 million m³	33

The potential for competition is limited by the number of customers declared eligible. France is adopting the directive's minimum requirement. Greece and Portugal, both eligible for derogation under their classification as emerging markets, have yet to decide on the extent of their liberalization. However, the majority of countries have provided for quicker and more extensive liberalization than required by the directive. The Commission expected 78 per cent of total EU gas demand to be eligible by August 2000 and 90 per cent by 2008.

Again, mirroring the electricity directive, there is no requirement for gas undertakings to establish the independence of transmission, distribution or storage activities, although accounting separation is required. Consumer organizations and independent market players have expressed concern that effective competition requires a clearer separation of transmission system operations from integrated undertakings, most recently at the Madrid Gas Regulatory Forum, 26–27 October 2000.

4. ECONOMIC PRESSURES FOR REFORM

Some sectors, most notably telecoms, are seeing established companies come under pressure from new entrants, even in the areas of network construction and operation that were previously thought to be natural monopolies. These pressures are leading to a reassessment of the role of regulation. However, the economic conditions of the telecoms sector are different from those in the electricity and gas sectors. Experience in telecoms is not therefore directly transferable to the energy sectors.

4.1 Competition in Telecoms

Telecoms networks use to be regarded as natural monopolies. The only way to promote competition was to provide third-party access to the network. However, in recent years this has started to change:

- *Competition between networks is developing*. For example, in the UK around 50 per cent of households now have a choice over the provider of fixed-link services to their house, that is, copper or cable. Moreover, the 25 million mobile phone subscribers have a choice between four competing networks.
- *Broadcasting, IT and telecoms technologies are converging*. As convergence occurs, the boundaries between these markets become blurred and the scope for competition is further expanded.

As the existence of monopoly elements diminishes and competition increases, the role of regulation and the requirement for a sector-specific regulator is brought into question. Many commentators regard regulation of telecoms as a transitional measure, before it emerges into the full glare of competition and becomes subject to little more than general competition policy. Price caps in regulation tend to be viewed as a remedy for market power that may become unnecessary in the future. The situation in electricity and gas is (so far) quite different.

4.2 Natural Monopolies in Electricity and Gas

Could natural monopoly elements in the electricity and gas industries erode to the extent that sector-specific regulation becomes unnecessary? As I explain below, the answer to this question is 'No', at least on current evidence. Regulation of electricity and gas networks (at least) must be regarded as permanent, not transitional. This has important implications for the form of regulatory institutions.

In economic terms, an industry is referred to as a natural monopoly when a given set of outputs can be produced more cheaply by one firm than if they are divided among several firms. To meet this condition, the industry must exhibit 'economies of scale or scope' or, more formally, when the industry cost function is 'sub-additive'.

By common agreement, natural monopolies exhibit other characteristics as well, as David Newbery notes in his recent lectures on the economics of regulation.[9] In particular:

- network investments are durable (so rents persist);
- capital investment in the network is large and irreversible (or 'asset-specific', to use the correct economic jargon); and
- networks are connected directly to large numbers of consumers (which increases transactions costs).

Natural monopoly in electricity and gas networks implies that some sector-specific regulation will continue to be necessary for the foreseeable future. This means that the economics of competitive markets are not relevant to any of these activities and that regulation must abide by the economics of natural monopoly. This distinction affects the choices of regulatory methods.

4.3   Economic Conditions in the Energy Sector

Most industries are subject to general competition law, not sector-specific regulation of their prices and terms of sale. Economic pressures in telecoms may be pushing the sector into the competitive arena. This suggests that governments need to take stock of sectoral conditions, to see whether sector-specific regulation is still required. Figure 7.1 shows a decision tree that NERA once developed for a European government client, setting out how to choose between sector-specific regulation and general competition law. Figure 7.1 might be too mechanistic for real policy decisions (the client certainly thought so), but it usefully describes the economic factors that suggest where energy sector regulation is headed.

Consider production (electricity generators and gas wells). Although production is characterized by sunk costs and long lives, the current state of

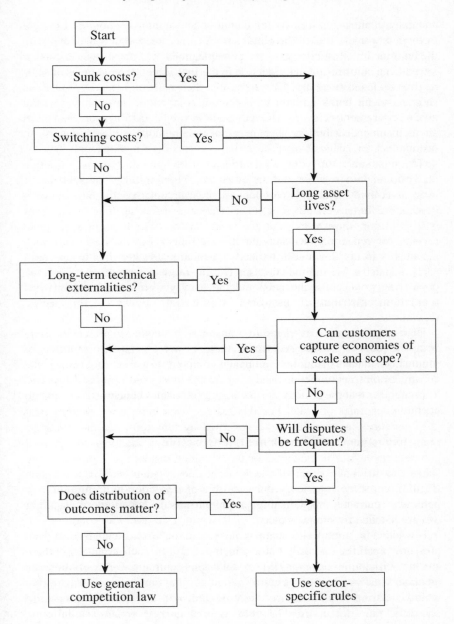

Figure 7.1   Decision tree for choosing between general competition law and sector-specific regulation

technology allows customers to capture the implicit economies of scale through wholesale trade. The elimination of major economies of scale, with the introduction of smaller gas-fired power stations, was one of the reasons for introducing competition in production in the first place. (If economies of scale re-emerge, legislatures may have to rethink their position.) Hence, production should end up being governed by general competition law. However, not every government of every Member State is prepared to abandon concerns about income distribution, such as protection of domestic coal miners, so residual controls persist.

The situation in low-voltage (electricity) or low-pressure (gas) distribution networks is also relatively straightforward. They suffer from sunk costs, long asset lives and large economies of scale relative to the size of a typical customer. Disputes will be frequent, because long asset lives will confront short-term contracts and tariffs (which require frequent revision or renegotiation) and the most efficient way to deal with such disputes is to lay down sector-specific regulations, rather than to approach each dispute as an individual case. Hence, even if protection of specific population groups like the poor and the elderly were not an objective of regulation, distribution networks would fall under sector-specific regulation.

High-voltage and high-pressure transmission networks present a more complex picture. In the gas sector, there is a long-standing tradition of production and distribution companies coming together to arrange the construction of new pipelines and to share the associated costs and benefits. This suggests that the customers (that is, the companies concerned) are able to capture economies of scale. For this reason, some regulatory systems treat large pipelines as a matter to be governed by long-term contracts under a regulatory scheme that is akin to (if not always identical to) general competition law. For example, in the US long-distance gas pipelines are subject to the jurisdiction of the Federal Energy Regulatory Commission (FERC), but some contracts reduce the role of regulation to arbitration over particular contract terms. Offshore gas pipelines in the UK sector of the North Sea are handled by similar means.

However, in some cases there is no separation between high- and low-pressure pipelines (as with Lattice in the UK). In such conditions, there are no distribution companies to take on contracts for high-pressure pipelines; instead, Lattice serves a myriad of final consumers. Furthermore, where existing high-pressure systems are not covered by long-term contracts, the owners may be able to exploit their economies of scale to earn an additional profit. In systems where anyone can build a pipeline, it would be unfair to characterize such profits as due to a monopoly; nevertheless, regulators may feel that it is in consumers' best interests to reduce profits by capping prices, essentially for distributional reasons. In both cases, high-pressure gas pipelines will end up under sector-specific regulation.

Hopes for a decentralized, contractual approach to electricity transmission have so far proved to be illusory. The main problem is the existence of technical externalities, such that one person's transmission line affects the capacity of other connected lines. In addition, the system operator possesses a real-time informational advantage over other users. These factors reinforce the economies of scope and natural monopoly characteristics of network operation. However, given a process for coordinating the design and specification of transmission projects, construction can be decentralized by any number of competitive methods, as evidenced by the number of 'national' grids in Europe that incorporate assets built and owned by different companies.[10]

4.4   Implications for Regulation and Competition

It follows from the above that some segments of the energy sector will remain subject to sector-specific rules for the foreseeable future. The economics of competitive markets will be irrelevant to the choice of regulatory method in these segments and affect the design of regulatory institutions, as discussed in sections 8 and 9.

In contrast (and *pace* the telecoms industry, which may have a different perspective), the shorter lives of investment in telecoms networks (say, ten years rather than 40 years) mean that the scope to exploit any natural monopoly is only temporary, as evidenced by the recent quickening of competition. The telecoms sector may therefore soon proceed down the left-hand side of Figure 7.1 towards regulation as a competitive sector – once distributional concerns about basic telephone services for the poor, the elderly or remote areas are made redundant by the sheer cheapness of the service.

So, if energy networks continue to be subject to natural monopoly regulation, regulators face several challenges if they want to introduce competition in the supply of electricity and gas as a commodity. The key challenges that I shall discuss are:

- unbundling;
- real-time balancing; and
- cross-border trade.

Later, I shall discuss the challenges presented by the recognition that natural monopoly regulation is permanent.

5. UNBUNDLING

5.1 Unbundling Services to Create Competition

Many European utility companies are vertically and horizontally integrated. The natural monopoly they possess in distribution networks may also give them equivalent power in markets for related services. For example, the advantage of possessing a network may extend into energy markets, new connections, system support services (ancillary services) and metering. Hence, natural monopoly in networks may act as a barrier to efficient competition in other services. This raises the question – should these other services be unbundled, and opened to competition? The solution to this problem is not straightforward.

In the UK, there has been a tendency – and indeed it has been a legal duty of regulators[11] – to promote competition in these related areas. To fulfil this requirement, UK regulators have often demanded extensive unbundling of management and ownership. They have occasionally reallocated costs from networks to competitive businesses, in order to create 'a level playing field'. However, not all demands for unbundling are efficient or (therefore) pro-competitive.

To begin with, I wish to discuss two different aspects of competitive unbundling:

- outsourcing by competitive tender; and
- allowing customers to choose their supplier of peripheral services.

5.2 Single Buyers – About to Rise from the Dead?

The single-buyer model (SBM) described in the European electricity directive seems to be a dead duck, since it is equivalent to TPA. As a consequence, the SBM for wholesale electricity offers none of the advantages of monopoly that made it attractive to some Member States. However, the rationale for such models persists in other parts of the energy sector.

Competitive tendering for power stations

The purpose of the single-buyer model was to ensure that new power stations were procured efficiently, even if the incumbent sold the output to consumers. Regulation would be required to ensure that the monopoly could not set prices higher than necessary. However, investment in generation did not need to be carried out by a monopoly. The directive would have allowed Member States to adopt competitive tendering as a means to identify the most efficient producer.

Experience of this approach has not been conspicuously successful. The design and volume of power station construction is a big determinant of future efficiency, and would not be subject to the same competition pressures, since the single buyer specifies the terms of the tender. The Public Utilities Regulatory Policy Act (1978) set up a similar system for the USA, but this did not work well in some states, because utilities, regulators and other interests conspired to favour inefficient forms of production. In some states, this meant favouring local sources of coal (a story that is familiar to Europeans). On the West Coast, high-cost 'renewable' energy sources were also an important feature of energy procurement.

Competitive tendering for standard projects
In some cases, the variation in service volume and specification is a relatively minor determinant of overall efficiency, especially where the services involved are subject to common standards. The construction of new connections for electricity consumers is a case in point. Here, the major efficiency gains can be captured by competitive tendering for construction of the facilities, even if operation (and even ownership) reverts to the monopoly network at the end of the project. The same is true of many projects to build electricity lines and gas pipelines according to a defined specification.

Regulators may demand (and indeed have demanded) further unbundling, by letting consumers choose who operates and maintains such facilities. However, the additional gains to be achieved (compared with normal incentive regulation) tend to be small. In the case of connections, each new connection immediately creates a small, localized natural monopoly that demands to be regulated; if each is run by a separate company, the task of regulating them will quickly spiral out of control. The loss of economies of scope in operations and regulation translates into inconvenience and transactions costs for the consumers concerned. In Railtrack's case, it seems that outsourcing maintenance may have created severe problems for scrutiny of contractors' performance – known to economists as the 'principal–agent' problem.

Hence, in some instances the gains from unbundling are limited, and the disadvantages are significant, in which case one should expect to see demands for reintegration. The combination of (1) political concern over safety and (2) economic factors probably explains the undiminished clamour at the time of writing for Railtrack[12] to take a more active role in maintaining its own track.

In the electricity and gas sectors, the proper scope for unbundling may be confined to competitive tendering of construction projects, where gold-plating and over-building are not major sources of inefficiency. Incidentally, if changes in technology ever place power generation into this category, we should expect a resurgence of the single-buyer model.

5.3   Unbundling to Remove Discrimination in Wholesale Energy Trade

The largest potential benefits arise out of competition in wholesale energy markets, because independent investors in power stations and gas wells can achieve big efficiency gains over monopolies when they are driven by competition pressure. However, in many European Member States, independent investors still have to deal with network companies integrated with wholesale trading activities. Unregulated integration of trading and network activities tends to conflict with efficient competition, since the incumbents can discriminate against efficient new entrants in (1) network access and (2) services ancillary to trading, including balancing. The UK and some other MSs have already separated out their national grids to remove conflicts of interest between integrated and independent traders. However, several European regulators (still) face the challenge of deciding whether integrated utilities should be required to separate out their networks and, if so, how to do so efficiently. Others have essentially given up the task of motivating a privately owned transmission company to behave in a non-discriminatory manner, and have opted for public ownership. Table 7.3 summarizes the current situation (or likely changes in the near future).

Completing a table such as Table 7.3 is difficult, because there are so many different degrees of unbundling – and because the situation keeps changing. The UK, Finland, Sweden and Norway have separate grid companies owned independently of producer interests (that is, owned by the state in all but the UK). In Spain the electricity grid is effectively an independent company, but ownership rests in whole or in part in the producing companies. In Portugal and (soon) in Greece, the electricity grid company is a separate business or subsidiary under one holding company. Looking at this variety of experience, what can one recommend?

It seems likely that efficient competition will not happen if particular producers retain a significant and influential influence over the transmission company. On the other hand, the solution of nationalization (as favoured in Scandinavia and as about to be adopted by the Netherlands) runs counter to the belief that privatization best serves consumers' interests, because the profit motive is an essential component of all incentive regulation. In the Netherlands, the government has recently determined that electricity companies must separate their networks into businesses that are independent of shareholder influence. The Dutch proposals do not provide scope for shareholders to encourage efficient management (and proved unsatisfactory in the UK, when applied to REC ownership of NGC from 1990 to 1995). Opinions on nationalization may depend on ideology, but it is hard to think of good economic reasons for the negation of shareholder control.

Europe might learn from recent developments in the USA, where the

Table 7.3 Ownership and status of EU energy transmission businesses

Country	Public ownership?		Legal Separation?	
	Electricity	Gas	Electricity	Gas
Austria	Yes	Yes	Some	No
Belgium	No	Yes	No	No
Denmark	Yes	Yes	West: Yes East: No	No
Finland	Yes (12%)	Yes (24%)	Yes	No
France	Yes	Yes	No	No
Germany	No	No	No	No
Greece	Yes	Yes	Within holding	No
Ireland	Yes	Yes	Yes	No
Italy	Yes	Yes	Yes	From 2002
Luxembourg	Yes		No[a]	No
Netherlands	Partial(2000)/full(2001)	Yes (50%)	Yes	No
Portugal	Yes (50%)	Yes	Yes, within EDP	No
Spain	Yes	Yes	Yes	Yes
Sweden	Yes	Yes	Yes	No
UK	No	No	Yes	Yes
Norway (not EU)	Yes	n.a.	Yes	n.a.

Note: a In practice, the Luxembourg grid relies on imports, and is therefore not integrated with production to any great degree. However, the network companies still handle the bulk of wholesale trade.

Sources: Various.

FERC has to face similar questions. Given a disaggregated industry with many grid companies, limited powers to enforce restructuring, and a long-standing commitment to 'interstate commerce', FERC has been looking for ways (1) to facilitate access over multiple networks and (2) to enhance the efficiency of operations. FERC's *Order 2000* (22 December 1999) sets out a framework of 'regional transmission organizations' (RTOs), which combine the grid companies of several states to provide integrated operations and tariffs over a wide area.[13] Companies had to file proposals by mid-October 2000. The overwhelming majority have chosen to create profit-driven 'transcos', that is, self-managing grid companies in the image of NGC and Lattice, rather than 'independent system operators' driven by stakeholder committees in the Californian model. These proposals offer independence from any particular producer interest, combined with a profit-oriented incentive to be efficient. Experience with RTOs is limited, but offers a possible solution where European utilities are unwilling to sell off their networks.

To summarize, it seems likely that accounting separation is insufficient and that further unbundling of key networks will be desirable for promotion of competition. Such unbundling represents an infringement of the property rights of the original investors over their networks, which they intended to use themselves. Several EU Member States regard such infringements of property rights as undesirable, or even unconstitutional. However, the long-term advantages of allowing more efficient competition in production may outweigh the disadvantage of undermining property rights – as with any 'essential facility'. The remaining challenge is to unbundle networks without eliminating the profit incentive that encourages efficiency; a multi-utility – or even multi-state – RTO model may provide a means of diluting individual influence whilst preserving the benefits of shareholder power in general.

5.4   Unbundling to Promote Retail Competition

Several Member States have already opened up retail trade to competition and are facing (or have already faced) questions as to the proper degree of unbundling between retail supply and distribution networks.

In the UK, such unbundling is taken for granted, since the creation of the necessary institutions to facilitate retail choice in gas and electricity took place back in 1998–99 (although it was known as the '1998 process'). UK observers might expect other MSs to follow the same path, but there is good reason to think that they might not, for economic as well as political reasons.

Memories being short,[14] most industry personnel will already have forgotten that the whole '1998 process' was estimated to cost around £1 billion for new software systems, with running costs of £100 million per year. This estimate omits several costs incurred by independent traders. It also omits the transactions costs of consumers. If every one of 25 million consumers spends one hour per year deciding which supplier to adopt, and if we price that time at the minimum wage (say £4 per hour), consumers' own transactions costs amount to another £100 million per year.[15]

The regulator's papers occasionally argue simply that such costs of '1998' were small compared with the size of the industry, but this is not valid without some consideration of the cost–benefit ratio. When challenged by the National Audit Office to produce a cost–benefit analysis, Ofgem was unable to produce a convincing one.[16] Some of the benefits were in fact transfers (which economists exclude from cost–benefit analysis) and some might have been achieved anyway by regulation. In any case, the electricity sector may be big, but a billion here, a billion there – pretty soon that adds up to serious money.

Other MSs will be less willing to spend a comparable amount on retail competition. Retail supply was liberalized fully in Norway from 1991, but the Norwegian regulator (NVE) adopted a piecemeal approach, solving problems as they arose. So far, NVE has abolished administrative charges for switching supplier and has introduced a single load profile for all unmetered demands within each distribution network (as an alternative to fitting hourly meters). The amount of customer switching in Norway has been less than in the UK, but Norway – a country of only 4 million people – has avoided major expense on information systems without retail competition falling into disrepute.

5.5 Conclusion

Unbundling is essential to avoid conflicts of interest, where the conflict reduces efficiency overall. Efficiency gains from competition are real – but need to be compared against the loss of economies of scope due to unbundling and any increase in transactions costs. UK regulators have a legal obligation to promote competition, which they interpreted as justification for major expense on systems designed to facilitate customer switching. Other Member States are unlikely to reach precisely the same conclusions. Hence, there is no reason to expect unbundling to proceed to quite the same extent as seen in the UK. A tentative recommendation, combining experience from various sources, would be:

- encourage network companies to form profit-driven multi-utility gridcos ('transcos'), subject to limited (or no) influence from individual producer interests;
- require network companies to offer standard projects for competitive tender, where principal–agent problems are minor;

- adapt retail supply conditions stepwise to meet specific problems where benefits exceed costs.

In addition, any consideration of competition and conflicts must include the need for independent operation of the real-time balancing system, to which I turn next.

6. REAL-TIME BALANCING

Electricity and gas trading is never exact. Flows always differ from the sales that traders make in their contracts. There is always a need for two monopoly functions:

- organizing real-time balancing – adjusting energy production or consumption to make up inadvertent shortfalls or to absorb inadvertent surpluses; and
- charging for imbalances (making sure no one without a contract can take free energy merely by flicking a switch).

The European directives are silent on this aspect of liberalized markets, but it is already proving to be a major focus of interest, especially in countries that have not unbundled grid operations from wholesale trading.

6.1 The European Situation

In the gas sector, balancing tends to be managed by contractual penalties for departing from pre-specified flows. Such penalties work well enough at the wholesale level, because wholesale gas traders are normally able to keep gas flows within acceptable bounds. However, electricity is not so amenable to decentralized control, and nor is retail trade in gas. In the electricity sector, and in fully liberalized gas sectors, the price for inadvertent flows ('imbalances') is therefore a subject of much debate.

In the electricity sector, one can observe two different approaches in Europe:

1. The incumbent utility sells or absorbs imbalances at a tariff rate, as seen for example in the Netherlands (at least until 2001), Portugal (where the 'integrated system' performs balancing for the 'independent system'), and Germany (under the latest 'Verbändevereinbarung').
2. An independent market operator (often the same as the independent system operator) who provides a competitive market for real-time

balancing (or 'regulation power') and who puts a price on imbalances (the UK, Scandinavia, Finland, Spain and the Netherlands from 2001).

National regulators will only accept tariff schemes on the understanding that the tariff is monopolistic, must be cost-reflective and will be subject to regulation. However, as our recent (German-language) report on the German system[17] shows, such schemes use a monopoly to favour incumbents without good reason. The German system currently limits the provision of regulation power to incumbents, and settles imbalances at (asymmetric and fixed) tariff rates. The possibility of incurring a large capacity charge (per kW) for deficits causes independent traders to run a permanent surplus, which incumbents absorb at a very low tariff (per kWh) for 'spill'. This system creates costs and risks for traders that only incumbents or large companies can manage. Such tariffs unnecessarily put small new entrants at a competitive disadvantage to incumbents and other large companies.

6.2 Future Developments

The prospects for tariff-based systems are not good. The Netherlands is switching to a regulation power market from 1 January 2001, with the market being operated by the independent grid company, TenneT. As a condition of their proposed mergers, RWE/VEW and E.On, the two biggest German utilities, must comply with a demand from the Federal Cartel Office to develop similar regulation power markets over the next two years. They must open up the supply of regulation power to all capable producers and traders, and they must move to a system of kWh prices based on market rates. (They have begun by conducting competitive tenders for six-month contracts, and will gradually switch over to a daily process.) Other German companies are expected to follow the example of their bigger brothers and the rest of Europe will follow.

6.3 Conclusion

Electricity traders know that the terms for real-time balancing and the charges for imbalances effectively determine the value of electricity as a commodity and the ability of traders to compete. Systems that bias competition in favour of some suppliers (particularly incumbents) can expect to face an onslaught of complaints. Even the German system, which nominally addresses complaints via general competition policy, has used the recent mergers to impose sector-specific rules for the procurement and pricing of power in real time. Other regulatory regimes, more open to sustained pressure and better able to impose common solutions, are unlikely to resist similar pressures for long.

7.   CROSS-BORDER TRADE

The stated intention behind the EU directives was to liberalize national markets and create a single market for energy. However, they say little or nothing about cross-border trade or the need to promote efficient inter-country choices. Several problems have emerged as a result, and the Council of European Electricity Regulators (CEER) and a Gas Regulatory Forum were established, taking place every six months in Florence and Madrid respectively, in order to develop a common position on these issues. Detailed below are some of the problems addressed by the Florence Forum.

7.1   'Pancaking'

The original concern raised by the European Commission was the accumulation of transmission charges from several grids on long-distance trade, in a manner unrelated to the marginal costs of any energy flow. This phenomenon is known in the USA as 'pancaking', that is, piling up charges. It represents the initial rationale for forming RTOs that cover a wider area.

The CEER regards pancaking as a 'barrier to trade'. (Economists might say that the addition of multiple charges based on sunk costs is simply inefficient.) The CEER has therefore been trying to find ways to remove such impediments. In practice, the CEER and the European Association of TSOs (ETSO) are finding it hard to design an efficient system, and are solving problems step by step.

7.2   Transmission Charges Paid by Generators

The proportion of transmission charges levied directly on generators (as opposed to consumers and other traders) varies significantly across Europe, from 0 per cent in Spain and France to 30 per cent in the UK and, under recent proposals, to 50 per cent in Greece. The CEER noted early on that differences between these percentages could distort competition between generators located in different countries. In particular, they could damage the efficiency of plant location (kW charges) and despatch (kWh charges), and might act as a barrier to (efficient) trade.

Early discussions in the CEER established that transmission charges were largely a matter of recovering sunk costs, and should therefore be charged to the most inelastic demands – meaning consumers rather than generators. However, some systems (including the UK) use generator charges as a means to encourage efficient location of generation plant. The latest proposals from the CEER suggest that generators would pay up to 25 per cent of total transmission charges as a means of providing incentives for efficient location.[18]

Signals to encourage efficient location of generation can derive from sources other than transmission charges (strictly defined). Many electricity markets set different prices for different locations – either different areas of the grid ('zones') or different points on the grid ('nodes'). Gas networks in the US offer short-term and long-term signals about the value of transmission capacity (and hence of gas in different places) by creating tradable rights to use defined routes.

If European electricity markets were to introduce such schemes, it would no longer be necessary or efficient to allocate a share of network charges to generators. However, European institutions seem unable to achieve a consensus on the treatment of constraints within European networks.

7.3 Allocation of Congestion Costs

Within the interconnected European electricity system, some grid companies experience high levels of congestion due to transit flows (that is, flows between two other states that cross their network). These grid companies have complained about the costs of reinforcing their grids for transit, which must currently be borne by their own customers. The ETSO has developed a short-term proposal for compensation payments between grids within the integrated UCTE (continental European) system:

- TSOs must contribute €2 per MWh for all exports to other UCTE Member States;
- TSOs receive a share of the revenue proportional to the role of transit in their domestic power flows (that is, maximum of exports or imports, relative to domestic consumption).

At the Florence meeting of 9–10 November 2000, the scheme received broad approval for one year, allowing for total compensation payments of around €200 million. However, France, Belgium and Germany wished to levy the charge of €2 on actual exports, whereas the other states involved (Portugal, Spain, Italy, the Netherlands, Luxembourg, Austria and Denmark[19]) preferred to recover it from all users. The European Commission indicated that adoption of differing systems would be unacceptable, and offered to speak to the French, Belgians and Germans. The resulting scheme therefore has yet to be decided. In any case, it is not intended to operate for longer than one year, after which some alternative will be needed. Ultimately, it may prove most efficient to internalize these costs of congestion by forming proper RTOs spanning several states, as in the US model.

7.4 Access to International Interconnectors

Questions have arisen over access to international interconnectors. Some parties treat them as the property right of incumbents. Others regard them as part of a network that, under the directive, is subject to TPA.

Recent developments regarding the Skagerrak, the sub-sea interconnector between Norway and Denmark, provide a potentially useful way forward. The capacity of the line had been tied up in long-term contracts with 20 years to run. However, in June 2000 the holders of these contracts (Elsam, Statkraft and PreussenElektra) agreed to convert these physical contracts into financial contracts. Instead of benefiting from the link by moving power from low-price markets to high-price markets, these companies will now receive a rental fee, equal to the difference between Norwegian and Danish spot market prices. Any trader prepared to pay the difference will be able to trade between the two markets, as currently happens within Nord Pool. This approach both opens up competitive access and allows the current contract holders to earn a reasonable return on their investment.

At the European level, the CEER is discussing the possibility of auctioning congested capacity. However, such schemes must be reconciled with the contractual rights of existing users, to avoid accusations of expropriation. European regulators will not benefit consumers by expropriating investors' rights and the Skagerrak solution provides a useful and efficient alternative. It becomes feasible, once real-time spot markets operate efficiently at either end of the connector.

7.5 Conclusion

European discussions face the same problems of transmission pricing and access as national markets, but with more discussion of congestion and the associated variation in electricity prices. These problems have been studied at length for the USA and, recently, in the UK, in the context of NETA. Any permanent solution will have to have the following characteristics:

1. Real competition means facing up to physical realities, including real transmission constraints and the associated differences in price between different locations. Attempts to create a single European market without recognizing such factors are doomed to failure. In the USA, the FERC is pushing for more segmentation of electricity markets.
2. Congested capacity can be rationed by price (long- or short-term auctions) or by quantity (awarding contractual rights to use a certain amount of capacity). There are no efficient alternatives.
3. Reallocating rights leads to windfall gains and losses for investors

in long-lived irreversible investments – including generators and factories, as well as the interconnectors themselves. European economies will not prosper if regulation routinely undermines property rights in such a fashion. Any scheme must therefore give due consideration to the existing rights of incumbents. Failure to respect property rights will not promote efficiency or consumers' interests.

This last point begins to bring in some of the economic constraints on regulators' freedom of action and it is to these constraints that I now turn. However European regulators choose to unbundle their energy sectors, to set up real-time balancing markets or to solve problems of congestion, they will face a number of economic constraints. Existing regulatory institutions in Europe may or may not incorporate these economic constraints; the sooner they do, the better for consumers and for European economies at large.

8. COST RECOVERY (1): STRANDED COSTS

As the previous section indicates, a major concern of investors is (and of reformers should be) the treatment of sunk costs of past investments. When it proves impossible to recover these costs in a liberalized market, they are termed 'stranded costs', but the same principles apply both to liberalization of markets and to regulation of the remaining monopolies. In the following sections, I examine both the temptations facing governments and the economic factors that should constrain their actions. It remains to be seen whether regulatory institutions in Europe offer the procedural constraints needed to ensure that decisions are driven by a concern for efficiency (not transfers), and that true competition results.

8.1 Regulatory Policy as a Game

Introducing competition can be merely an opportunistic tool to deny cost recovery by incumbents, if market prices are lower than regulated prices. As with any opportunistic tool, using liberalization to cut prices immediately appeals to governments and regulators who have only a narrow section of the public interest at heart (for example, consumers' short-term interests). However, such choices open up the possibility of an inefficient regulatory 'game', as shown in Figure 7.2.

Assume that regulated prices reflect average costs. In this example, the government follows a simple 'myopic' policy:

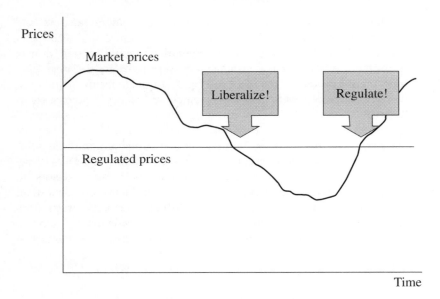

Figure 7.2   Schematic of an opportunistic regulatory cycle

- if market prices are lower than average costs, liberalize;
- if market prices are higher than average costs, regulate.

The result of such behaviour is to create a regime over the long run in which it is practically impossible for an investor to recover total costs. If they anticipate such a regime, investors may keep existing facilities in operation until they break down. However, they would be wise not to engage in new investment within the regulated sector. The result would be a gradual (or catastrophic) decline in service quality that could only be offset by offering very high regulated prices (that is, accelerated cost recovery) to cover the increase in the required rate of return.

8.2   Pressures for and Safeguards against Opportunism in Europe

Is such a development likely in Europe? Certainly, European institutions will favour liberalization where it reduces prices, and not otherwise. They may also follow the example of California, and attempt to reimpose controls the minute that market prices rise above certain levels. In California, the consensus seems to be moving (in November 2000) away from demands for re-regulation and in favour of reforms to the market rules (in particular, a move towards nodal spot pricing and more transparent treatment of congestion). European regulators might adopt the same attitude – but investors have been warned!

The main safeguard against the opportunism described in Figure 7.2 is a legal prohibition on legislation or regulatory decisions that prevent long-term cost recovery without good reason. (Observing that market prices this year would be lower than regulated prices would not count as a good reason.) This provision would give investors some protection against the expropriation of their investments through the creation of stranded costs. The European Commission (in the person of Sr Mario Monti) is currently considering the Spanish system of 'compensation for the transition to competition' (CTC) and his decision may set the standard. However, European investors will also look to the European Convention on Human Rights for higher-level protection, if individual decisions threaten their viability and hence their ability to raise capital for investment in the sector.

9.   COST RECOVERY (2): REGULATORY INSTITUTIONS

9.1.   Economic Principles of Regulation

The issue of stranded costs is only one of many where regulators have the ability (if not always the power) to prevent recovery of certain costs. In many cases, regulators prevent recovery of costs that were incurred unnecessarily or imprudently, in order to provide an incentive for efficient decisions by the regulated company in the future. However, all regulatory regimes contain scope for opportunistic decisions to deny cost recovery in ways that act against consumers' long-term interests, but which serve the interests of a narrow section of the population.

Recall the fundamental characteristics of natural monopolies – that they consist of long-lived, irreversible investments. In the absence of legal or procedural constraints, it is easy[20] for any single regulator (whether an individual or body) to cut prices now, by denying recovery of sunk costs. The regulator will receive praise for the immediate benefit to consumers, and the company will continue to operate its existing facilities as long as prices exceed operating expenses. By the time the quality of service starts to decline, because the company is no longer willing to commit funds to new irreversible investments, the offending regulator is long gone.[21]

Such regulatory opportunism is bad for consumers, damaging to efficiency and hence – according to section 1.1 – inconsistent with the promotion of competition.[22] The only safeguard is a set of regulatory institutions (laws, procedures and bodies) that protect investors against opportunism over the long run. These institutions do not need to guarantee cost recovery (which would be inconsistent with incentives for efficiency). However, they should not deny the possibility of cost recovery. To summarize the combination of these two principles, one might say that regulatory institutions must offer investors a 'reasonable prospect of cost recovery'.

9.2 Regulatory Institutions in Europe

Europe is unfamiliar with the need for institutions to constrain opportunism and to protect investors in the energy sector, for several perfectly understandable reasons.

There is a history of public ownership where government supervision acts in place of shareholders and the profit incentive. The government can afford to act opportunistically with companies that it owns, since such behaviour will not damage the (already weak) incentives for efficiency. Under private ownership, the effect of economic regulation is quite different. Regulators are no substitute for shareholder control of management. All they can do is to adjust the company's incentives, so that shareholders earn more profit when management improves the company's efficiency.

Misunderstandings about this role abound, for example where regulators imply that cutting revenues will in itself make companies more efficient. Regulatory institutions with a history of public ownership tend to underestimate the role and need for profits in encouraging efficient operations and investment. Public agencies might conceivably become more efficient if their budgets are cut, if they have incentives to spend. Private companies have an incentive to maximize profits and will cut costs and become more efficient whenever they can make more profit by doing so. Simply cutting revenues does not enhance incentives to be efficient. It might place the company under a cash constraint, but the resulting cost cutting is unlikely to be efficient.

The basis for incentive regulation is unfamiliar. Many European systems operate with a variant of cost pass-through (or do not relate prices to costs because the sector is publicly owned). As part of a major restructuring, regulators will often pick up the worldwide trend towards use of price caps, but may not recognize that effective incentive regulation is still cost-based. Again, misunderstandings abound, for example where regulators insist that competitive markets provide some guide to pricing for natural monopolies.[23] I have recently encountered statements that competitive markets set prices equal to efficient costs, and therefore so should regulators. Both halves of the statement are incorrect: efficient companies earn super-normal profits precisely because prices are set by averagely efficient companies; offering a reasonable prospect of cost recovery means assuming average efficiency, not exceptional efficiency.

There is no explicit constitutional protection of investments. Western economies are founded on the premise that property rights (and competitive markets) work better in most conditions than government ownership (and control). This was the rationale for privatization. Otherwise, there is no reason why the utility sector could not have continued to receive the necessary capital from government borrowing. Normally, European governments are careful not to trample on property rights without good reason. Regulation by government can undermine property rights. There is no good reason to allow opportunistic decisions that undermine the property rights of investors in utilities. However, the impact of regulatory decisions on property rights is not immediately apparent, and will only emerge from protracted discussions.

9.3 US Precedents

Much is made of the 'constitutional protection of property' in US regulation. However, anyone perusing the 200-year-old US Constitution will be hard put to find an explicit safeguard against opportunism in the regulation of electricity, gas and telecoms sectors. In fact, the protection offered to investors is not explicit and has three components:

1. The Fifth Amendment of the Bill of Rights prohibits government from 'taking without due process' (that is, from depriving citizens of their life, liberty and property without following due process of the law).
2. Supreme Court Decision on *Bluefield Water* (1923):[24] regulators must allow investors to earn a rate of return comparable with that earned by investors in other sectors, or else the decision constitutes a 'regulatory taking' (expropriation of investors' property).
3. Supreme Court Decision on *Hope Gas* (1944):[25] regulators must allow investors the opportunity to earn the comparable rate of return after recovery of operating costs and depreciation (return of capital).

Application of these principles applies to the rate of return earned on past investments (that is, recovery of sunk costs) as well as to the rate of return promised for future investments (that is, recovery of avoidable costs).

I should point out that these principles allow for a wide range of regulatory methods. These legal constraints do not 'guarantee' any particular rate of return. Regulators can design incentive schemes in which the rate of return rises or falls in line with the efficiency of the regulated business, so long as the general level of return on offer is comparable with that in other sectors. The US Constitution does not require pass-through of all costs. US regulators frequently impose the kind of price caps and other forms of incentive regulation found in the UK.

What is more, these principles do not rule out disallowance of investment costs – provided that due process shows such disallowances to be beneficial to consumers (and not just a regulatory taking). To meet this requirement, regulators have to show, broadly speaking, that the expenditure was inefficient, imprudent or unnecessary, in the light of information available at the time of the decision to incur the cost. Such disallowances encourage efficiency in the future; other disallowances would not.

As this last point illustrates, the ultimate safeguard against opportunism is the requirement for due process – regulators who want to infringe investors' property rights must show that they have a good reason for doing so. The most obvious reason for disallowing costs (that it results in lower prices in the immediate future) is not good enough.

9.4   Implications for the Promotion of Energy Competition in Europe

European observers should note immediately that the 'constitutional protection' of US investors does not rest in any explicit constitutional or legal treatment of utilities that is specific to the USA. Points 1 to 3 above are general lessons derived from economic experience within the framework of a particular legal system.[26] Economic principles (unlike laws) know no boundaries; they merely await discovery by different means in different legal systems. The USA took roughly fifty years to establish these principles; European consumers will be better off if their institutions discover and adopt the same principles more quickly.

Some Member States already have public procedures that allow all arguments to be subject to detailed scrutiny, and regulators in these States are already constrained by due process. (I am working with a procedure of this type in the Netherlands.) However, some MSs are more used to political negotiations with utilities and would find it more difficult to adapt to open procedures. Moreover, due process alone may not immediately result in the adoption of the three economic principles set out above, or of any similar variant. Where they are not already entrenched in the law, they will need to be rediscovered through a process of discussion and dispute. Whilst this process continues, investors will be unsure of their rights, investment will be discouraged, and the full benefits of efficient competition will not be achieved.

Within the UK, it will be interesting to see what difference the repatriation of the European Convention on Human Rights will make to UK government procedures. The EHCR may impose new procedural requirements, including a requirement for substantive appeals in 'criminal' cases (for example where Ofgem penalizes companies for breach of a licence). Only time will tell how this affects our regulatory institutions.

10. CHALLENGES FOR EUROPEAN REGULATORS

This brief survey of European energy markets draws on my experience (and I make no apology for focusing on the electricity sector, with which I am most familiar). However, my findings depend on analysis of general economic factors and their effect on the development of competition.

It seems to me that the telecoms sector does not provide a useful indicator of the way ahead for energy sector regulation, because it is significantly less prone to natural monopoly conditions. In telecoms, regulation might just be viewed as a measure to mitigate market power until competition reduces the dominance of certain players. Competitive markets may even provide a paradigm for the design of such measures. In electricity and gas, however, natural monopoly is so prevalent that (a) regulatory interventions will be required to promote competition and (b) regulation of the natural monopolies must be regarded as permanent.

The measures required to promote competition should follow the principles of the 'essential facility doctrine'. Networks are the property of investors who intended to use them. Regulators may require such networks to be made available to others, when the efficiency gains coming from competition among network users more than offset any loss of efficiency due to loss of economies of scale and scope, or any disincentive to invest in networks. To avoid creating such disincentives, European regulation may need to give more detailed consideration to (and may require more institutional safeguards of) the need to offer a reasonable prospect of cost recovery.

In the meantime, European electricity and gas markets will require regulatory measures that are by now familiar to a UK audience:

- unbundling of transmission networks, preferably as profit-driven independent 'transcos' in the style of NGC and Lattice; and
- unbundling of an open and competitive market for real-time balancing ('regulation power').

For good economic reasons, European regulators probably should (and will) be a little more selective than in the UK when adopting measures to promote competition in other parts of the system, including:

- measures to facilitate retail competition; and
- unbundling or outsourcing of peripheral services.

Within any energy liberalization process, the biggest economic problem facing European regulators, utilities and traders alike in the immediate future will be the design of efficient transmission pricing. Sustainable solutions should take the following economic principles into account:

- ignoring physical realities does not promote efficient competition;
- The physical reality of any transmission system (gas or electric) includes real congestion over capacity that must be rationed by price or quantity;
- segmenting markets will lead to changes in prices and windfall gains and losses in the value of long-lived investments in production and consumption;
- efficient investment in networks will only be forthcoming if regulated revenues offer a reasonable prospect of cost recovery, and so regulation should offer reasonable protection against (or compensation for) investors' windfall gains and losses.

Where private investment is important, regulators need to be sensitive to the need to attract capital for continuing investment. Regulatory institutions will therefore need to restrain the tendency or temptation to indulge in opportunism – both when deregulating markets and when regulating the remaining monopolies. Given the importance of future investment for competition, efficiency and consumers, the need to develop such institutions may overtake transmission pricing as a higher priority for Europe in coming years.

NOTES

1. Council Directive 90/547/EEC of 29 October 1990 on the transit of electricity through transmission grids.
2. John Rhys, Graham Shuttleworth and Leigh Hancher (1995), *Evaluation of the French Proposal for a Single Buyer Model*, London, NERA.
3. 'Electricity prices for EU industry on 1 January 2000: downward trend' and 'Electricity prices for EU households on 1 January 2000: downward trend', Eurostat, *Statistics in Focus, Environment and Energy*.
4. For example, see 'Florence Forum: The threat of new regulation', *EU Energy Policy*, 31/10/00.
5. Negotiations over network access are effectively regulated by the adoption of common agreements between 'associations' of the industry and its customers ('Verbändevereinbarungen'), with arbitration over details by the Federal Cartel Office.
6. From 19/2/99 almost two-thirds of electricity consumers in Europe were, in principle, free to choose their supplier.
7. See 'TPA conditions of major European gas transmission operators', draft discussion document prepared by the EC, 09/11/00, www.europa.eu.int/comm/dgs/energy_transport/index_en.html.
8. For example, see 'EC set to introduce unbundling decree', *Gas Daily Europe*, 09/11/00.
9. D. M. Newbery (2000), *Privatization, Restructuring, and Regulation of Network Utilities; Walras–Pareto Lectures at the École des Hautes Études Commerciales - Université de Lausanne*, Cambridge, MA: MIT Press.

10. The 'national' grid company leases assets from others in the Netherlands, Norway, Spain and Sweden.
11. The Electricity Act says the DGES must 'promote competition in generation and supply' (energy retailing); further unbundling has been imposed to facilitate the latter. The Gas Act 1986 contained a secondary duty to 'enable persons to compete effectively in the supply of gas through pipes at rates which, in relation to any premises, exceed 25,000 therms a year'. The Competition and Service (Utilities) Act 1992 required effective competition 'between persons whose business consists ... of the supply of gas' without the restriction to the market for more than 25 000 therms per year. The Utilities Act 2000 adds a general duty to protect consumers' interests, bearing in mind the scope for competition.
12. After the time of writing, Railtrack disappeared from the scene. However, pressure for reintegration of activities continued unabated in the rail sector.
13. See Gene Meehan and Walter Surrat (January 2000), *Order 2000: FERC's Final Rule on RTOs?*, Energy Regulation Brief No. 4, NERA.
14. The costs of '1998' may have been forgotten, because another £1 billion is being spent on the new electricity trading arrangements.
15. If consumers decide not to incur these costs, by never switching supplier, the costs will translate into a price advantage for their current supplier, so they bear the costs anyway.
16. See FT Energy Economist, 20 February 1998, *An Unanswered Question*.
17. Graham Shuttleworth and Enese Lieb-Doczy (August 2000), *Wirtschaftliche Effizienz und Wettbewerbliche Aspekte der Bereitstellung von Regelenergie in Deutschland* (*Economic Efficiency and Competitive Aspects of the Provision of Regulation Power in Germany*), NERA.
18. Unlike earlier drafts, recent documents from the CEER do not link the imposition of generator charges to the need to provide locational signals. The absence of such a link may have been imposed by the Dutch regulator, who recently assigned 25 per cent of transmission charges to generators, without offering any locational signals.
19. Ireland, Finland, Greece, Sweden and the UK fall outside the interconnected UCTE system.
20. Cutting prices is sometimes called 'tough regulation'. It isn't. Cutting prices is the easiest thing for a regulator to do, given the likely degree of public support. 'Tough' regulation is ordering a price increase when costs go up!
21. Part II of the Utilities Act 2000 obliges gas and electricity regulators to 'protect consumers' interests' and explicitly defines consumers to mean 'existing and future consumers'. Hence, actions that put the interests of future consumers in jeopardy, in return for temporary, opportunistic gains, may already be illegal under UK law.
22. This idea can be found in numerous academic texts. For a recent contribution see Newbery (2000), note 9 above.
23. Such statements can be found in documents recently issued by the Dutch energy regulator, DTe, along with other statements that incorrectly describe how prices are set in competitive markets. DTe's attempt to apply these (incorrect) principles has provoked a number of disputes that may result in court proceedings.
24. *Bluefield Water Works & Improvement Co.* v. *Public Service Commission of West Virginia* (262 U.S. 679, 1923).
25. *Federal Power Commission* v. *Hope Natural Gas Company* (320 U.S. 391, 1944).
26. Canada has adopted the same principles of regulation, without being subject to the US Constitution, on the basis of UK-style common law.

CHAIRMAN'S COMMENTS

Clare Spottiswoode

I believe more in the ability of the market to deliver than does Graham Shuttleworth. Furthermore, I am not a professional economist and therefore, not surprisingly, I take a slightly different view of some things – though I agree with most of what Graham says in his chapter.

Graham says his primary purpose is to find out whether competition will promote efficiency; if it does not do this, it is pointless. I agree with this in general, but I believe that we can create competition in a way that is guaranteed to promote efficiency. We should start from what will promote efficiency – in other words what parts of the market are genuinely a natural monopoly, and what can be made competitive. It is this that dictates how one should deregulate, and how one should regulate what remains as the regulated natural monopoly.

Graham brings up telecoms: 'the state of competition in gas and electricity markets contrasts strongly with the situation in telecoms. Consumers readily switch between telecoms suppliers and there is competition developing between competing networks. Developments in technology and economic pressures are driving telecoms markets away from natural monopoly and into the competitive arena.' This is an interesting comment, and expresses a view shared by many. What appears at first glance surprising is that it is not true. There has been substantially more competition in gas than in telecoms, and I think it is worth considering why.

Stephen Littlechild says that at least seven to eight competitors are needed for a market to be competitive. In telecoms there is some competition in infrastructure – but nowhere near enough. That means we need to continue to regulate the infrastructure as there are still real monopolies/oligopolies. Competition will not be created without this separation of infrastructure and regulation.

We need, I think, to go through what is required to get competition to work effectively, which is not quite the same as Graham's approach. I made these proposals to the European Commission back in 1995, and it is interesting to see what they have put into the gas and electricity directives, and just how far it falls short of what is needed for competition to thrive. Competition is a matter of choice for individual governments in Europe – they have a choice of whether to go further than the directives to promote competition, or whether to go with the minimum requirements. If they take the latter course, competition will not happen – except at the fringes where there are such large opportunities for others that they can overcome the anti-competitive barriers put up by incumbents.

I hold strongly that competition is good because competition, properly done, encourages innovation and hence efficiency, to such a degree that there is no question of whether the benefits are worthwhile. They clearly are when you take a dynamic view of competition. I'll come to the costs in gas later.

Separate accounts are not enough. Our licence condition on British Gas (BG) for separation was a very important step based on Michael Beesley's ideas. It was so tough that eventually BG decided to separate of its own accord. But in the EU directive separation is too weak to be effective, the discrimination clause is weak or absent, and the investment clause non-existent.

Competition is a matter of choice for governments and regulators – whether they are prepared to do what it takes to make competition happen. In that context, I would argue the following:

- Competition for the market (as opposed to 'in' the market) – where there are monopolies it is good regulatory practice (and good commercial practice – the two are usually coincident) to market-test, tender and contract out services where a good service-level agreement can be written. Where this is not possible it is difficult to outsource effectively, as it is when the outsourcer has a great deal of capital and assets which have to be replicated when a new organization wins a bid. In these circumstances it would be best for the original company to control the use of these assets.
- Graham says that unbundling 'represents an infringement of the property rights of the original investors over their networks, which they intended to use themselves'. This issue itself needs unbundling. Provided that the infrastructure business is unbundled, and then incentivized to carry more products, there is no loss of property rights. The issue then is whether there is any loss of property rights in the newly competitive businesses. Here the analysis is much more complicated. But, as British Gas shows, unbundling can be very good for shareholders as well as customers – a clear win–win solution.
- The real issue is the unbundled newly competitive piece, which is not the monopoly network – that is, production or retail. Here it depends on how the demerged company performs. In 1994 which would have been considered the dog and which the star performer, BG or BT? In the UK BG has done much better by shareholders as a result. BT is showing signs of poor performance. It has spent too much time managing the regulator and defending its patch, and not looking forward.

- I view monopolies on essential facilities as an issue of principle as well as of property rights. Clearly, where there are licences, the rights and responsibilities are, at least partially, laid out. But where these companies are not licensed, I think governments have every right to ensure that essential facilities are used to the benefit of the country and its economy – subject of course to a fair return and reward on investment.
- Once unbundled, the network is far easier to regulate and manage. There is less danger of mistakes, more focus, and a clearer regulatory remit.
- Cost of competition: in gas it cost £187m – the figure we allowed in the Transco price control to cover the whole of BG (both Centrica and Transco). So these were the direct costs as far as customers were concerned. Other companies could choose to invest and join the party; it was their risk. Presumably they would only do this if they felt that they would get customers by offering better value for money than British Gas, so, by definition, customers would be better off if they chose to move. The benefits of competition in gas were estimated to be £200m+ per year, and in the event they turned out to be of the order of £1bn, and sustainable and rising. We had no problem in persuading people of the merits of competition.
- I agree with Graham that Gridco should be encouraged to form profit-driven companies (but I question multi-utility). But it is very important that these companies are not subject to any influence from producer interests.

Cash constraints do work – compare the case of water. They work because games are played, and there is a natural tendency of managers to satisfice if they can. Why cut staff hard if you can satisfy shareholders to a reasonable extent, and no one else is showing how much can be done? No one wants to break out, and anyway everyone wants some extra left to cushion the next price control. Clearly, with game-playing, regulators are working to a large extent in the dark, and will therefore not get things precisely right. It is perfectly possible for regulators to be too tough – which brings me on to price controls!

I agree that there should be a reasonable prospect of cost recovery. The 1997 Transco price control does precisely what he is asking for, and ensures that there is a fair prospect of cost recovery – indeed it does so with very little risk for investors. I believe it is a very good model for all network price controls, provided the glaringly obvious mistake of this particular price control of using an unfocused approach is rectified.

- One brief note on our 1997 price control – it was unfortunate that the MMC referred to RAB, regulatory asset base, rather than our term of regulatory value, as our price control did not concern assets, but looked at how much shareholders had invested as the appropriate base on which to assess the provision of a fair return.

8. Concurrency or convergence? Competition and regulation under the Competition Act 1998

Tom Sharpe QC

In preparing this chapter I reverted to a book written by David Boies entitled *Public Control of Business* (Little Brown, 1977). In his chapter on the application of anti-trust laws and policies to regulated markets he says this:

> The interface between anti-trust and regulation is a veritable no-man's land for students and practitioners alike. Since the theories of anti-trust and regulation reflect differing assumptions about Government intervention into the marketplace, it is often difficult to rationalise their impact on particular industry behaviour. The anti-trust laws, to borrow a phrase, are a brooding omnipresence, with a pervasive, almost constitutional meaning in our jurisprudence. Direct economic regulation (which is entrusted to agencies rather than the Courts) may supplant the anti-trust laws and specific industries for carefully carved-out purposes. But at the edges, these purposes thin out and the anti-trust laws inevitably reappear in the background. At this point it is no small matter to blend the policies of the two conflicting regimes into an overall regulatory purpose that preserves the values of both.

Boies's comments are set in time and space: they were made at the beginning of the deregulation movement and concern the USA. At that time, the USA had an anti-trust tradition of nearly ninety years. US regulation is often described as inimical to competition, constituting instances of safe havens from the rigours of anti-trust scrutiny, erecting barriers to entry, and occasionally deploying different and more lenient standards 'in the public interest' than would be ordained by the anti-trust laws, especially mergers. There is some truth in this, although Fred Kahn's tenure at the Civil Aeronautics Board is an important and eloquent exception.

There are important differences with the UK. First, in the UK since the beginning, nearly every sector has been subject to a licensing regime and the enforcement of the licence has been a primary function of each regulator.

Second, each regulator has been charged, using various formulations, to 'promote and maintain' effective competition. Professor Littlechild made special note of this in his comments on Stelzer's chapter (Chapter 5): he interpreted this objective to mean that where competition was possible, it should be maintained or promoted. Some regulators have seen this provision as a means of encouraging competitors and, conversely, viewed from the perspective of the incumbent regulated utility, this provision often sees the regulator as unfairly favouring new *entrants* rather than *efficient competition*.

A third function of regulators, typically, has been to control prices or tariffs by way of variations of the RPI–X formula, at periodic intervals. The UK chose not to adopt 'out-of-service' regulation but adopted, initially at least, a form of incentive regulation.

The RPI–X incentive regulation regime, in its pure form, was undoubtedly a major innovation but, with the possible exception of water, or natural monopolies, it was always seen as an interim solution to a problem which would ultimately be solved by the advent of new competitors or by altering the structure of various industries or regulated utilities such that competition could be encouraged or introduced. It is perhaps trite that more than any other single factor, the underlying structure of the particular industry being regulated has defined the context in which regulatory agencies have operated.

The last element, and the subject of my chapter, is the application of what I shall call the general competition laws by the specialist regulator to the sector being regulated. From the beginning, regulators shared the power to make references to the (old) MMC, sometimes with the consent of the Secretary of State. The exception lay in mergers, the responsibility for which remained with the Secretary of State. So, a regulator could refer a particular practice or the structure of a utility to the MMC. An obvious example is found in the parallel reference of British Gas, under the Fair Trading Act (FTA), to the MMC, which culminated in the recommendations regarding the separation of the component elements of British Gas. Alternatively, it was possible for the regulator to refer utilities under the Competition Act 1980 in respect of any 'anti-competitive practice'. These powers were often threatened but seldom invoked.

The advent of the Competition Act 1998 has completely transformed the powers available not only to the Director General of Fair Trading (DGFT) but also to the regulators. The deficiencies of the old general competition law are too well known to require repetition here. It may be recalled that the Director General of Telecommunications (DGT) regarded his concurrent powers under the Fair Trading Act as insufficient to enable him to deal with the practices he anticipated would arise in relation to British Telecom and so, in 1996, he proposed modifying British Telecom's licence to include a 'fair trading condition' modelled very closely upon Articles 85 and 86 of the EC Treaty. British Telecom sought to challenge whether it was within the DGT's powers to 'arrogate' (the word is in the pleading) to himself powers parallel to those combined, at that time, in the OFT and MMC, and to acquire an essentially summary power, with no appeal, only judicial review, under the guise of licence enforcement, which would circumvent the review/appeal function of the MMC.

This litigation foundered on the fact that BT chose to assent to the licence modification and then subsequently to seek judicial review of the modification. The High Court told BT that it could not have its cake and eat it and, whatever conditions were either expressed or implied surrounding its acceptance of the licence modification, the fact of its consent was conclusive and disabled it from further challenge. The interesting point about the judgment of Phillips J. (as he then was) was that he expressly left open (indeed he seemed to cast doubt on) the possibility for the DGT to 'arrogate' powers and thus circumvent the existing statutory regime, with its checks and balances, especially the right to have matters investigated by the MMC.

The attraction of a licence condition, as opposed to the 'general competition law', is that a licence condition may be enforced virtually summarily and, until very recently, was only susceptible to judicial review, a mechanism which provided the regulator with a good deal of discretion in the exercise of his judgment. Historically, this discretion was usually upheld by the courts but this has not always been so, as Ofgem found out when confronted by Scottish Power.

Two developments are worth noting. First, the Utilities Act 2000 provides for financial penalties for breach of licence conditions and, perhaps prompted by the human rights background, the provision for appeal against such a finding. This has been enacted in modifications to, for example, the Electricity Act. It is doubtful whether the form of appeal chosen in the Utilities Act fully satisfies the requirements of human rights legislation in that it is unlikely (although the matter has yet to be tested) that the jurisdiction on appeal is 'full' enough to satisfy the requirements of an effective appeal against punitive sanctions. At present, there is a stalemate in that the regulators insist that the jurisdiction is 'full' and, perhaps not surprisingly, the regulated utilities insist to the contrary, with both sides waving QCs' Opinions at each other.

The second major change has been, as noted above, the introduction of the Competition Act 1998. As is well known, this Act no longer confers any reporting role on the (renamed) Competition Commission. The DGFT has the power to investigate and make decisions, and impose penalties equivalent to 10 per cent of UK turnover of any undertaking under investigation (with 'turnover' being defined opportunistically as the sum of the last three years' sales). This Act is very closely modelled on what are now Articles 81 and 82 of the EU Treaty, and Section 60 of the Act ensures that changes in EU competition law are binding upon the DGFT, the regulators and the courts within the UK. Moreover, the developing decisional practice of the

Commission constitutes matters to which the DGFT, the regulators and the UK courts must have regard. Decisions are subject to appeal to the new Competition Appeal Tribunal, which is formally part of the Competition Commission.

As stated, these powers are shared concurrently with all the sectoral regulators. They essentially possess exactly the same power as the DGFT within their primary sphere of influence. The scope of that sphere of influence is not without difficulty of definition, especially since, as in communications, the lines are very blurred as between different systems of conveying information and so on. One solution is to concentrate regulatory power in overlapping areas in one regulator – a form of regulatory convergence. For the moment an Order is in place empowering the Secretary of State to resolve any differences that may arise as between regulators: the most obvious source of difficulty may well be in relation to the multi-utility companies possessing water, electricity, gas and communications functions. The first problem arose in telecommunications, over a retail sale of fax machines, where the OFT took jurisdiction.

The arguments in favour of concurrence, endorsed by the Hansard Society investigation into utilities in 1996 and by the government since then, rest upon the need for the specialist regulator to have powerful tools of competition enforcement as an essential element of his armoury. Moreover, the sectoral regulator is deemed to have the necessary technical and other expertise, thus enabling the competition powers to be enforced more effectively. To the extent that jurisdictional disputes arise, these can be resolved if necessary by recourse to the Secretary of State but, preferably, by administrative concordats.

The above certainly has superficial attraction and would doubtless be considered apostasy if any material change were proposed. However, I have doubts.

It would be easy to say that the best definition of 'regulation' is that it is what regulators do and that further definition is unnecessary. This would be deeply unsatisfactory though probably quite accurate. What are the defining characteristics which distinguish a 'regulator' from a national competition authority?

I set out above four actions which, uncontroversially, regulators perform in fact. In my view, by far the most important function of a regulator is to act as a positive stimulant to introduce competition. For a time, certainly for Professors Littlechild and Carsberg, there is no doubt that this view was shared. I have a strong if mischievous suspicion that there might well have been a first draft of Professor Littlechild's report to the DTI which said that all that was needed to regulate British Telecom was complete liberalization, open licensing for competitors, the introduction of resale to encourage arbitrage and, possibly, the structural separation of BT in 1982. This, of course, is mere fantasy, but if such a report existed and is unearthed by some diligent researcher after the expiry of 30 years, I suspect none of us would be surprised. We might also find an original copy with Michael Beesley's annotations all over it suggesting that Professor Littlechild had not gone far enough!

Similarly, Professor Carsberg's tenure at Oftel is peppered (perhaps 'characterized' would be a better word) with attempts to introduce competition at every juncture and to elevate the introduction of competition and the facilitation of entry as key considerations.

Professor Littlechild is on record as describing (in his Wincott lecture, *Privatisation, Competition and Regulation*, IEA occasional paper No. 110, 2000) his efforts to introduce competition both in generation and in supply to industrial and then domestic customers. He took his legal power from the statutory injunction to promote and maintain effective competition and he interpreted this to mean seeking new opportunities to provide effectively structural remedies to enable competitors to enter. What is interesting is the apparent resistance he found from civil servants, interpreting the wishes of politicians, and his resort to subterfuge. A similar story could be told in relation to the introduction of resale in telecommunications and the development of a strong open licensing policy for new entrants, and in the progressive unbundling of British Gas. I refer, in particular, to storage, as well as supply.

The sustained pressure exerted by these regulators, and others, toward opening up markets and, I might add in the case of gas, ensuring structural separation which facilitated competition, should not be confused with the control of anti-competitive behaviour. The former are concerned with creating competitive structures. To some extent, they remedy the initial political defects in the opening privatization settlements. This is perhaps particularly true of electricity generation and supply; in relation to gas, the management of British Gas saw the opportunities to enhance shareholder value in separating gas transmission from domestic supply and also, perhaps with some encouragement, in relation to storage facilities. The progression has now been completed by the separation of gas transmission and oil and gas exploration. The transition from a vertically integrated monopoly, over which Sir Dennis Rooke presided in 1986, to the current situation has been a remarkable achievement, achieved (although neither side would probably ever admit it) by an uneasy partnership between management and regulator, each, at various times, wielding both carrot and a stick.

The position of BT is more delicate. The structural settlement of 1984, presided over resolutely by Sir George Jefferson, has survived but the management itself is seeking ways of effecting a divisional structure, retaining majority interests in each, at least for the time being.

I want, however, to address a fundamental issue where competition and regulation come together in the choice of structure. Competition laws are essentially about prohibiting anti-competitive behaviour. There are, of course, rare situations in which the behaviour is such that the only appropriate remedy lies in a structural solution. Such a solution has seldom been invoked successfully. In the UK, the MMC required divestiture of cross-shareholdings in the tobacco industry and found that the (then) monopoly in the manufacture of contraceptives by the London Rubber Company was contrary to the public interest and considered divestiture. (On noting there was only one production line, the MMC backed off, considering the production to be comparable to a natural monopoly.)

It is very unlikely indeed that the Competition Act 1998 would ever allow a structural remedy. Structure remains a matter for the Competition Commission to make recommendations about, in the course of a scale monopoly reference. This is why, I think, the FTA was not repealed in its entirety. In the end, the decision to divest is a political one. Similarly, in EU competition law, structural remedies have hardly ever been invoked, although, using different powers, EU law is soon to insist on local loop unbundling. By contrast, in the USA, the reconstruction of the telecommunications industry was the product of a consent decree administered by Judge Greene in the context of anti-trust proceedings brought by the Department of Justice. Something similar may emerge from the *Microsoft* litigation.

In the UK, in assenting to a licence modification in August 2000, BT consented to local loop unbundling, which required it to surrender exclusive use of 'metallic path facilities' from its exchanges to domestic and business premises. This also involved co-location of competitors' DSL equipment within or near to BT's exchanges.

BT consented to this structural solution notwithstanding the fact that, as Oftel acknowledged, more than 50 per cent of homes have access to cable, which could carry wide-band voice and data transmissions, and that for many, particularly dense city areas, BT's share of new connections was low and, as in the City of London, its market share was quite small in relation to its principal competitor. It also consented in the full knowledge that unlimited Internet access is somewhat secondary: I predict that wide band will be used mainly for voice conveyance. I mention this because a very respectable anti-trust defence could have been erected if the Competition Act 1998 had been invoked. The *ENS*[1] judgment of the Court of First Instance in 1998 marked a legal watershed in determining what a competition authority should have to prove to competitors before parting with resources.

New structures such as that represented by unbundling create significant problems of supervision. For example, what obligation does the incumbent owe to its competitors if, for example, its own demands on its own facilities are such that there is no surplus capacity available to facilitate entry by the competitors? Must it rein in its own plans or, if the regulator was satisfied that the claims on its own resources were justified, should the competitors be obliged to live with it? The 'regulatory' solution may be to encourage entry by disabling the incumbent from utilizing its own resources for its own genuine purposes. This would be to elevate the 'promotion' of effective competition over any other value, including 'efficiency'.

It is by no means clear that a competition authority would arrive at the same conclusion, although the analysis would be based upon the necessity for access to the facility to be so absolute as to enable any form of competition before any obligation to a third party could crystallize. While it is clear that a dominant incumbent would run grave risks if it refused facilities to a competitor, when such facilities were essential to competition and if spare capacity existed, it is by no means clear that a competition authority would oblige a dominant undertaking to cut back its own facilities and services in order to achieve this.

Nearly all of the cases, perhaps with the exception of *ENS*, involving railway paths through the Channel Tunnel, have been instances where no issue of scarce capacity appeared to have arisen. Moreover, EC cases such as *Bronner* appear to impose a heavy burden upon the applicant to show that the resources could not be duplicated. In other examples, such as the compulsory licensing of intellectual property rights – as in *Magill* (the TV listing case) – no issue of scarce resources arose. In relation to local loop unbundling, and this is a very live issue in which I declare an interest, it would be strange indeed if BT were required to curtail its own efforts (after such public encouragement from the Chancellor of the Exchequer and others) to make way for other parties.

But assuming that such an obligation exists, is it suggested that the applicant or competitor should be furnished with the facilities for free? Hardly. But what is the proper basis of charging? It seems to me that there are two extreme cases: the first represents the opportunity cost of providing such facilities, using the unmodified Baumol–Willig rule, capitalizing monopoly profits; the second is that the resources should be furnished at some measure of cost, allowing only a 'competitive' rate of return, irrespective of the actual rate of return.

This choice is fundamental and goes to the heart of a difference between regulation and competition. Regulation, with its stress on promoting effective competition, may nevertheless concede that if the basis of charging should be opportunity cost, where the new entrant's choice should be between taking the resources and building them for itself, it is likely that the end result would be no entry and consequent frustration of the regulator's ambitions.

The latter case, of a compulsory contract at some measure of cost, runs the risk of endangering the survival, maintenance or renewal of the assets if the rate of return is too low or regulatory uncertainty too high. This resolves into a question of what is the appropriate 'cost' – should this be long-run or short-run cost, average or incremental cost, or average incremental cost? Should it seek to simulate or mimic what the price would be in a competitive market when, by definition, there is no competitive market? In a competitive market, price tends to the level of costs and therefore the competitive price must relate to cost. But then, I am told by experts, this is not so because price reflects 'option values'. I am also reminded that there is uncertainty in this world and this should be reflected in a premium over cost; I am also told that in the long run all costs are variable and this too should be reflected in the cost calculation. I am reminded of trying to get to grips with Lange and James Meade and recall why Pareto gave up economics (and why I did so too!).

So, should regulators be trusted with the development of competition law? Is it their *métier*? I am not sure it is. I understand and appreciate arguments based upon speciality and expertise, but this argument works both ways. To express it at its most generous, our public agencies are not over-endowed with staff who have a clear appreciation of competition law and proper policies. I acknowledge the great efforts being made by the OFT, which remains in very good hands, in the training of its staff, and applaud its efforts. But the problem goes beyond the difficulties created by spreading talent over so many agencies.

First, there are obvious difficulties in seeking to combine two distinct philosophies. In the main, regulation is about structure, encouraging new entrants, remedying examples of market failure other than abuse of a dominant position, as well as putting in place formulae for price controls. It is also about constant political pressure to introduce new opportunities for competition and innovation.

Chapters 1 and 2 of the 1998 Act are about conduct or behaviour. Competition specialists should be quite modest. I would be the first to acknowledge that the mere absence of anti-competitive behaviour does not inevitably mean (without more) the presence of a competitive market. The role of competition law in forcing people to compete is negative rather than positive.

When the Competition Bill was first introduced, it set out to endow the regulators with concurrent powers and stated that the regulators, in exerting these concurrent powers under the Competition Act 1998 should have regard not only to their duties under the competition legislation but also to their disparate statutory objectives laid down in sectoral regulation statutes. The competition legislation would have primacy. I was not alone in regarding this formulation as inherently unstable: the regulators could hardly ride two bicycles, especially, as events have shown, as they may be going in different directions. Happily, the government relented and formally at least 'broke the bridge' between the sectoral statutes and the competition provisions. But I think we should be realistic in assuming that a regulator cannot turn off and ignore long-cherished regulatory objectives if the Competition Act 1998 offers an opportunity to achieve those objectives. My concern is that this will result in violence being done to the development of competition law at this especially sensitive stage and, moreover, the resulting appeals, successful or otherwise, will seek to frustrate the effective development of the law.

Second, there are issues of consistency between the regulators. Plainly, men and women of the distinction of the regulators we have appointed will have different views about the proper application of competition laws, as well as their own regulatory remit, and I anticipate profound differences in approach, the risk of which is unnecessary. The OFT has published an extensive set of guidelines to the application of the Act. The regulators, too, have produced their own guidelines in specific matters, in consultation with the OFT. It is interesting to note the differences of emphasis and approach in these documents. For example, in telecommunications, the regulator is not content with the conventional approach toward predation, as laid down in the EC *Akzo* judgments of the European Court of Justice (ECJ), but has developed new criteria based upon the specific situation found in network industries where fixed costs are very large and where marginal costs are very small (following the EC Commission's Telecommunications Access Notice, which I understand was largely prompted by the UK authorities, and need not be followed by the EC competition authorities or by the UK competition authorities).

Similarly, in relation to energy, the distinctly different situation relating to electricity, a commodity which cannot be stored and where the system must always balance, gives rise to specific problems which are addressed by the regulator in a specific way. But, even acknowledgement of such differences in the 1998 energy guidelines was thought insufficient by the energy regulator because he judged his powers under the 1998 Act to be inadequate to deal with what he regarded as untoward practices conducted by some of the generators; hence his attempted introduction of the 'market abuse licence condition' (MALC).

As is well known, two companies refused to accept any modification to their licence to include such a condition. The matter was referred to the Competition Commission, which has now reported.[2] Ofgem's press release gives details of the contents of the report. The Competition Commission found that the two parties had no power to effect the short-term price spikes and market manipulation which formed the core of his argument that the MALC was necessary. Accordingly, no revision to their licences was required. What is perhaps surprising is Ofgem's subsequent decision to seek to amend the licences of the parties that had accepted the introduction of the MALC, some of which, if the issue had been tested, might have been found to possess market power.

In the course of the Inquiry, the regulator's position was not only that the MALC is necessary, having regard to the position of the generators under investigation, but also that the general competition law is inadequate for his purposes. This was because, as he was advised, the courts are unlikely to hold any generator possessing sufficient ability to cause significant short-term price increases to be in a dominant position owing to the relatively low market shares of such companies, both absolutely and relative to their competitors.

British Energy took a different view. Again, this is one of those cases where one QC was matched against another (in doubtless unequal combat) and, uniquely, where the Opinions of both were posted on the Internet for the inadequacies of at least one of them to be revealed to all. It is a curious reprise of the situation when the telecommunications regulator sought such a power in the absence of tough and effective general competition law; the energy regulator sought such a power because he had been advised that the new tough and effective laws were nevertheless inadequate for his purposes.

The inadequacies of general competition laws in the eyes of the regulators are not a new theme. Again, in relation to telecommunications, the history of EC and UK regulation has been to impose standards on undertakings deemed to have something called 'significant market power', 'market influence' or 'well-established operator "status"', all defined administratively, that is, without any necessity to adopt and observe the principles set out over the last 30 years by the ECJ to define a dominant position. It is a case of when in doubt, change the rules, in order to achieve the 'legitimate' regulatory objective.

Earlier, I hinted elliptically that the bicycles may be heading in different directions. What I have in mind is the current statutory objective of achieving consumer benefits. When this was first proposed, when the present government was in opposition, I regarded it simply as a not unwelcome but nevertheless cosmetic device to focus regulators' attention on consumers and their interests, and perhaps to be less forgiving of the regulated utilities and the problems of their management. I was in good company, judging by my conversations with various regulators, who always thought that in the long run their actions were directed toward improving the lot of consumers. Of course, I was wrong in this. It seems that short-term consumer benefits are what the government had in mind.

As George Yarrow pointed out so persuasively in his lecture last year, there is a fundamental difference, actually or potentially, between the short-term interests of the consumer and economic efficiency. As he cogently argued, there will be situations where the regulator will seek to enforce the 'consumers' interest' at the expense of economic efficiency, where the latter would involve price increases or other benefits to shareholders, including a higher rate of return on capital. I had assumed, in my *naïveté*, that the primacy of market solutions was equivalent to maximizing benefits to consumers. This is wrong. A hard struggle to make competition law accord with basic economics is therefore being questioned.

I cite one very thoughtful example contained in Oftel's strategy document of January 2000. The document cites 'competition plus' as the guiding principle, in that it recognizes that there are circumstances where some formal or informal regulatory action is needed to protect consumers' interests in addition to the achievement of effective competition. The provision of universal telecommunications service is given as an example. I took this to mean, at first, that there are acknowledged market failures and what was being considered was a policy of promoting competition subject to remedying obvious market failures. If this is so, it is not clear on a closer reading of the document. As the document states (at 2.17):

> The starting point for the re-assessment is as follows:
> - Competition between telecom suppliers is likely to be the best regulator *provided it is effective in delivering benefits to customers*;
> - 'Effective competition' will not always be present and, *even if it is*, there are some circumstances where it cannot deliver the best deals to consumers.
>
> Consequently, even in the longer run, there is likely to be a residual role for sectoral regulation. (Emphasis added)

This marks, to me at least, a significant development away from the stress placed upon competition and goes well beyond an acknowledgement of the well-known (but occasionally exaggerated) limitations on competition by way of market failure, such as information failures to consumers, and so on. It sets out something called the consumers' interest yet does not offer any criteria indicating when the consumers' interests (or 'best deals') will be furthered other than by the existence of effective competition, or in other words the basis for predictable intervention. In the absence of either recourse to the market or clear and predetermined principles of intervention, recourse to the 'consumers' interest' is a recipe not only for *ad hoc* intervention but regulatory survival. Or to put it another way, when faced with a demand by a regulator to do something, an appeal to efficiency based upon the existence of competitive markets and the absence of anti-competitive conduct will, by definition, be insufficient in certain circumstances. But those circumstances are at present unknown. Regulation is thus guaranteed a long life. I do not regard this as a satisfactory situation.

In these circumstances, it is probably sensible for a creative institutional tension to exist between the OFT and the regulators. The former will uphold competition, in the light of the developing case law in the UK and the EU. The latter will be able to qualify such an objective by references to whatever principles animate regulators. As David Boies suggested in my opening quotation, competition and regulation reflect different assumptions. There can be no harmony if, wearing one hat, the regulator has, by statute, the ability to intervene and impose provisions based upon very loose and thus far unspecified criteria detached from competition. If both policies are pursued by the same individual or agency, the 'looming omnipresence' of competition laws, even in the UK setting, will be evanescent and ineffective. There will be no counterpoint to random intervention getting better short-term deals 'in the interests of the consumer', notwithstanding the fact that markets may, in fact, be competitive (where no criteria for intervention are proposed save random periodic checks) or, more pertinently, where there is a complete absence of anti-competitive conduct.

As a rational pessimist, I have to say I am certain that no changes will be made. The regulators will continue to perform a dual and conflicting role. There are opportunities for regulatory games to be played, using whichever powers are most apt, and least reviewable. When faced with the possibility of appeal by recourse to established principles of competition law, which might frustrate their ambitions, as in energy and communications, regulators will invariably adopt 'regulatory' solutions requiring licence enforcement or modifications, occasionally, as with the 'market abuse licence condition' and 'market influence' tests, moving goal-posts away from established notions of dominance in the process. Even under the new 'appeal' process in licence enforcement, such an appeal can only be conducted by recourse to principles which are as yet unspecified.

I think I can hear Michael Beesley offering a wry chuckle from the grave.

NOTES

1. Case T–384/94, European Night Services Ltd v Commission (1998), ECR 215.
2. The energy regulator accepted the report and withdrew his attempt to impose the MALC on the two companies. However, the DTT is apparently seeking to impose a similar condition in new licences.

CHAIRMAN'S COMMENTS

Geoffrey Horton

The chuckle from beyond the grave is easy to imagine. I had many long entertaining arguments with Michael Beesley. They could also be quite hard work because sometimes I had to translate what he was saying into my own terms, think about it, and then translate the response back into 'Beesley'. However, it was always worth the effort and could even result in a thing of beauty. On one occasion Michael and I were arguing about price control at the OFFER board table in front of Stephen Littlechild (who used to pretend not to understand when we tried to involve him in the argument) and various other OFFER directors. Finally we reached an agreement and stopped. Stephen's deputy, Peter Carter, said, 'That was marvellous. It was like something you used to hear on Radio 3 late at night. Did you conclude anything?'

On that occasion we did, but often we didn't and, at this early stage, this may well be the case with 'Concurrency or convergence?'. Tom Sharpe has, as usual, set out an important topic with great clarity and I agree with the vast majority of it. However, there are four points that I wish to make.

The first point is to question the degree of conflict between his second regulatory objective of promoting competition and the fourth one of the application of general competition law. The promotion of competition mainly concerns structure, while competition law mainly concerns conduct, but the two are closely linked. Indeed, many forms of anti-competitive conduct are intended to maintain a market structure in which there is market power.

Industries where there is a need for a sectoral regulator are different from other sectors, which is why they have been deemed to need a separate regulatory system. This may be because they contain a natural network monopoly (such as electricity wires, gas pipelines or railway lines) or because there has recently been a statutory monopoly in what should be a competitive activity and an incumbent is starting with a 100 per cent market share. The ideal solution would be for the regulator to separate the monopoly from the competitive activities, help the latter to achieve effective competition, and then withdraw from the competitive activity. At that point competition can be regulated as in other sectors, but it is surely not unreasonable for there to be a different approach before then.

Having said that, it is the case that regulators have to use their Competition Act powers separately from their other duties. Tom's image of the broken bridge on which regulators must ride two bicycles simultaneously gives an unpleasantly accurate indication of the complexity involved.

Given the model that I have in mind, it is important that separate regulation is not introduced in industries where that is not appropriate and that regulators withdraw when competition has been introduced. Telecommunications, which provided several of Tom's examples, is more difficult than most sectors under this model. It is a network industry but with the possibility of a number of competing networks. In the UK a vertically integrated company was intended to compete with others in most of the different markets, including local and national networks. Other countries have adopted different models and Mark Armstrong's paper[1] in this lecture series three years ago questioned whether the UK's model was the best. He said that other countries would watch with interest the outcome of this experiment in industrial policy. The jury is still out, but it is not surprising that there have been particular problems with competition in the industry.

Second, the nature of the industries that require individual regulation means that the treatment of essential facilities is a key feature. They involve bottlenecks where there is a natural (and sometimes statutory) monopoly, or at least significant natural market power. Firms controlling these bottlenecks have often also been firms with 100 per cent initial market shares in the competitive market. In such circumstances it is important to ensure that would-be competitors can gain access to the essential facility and that pre-emption is not used by the incumbent to retain market share in the potentially competitive market. Depriving the incumbent of the use of a part of the facility is an obvious response in such circumstances. It is a tempting response in other cases. The difficulty of obtaining planning permission for new bus depots in London means that ownership of 'pre-empted' present depots probably gives local bus operators market power in parts of London. This is not a regulated industry and so would not at first sight qualify for deprival, but there is a monopsony franchise regime under the Greater London Authority Act under which depots can perhaps be separately purchased and made available to others.

Baumol and Willig's efficient component pricing rule (ECPR) is not easy to use to set a price for compensation for deprival. This is particularly the case when the essential facility whose use is being removed, or the retail service provided by the incumbent when using the facility, is price controlled, as will often be the case in regulated industries. ECPR gives the incumbent the difference between the price charged and its marginal cost as compensation for lost profit. However, it is in a position to rebalance prices under its price control and allocate costs within its accounting conventions to manipulate this sum to its own advantage. Oftel recognized this in 1994 and did not use ECPR for that reason.

However, given that there is likely to be a deficit between the revenue that would be recovered from marginal cost pricing of networks and the total revenue deemed in a price control review process to be required to cover costs (including the cost of finance), an access deficit charge will often be needed.

Ramsey–Boiteux seems the obvious response (and has other advantages over ECPR) but it is not generally used in the UK.

My third point is to share Tom's concern when regulators seek to insert in licences conditions to control anti-competitive conduct (or 'market abuse') which then use different criteria to assess anti-competitive conduct and more one-sided procedures to determine whether it has occurred. It is of particular concern when the market is one where competition has been introduced but the response of the regulator is not then to withdraw but to set up a system that will require perpetual specific regulation.

When the Competition Act guidelines, which are published jointly by the OFT and the industry regulators, were being written, there was concern that the market share figures quoted in them (as indicators of dominance being unlikely or an agreement having an appreciable effect) would not be appropriate in regulated industries, in particular for electricity where short-term demand is inelastic. I thought then that the figures should be omitted but, on reflection, there is no point in ignoring existing jurisprudence and it probably is right to quote figures subject to the caveats given in the guidelines.

It may well be that, when markets have been appropriately defined, dominance or appreciable effects of agreements can be established under existing jurisprudence if market power is abused in electricity generation. If substitution is difficult, the market is likely to be narrowly defined. If a company with a small share can still affect the price, then dominance will have to be considered and joint dominance may be an issue, although the possibility of rapid entry to the market would also need to be entertained. If there is a real danger of abuse that cannot be dealt with under the 1998 Competition Act, there is a general problem with competition regulation that needs to be generally addressed, perhaps just in new case law, rather than by special measures for each industry. Electricity generation should not be a special case. It is an example of an industry where capacity is fixed in the short term and demand is comparatively inelastic in the same period.

Finally, Tom was if anything too restrained about the dangers of regulators promoting consumer benefits that it is claimed could not be provided by effective competition. This last is a fairly broad concept and presupposes that consumers are able to make sensible choices between products, so that any consumer information problems are resolved through modest consumer protection such as the general prohibition of unfair contract terms or disclosure requirements that may be particular to the industry.

Pursuing aims other than to enable customers to choose effectively between competing products can be wasteful. However, other types of duty are laid on regulators. They can be placed in three broad categories that relate to:

- external costs and benefits, such as on the environment;

- distributional effects, when a particular group of consumers might be adversely affected;
- achieving a particular outcome said to be for the benefit of consumers, such as on energy efficiency or unmetered Internet access.

In general, external costs and benefits should be dealt with through the price mechanism by general taxes and subsidies or by assigning property rights that can be bought and sold. Piecemeal measures at the level of the individual regulated industry are unlikely to be efficient.

The same sort of argument is often made where distributional effects are concerned. Piecemeal attempts to achieve distributional outcomes through subsidizing consumption of particular goods and services are likely to distort the market and produce inefficient outcomes. However, tax and benefit systems are also distorting, and there may be occasions when the product is of sufficient importance to a particular group and their demand sufficiently inelastic that a cross-subsidy may be appropriate. This can be done by pricing in monopoly networks, but should be the exception rather than the rule.

Second-guessing the customer is rarely sensible. There is a large literature[2] describing the folly of supposed experts' attempts to promote energy efficiency by subsidy or price manipulation to change consumer behaviour to something allegedly more to their own advantage. It is to be hoped that the present pressure on the structure of telecommunications charges will not provide another set of examples.

I hope Tom is being unduly pessimistic when he speaks of creative tension between regulatory offices and the OFT. When I headed the consumer protection half of the OFT there was a degree of tension between it and the competition policy side and perhaps it was sometimes creative. Industry regulators, however, should be working hand in hand with competition policy to promote effective competition and regulate monopolies where competition cannot be introduced. Competition law is not itself sufficient for the sectors in which they operate; hence their presence and the need for more pro-competitive action than is required in unregulated industries. But, if they end up pursuing other aims to the extent that there is a tension between their activities and competition policy, something will have gone wrong.

NOTES

1. 'Local competition in UK telecommunications' in IEA readings 48, *Regulating utilities: understanding the issues* (ed. M. Beesley).
2. P. Joskow and D. Maron, 'What does a negawatt really cost?' *Energy Journal*, April 1992 is a well-known example.

9. Ten years of European merger control

Paul Seabright

1. INTRODUCTION

European Union merger control is ten years old this year. An infant 16 years in the gestation has grown to maturity in far less time. Such an anniversary inevitably invites an assessment, but it is not always obvious what questions one may reasonably ask. The birth of the infant was attended by considerable scepticism that it could cope with even the simplest practicalities of life: would the Commission's resources prove adequate to the workload; would the European system really ensure speed, a one-stop shop and the legal certainty that the Commission's procedures in other areas of competition policy had so conspicuously failed to provide? So it is tempting to confine my assessment to an expression of considerable admiration that the infant has survived at all (not to mention displaying a nimbleness and agility one might not have anticipated from an observation of its parenthood), while noting the various remaining areas of procedural contention regarding its future role in life.

Although I shall devote a section of this chapter to noting some of these areas of contention, procedural questions will not be my main theme. This is not because such questions are dull or of secondary importance: indeed, some of them raise profound constitutional issues regarding the distribution of power between the European Union and its Member States;[1] the proper role of philosophical divergences between Member States in their regulation of market transactions; and the place of sheltered technocracies in a modern democratic society. Rather it is because such procedural questions have dominated discussion of EU merger control to date, at the expense of a number of other questions whose importance I should like to affirm. Briefly, in discussing ten years of EU merger control I should like to point to some intriguing questions about the nature of mergers without ignoring more familiar questions about the nature of control.

The European Commission has been highly active, and the pace of its activity has been accelerating. Table 9.1 divides the ten years into two periods, one comprising nearly three-quarters of that time (from September 1990 to December 1997) and the second barely over a quarter (from January 1998 to

Table 9.1   Ten years of EU merger control, 1990–2000

	1990–97	1998–2000
Number of notified cases	701	758
Cases withdrawn	30	30
Commitments in Phase 1	14	55
Commitments in Phase 2	23	23
Prohibition	8	5
% openly influenced by Merger Regulation	10.7	14.9

Source: European Commission.

August 2000). There have been slightly more cases notified in the second period than in the first, so the acceleration has been remarkable. Although only 13 mergers have been prohibited in ten years, many more have seen their approval subject to conditions, either after the four-month Phase 2 investigation or to an increasing extent after the one-month Phase 1. A further 60 cases have been withdrawn after notification, most of these because of fears that the Commission would prohibit them or because modifications were demanded that the parties were unable to accept. Chiefly because of the increase in Phase 1 conditions, the proportion of cases that can be said to be directly influenced by the operation of the Merger Regulation has risen from a little over 10 per cent in the first period to nearly 15 per cent in the second.[2] Since the cases under review involve all the largest corporate transactions in the European Union, this must count by any standards as a great deal of influence. In terms of the Commission's lasting impact on the operation of European markets, merger control dwarfs the remainder of its activity in all other areas of competition policy combined.[3]

How has this influence been exercised? In particular, can we say anything about the role mergers are playing in the overall portfolio of strategies available to Europe's businesses, and the way in which EU merger control interacts with their choice of strategy? The last ten years have taught us a good deal, theoretically and empirically, about the point of mergers in a modern economy, and I want to suggest that these lessons can fruitfully inform our understanding of the point of merger control.

The outline of this chapter is as follows. In section 2 I shall describe some basic facts about the Commission's activities and about their setting, the evolution of merger activity within the EU. I shall mention, without giving them more than superficial comment, some of the remaining difficult questions about the Commission's procedure and their constitutional place in the institutional structure of the European Union. Then in section 3 I shall outline two of the last decade's major advances in our understanding of the role mergers play in a modern economy: the contribution of the theory of incomplete contracts to the theory of the firm; and the empirical analysis of productivity change using census panel data. In section 4 I shall conclude by saying why I think these advances help us pose sharper questions about the future of European merger control. I shall not in this chapter presume to try to answer them.

2.   THE MERGER REGULATION AND EU MERGER ACTIVITY

On 21 September 1990, Council Regulation 4046/89 of 21 December 1989, on the control of concentrations between undertakings (the 'Merger Control Regulation')[4] came into force, introducing into Community law a legal framework for the systematic review of mergers and other forms of concentration. From the outset, the Commission has considered the Merger Control Regulation a 'vital additional instrument made available . . . to ensure a system of undistorted competition in the Community'.[5] Over the intervening decade, the Commission has dedicated significant resources and energy to ensuring its effective application, improving its jurisdictional, substantive and procedural rules, and winning the approval of Member States and the business community for its four fundamental principles: the exclusive competence of the Commission to review concentrations of Community dimension; the mandatory notification of such concentrations; the application of market-oriented, competition-based criteria; and the provision of legal certainty through rapid decision-making.

In contrast to the Commission's broad interpretation of Article 81, where it has considered a large number of agreements to be anti-competitive, the Merger Control Regulation is based on the premise that major concentrations are 'in line with the requirements of dynamic competition and capable of increasing the competitiveness of European industry, improving the conditions of growth and raising the standard of living in the Community'.[6] In the decade since its adoption, the Merger Control Regulation has evolved into an integral part of Community antitrust practice. Unlike other areas of Community competition law, where few formal decisions have been adopted,[7] the Merger Control Regulation has produced a rich and extensive juris-prudence that provides invaluable guidance on a variety of issues, including market definition and the substantive assessment of transactions affecting a broad array of markets. Of the operations notified, the largest proportion has involved joint ventures (around 48 per cent of all notified transactions), with the remainder comprising acquisitions (38 per cent), takeover bids (8 per cent), and other forms of concentration (8 per cent).[8] As to the market sectors examined, over 260 cases (representing more than 20 per cent of all notified operations) have involved oil, gas, mining and chemical markets; more than 250 operations (around 20 per cent of all notifications) have concerned consumer products; over 150 transactions (equivalent to 10–15 per cent of all notified operations) have concerned financial and insurance markets; and over 125 transactions (around 10 per cent of all notifications) have involved the wholesale and retail trade. The single largest other major categories have been telecommunications, media and transportation.

The Commission has adopted a pragmatic and comparatively informal approach to the Merger Control Regulation's application. It has made extensive use of pre-notification meetings to clarify threshold legal issues, discuss the scope of any filing required, obtain a preliminary understanding of the relevant markets, and consider procedural questions. Such meetings have undoubtedly made the procedure more business-friendly, with both the advantages and the risks that implies (see Neven et al., 1993, chs 5–7). The Commission has also acted swiftly to address shortcomings in the original form of Merger Control Regulation adopted in 1989, abandoning the distinction between 'concentrative' and 'cooperative' joint ventures, correcting the lack of explicit authority to accept undertakings at the end of Phase 1, clarifying the ambiguity surrounding the Merger Control Regulation's application to situations of collective dominance, formulating clear rules on ancillary restraints, and introducing a 'short-form' notification for unproblematic transactions.

Since the Merger Control Regulation came into force, the number of transactions notified each year has grown significantly: from 60 in 1991, to 110 in 1995, to 292 in 1999. The growing complexity of many transactions, increased expectations as to the detail and sophistication of Commission investigations, and changes in Commission practice have also resulted in increasingly extensive and detailed decisions. For perspective, the first decision rendered after an in-depth investigation, *Alcatel/Telettra*,[9] was 45 paragraphs long and filled seven pages of the *Official Journal*; in 2000, the Commission decision in *Volvo/Scania*[10] ran to almost 400 paragraphs and extended over 100 pages.

What about the merger activity the Commission is seeking to control? Table 9.2 shows the total number of M&A transactions (drawn from the AMDATA database) involving EU firms: it increased nearly threefold between 1987 and the end of the 1990s, though by 1998 the figures were not much above their peak in the previous merger boom in 1990. A different source (Securities Data Company) reports the annual number of transactions worldwide to have risen from 11 300 in 1990 to 26 200 in 1998, so transactions involving EU firms would appear to have declined as a proportion of the international total, from

Table 9.2   Evolution of M&A involving EU firms, 1987–98

Year	1987	1988	1989	1990	1991	1992	1993	1994	1995	1996	1997	1998
Number	2775	4242	6945	7003	6607	6005	5740	6334	6810	6327	7097	7600 (est.)

Source: AMDATA.

over half to around 30 per cent unless there are incompatibilities in the data. What is indisputable is an increase in transactions values, particularly in the late 1990s: Table 9.3 shows KPMG data reporting an increase in total world cross-border M&A from $237bn in 1995 to $797bn in 1999, and a fourfold increase in average deal size over the same period. These are large numbers, and it is worth bearing in mind that even in an era of globalization, cross-border transactions are in a minority, even weighted by value: on SDS figures cross-border transactions rose from around 24 per cent to only around 33 per cent of all transactions. Table 9.4 shows the industries in which such activity

Table 9.3   World cross-border M&A, 1995–99

Year	Total spending, $bn	Average deal size, $m
1995	237	38
1996	275	50
1997	341	59
1998	544	105
1999	797	157

Source: KPMG.

Table 9.4   Favourite global industries, 1999 and 1998 ($bn)

1999		1998	
Telecoms	159	Oil/gas	71
Chemicals	93	Banking	51
Oil/gas	75	Automotive	51
Banking	59	Telecoms	50
Food/related	53	Print/publishing	41

Source: KPMG.

has been principally concentrated: telecoms, oil and gas, banking, the automotive, food and publishing industries. As I shall discuss in section 3 below, these are all industries in which intangible assets play a large part in the creation of value, whether through research and development and its associated intellectual property rights or through advertising and the creation of brand loyalty.

Table 9.5 shows the total notifications of merger transactions to competition authorities (national and supra-national) in the EU for the period between March 1998 and December 1999. Interpolating from Table 9.2, around 15 000 transactions are likely to have taken place in the EU during this period, so something under 30 per cent would have been notified to competition authorities. Of the latter, only some 12 per cent were notified to the European Commission. A further 8 per cent were notified to two or more national competition authorities, indicating that the 'one-stop shop' principle is honoured two-thirds as much in the breach as in the observance.

One might conclude that a procedure which is amending only 15 per cent of the Commission's 12 per cent of the notified 30 per cent of all the deals that are taking place in the European Union cannot be having so great an influence after all: only one deal in 200 is visibly modified as a result of the process. Such a conclusion would obviously be misleading, if only because of a failure to weight for size: the one deal in 200 that is modified is certainly among the largest and most important. Its amendment may correspondingly have a value as a signal, to other firms and to other competition authorities, about the principles that are to govern merger control overall, and therefore to govern the regulation of the market for corporations in the EU as a whole. But – of course – this imposes a correspondingly daunting burden of accuracy: is the procedure selecting the one deal in 200 that truly needs amendment, and is it amending it in a defensible and constructive way? Even to begin to answer this question requires some hard

Table 9.5   EU merger notifications, March 1998–December 1999

Total notifications	Of which:			
	number notified to EU Commission	number notified to 2 national authorities	number notified to 3 national authorities	number notified to more than 3 national authorities
4303	494	294	31	39

Source: European Commission.

thinking about what is motivating the other 199 deals that the procedure currently allows to proceed.

Before returning to this question in section 3, let me sketch some of the procedural issues that remain outstanding and will certainly be debated over the next months and years:

- Table 9.5 is drawn from a report to the Council adopted by the European Commission[11] and is used to argue that 'too many mergers with cross-border effects still fail to meet the turnover thresholds set in the Merger Regulation as revised in 1997'. Even if this judgement is correct, it need not follow that the appropriate response is to revise the thresholds downwards, though that is one possible solution. Others include the introduction of rules to allocate responsibility to a 'lead' national authority, a procedure for triggering upward referrals to Brussels for deals with multiple filings (but without an explicit revision of thresholds), and a move towards more standardized filing and investigation procedures that would reduce the costs and uncertainty associated with multiple filings rather than reduce their number.
- The increasing decentralization of other areas of competition authority to Member States has highlighted not only that national authorities cooperate with the Commission, but that national courts are expected to apply EU law in these areas. National authorities do not, however, apply EU merger law. This may or may not be an anomaly but it will certainly be subject to increasing scrutiny. It will also raise the question of whether differences in regulatory philosophy between Member States are a problem with the system or one of its sources of strength.
- There has been discussion at various times about the desirability of making merger control a quasi-independent[12] activity as it is in Germany and is increasingly becoming in the UK. The analogy with monetary policy might be considered to militate in favour of such a development; growing concerns about the democratic accountability of the EU institutions might be considered to militate against it.
- A related issue concerns the relation between the Commission's investigative and decision-making roles, which are currently combined (albeit subject to judicial review) and which some think would be better separated.
- The growing willingness of the Commission to negotiate remedies to merger deals in the first month of investigation raises questions not only about the economic rationale for such remedies but also about their enforceability. The Commission does not have the resources to monitor remedies on a systematic basis.

- Cooperation with competition authorities outside the EU has generally been good but tensions that notably surfaced over the Boeing/McDonnell-Douglas case could re-emerge. Enforceability is a major issue here: if two major US firms whose merger had been cleared by the US authorities refused to acknowledge the legitimacy of a blocking decision by the Commission, the result might be very serious indeed.
- The accession of new members to the EU in the next few years will require not only additional resources but additional thought: does merger evaluation require modification to be adequate to the circumstances of economies so poor and so recently under central planning?

I now turn to questions raised by the merger process itself.

3. WHAT PART DO MERGERS PLAY IN A MODERN ECONOMY?

Mergers, acquisitions and the creation of joint ventures involve the transfer of ownership of corporate assets, so a reasonable way to ask what part these transactions play in a modern economy is first to ask what part ownership itself plays. The theory of incomplete contracts, whose pioneer was Oliver Williamson, which addressed itself to questions first posed by Ronald Coase and which has more recently been formalized and developed by Oliver Hart, John Moore, Jean Tirole and others, has emphasized the value of seeing ownership as primarily about the allocation of residual rights of control of productive assets.[13] These rights are described as residual in the sense that they operate in circumstances whose details have not been and could not be foreseen to the extent of being made the basis of contractual enforcement of rights and responsibilities. When contingencies cannot be adequately foreseen, someone must exercise discretion over the asset, and that someone is ordinarily described as an owner.[14]

So much for ownership in general: what is special about ownership of corporate assets? Typically corporations are large combinations of assets that have to be used in combination and are not suitable for dividing up among individual owners (even if they have individual owners they are typically too large to be managed by any single individual). The owners therefore have to work together, and much of the value of the corporation consists not simply of the individual component assets but of their ability to work together efficiently. This ability could not be contractually enforceable, otherwise ownership could be made an entirely individual matter (one individual might own the lathe, the other the maintenance equipment, the other the materials for processing and so on). This has a number of implications:

1. The rules governing the exercise of owners' discretion are more tightly drawn than for individual assets, typically because corporate owners need certain safeguards (such as those governing the rights of minority shareholders) to give them the confidence to cooperate efficiently.

2. We can consider any corporation as consisting of a combination of physical assets (machinery, buildings and so on) that could in principle be owned and managed individually, plus a combination of human assets that could not be so owned (since slavery is illegal), plus a combination of intangible assets which can be described as all the conditions that determine the way in which the physical and the human assets work together. These include the knowledge embodied in corporate rules and procedures, the corporate culture, the firm's reputation in the marketplace, and so on. The corporation itself formally owns only the physical assets and a very few of the intangible assets (those embodied in formal intellectual property rights such as patents and trade marks), but its value as a corporation consists primarily in the reasonable expectation that whoever owns the physical assets can benefit also from the human and intangible assets that are complementary to them and which may be called the non-tradable assets.

3. When one corporation buys another (rather than directly buying its physical assets) it is really buying the tradable assets in the hope that the non-tradable assets will come too. If it wanted just the tradable assets it could usually buy them directly; if it wanted just individual human assets it could hire them directly through the labour market. There are some exceptions due to indivisibilities: I cannot realistically buy half a mine, but if I buy the whole mine I typically buy a company and not just a site. But in most other contexts we can only understand the motivation for corporate mergers and acquisitions if we appreciate that the parties could just have exchanged tradable assets but chose not to do so. So paradoxically the key to understanding this kind of trade is to see it as a contractual exchange of assets, in which the assets enumerated in the contract are not the primary motive for the transaction. This explains why the sectors in which M&A activity has been prevalent are those for which intangible assets are an important component of overall value.

4. Buying and selling corporations is an intrinsically high-risk business, much more so than buying other assets. This is for reasons more fundamental than just the large amounts of money at stake; it is due instead to the fact that the principal contribution to value creation in the transaction comes from the non-traded assets. If I buy a house principally

for the view, the contract entitles me to the house and not to the view. But still, when I take possession of the house the view usually comes too (there are exceptions, but they are relatively rare). But if I buy a firm for the brilliance of its management or an investment bank for the brilliance of its M&A team, the management or the M&A whizzkids may choose to leave. Mergers in the banking industry in particular are littered with stories of just this kind. Or the human assets may come but simply be unable to integrate their culture with that of the acquiring firm. Likewise, I may buy a brand but I cannot be sure I am buying the brand's success in the marketplace: the cachet of Fortnum & Mason might not survive if it were bought by, say, Burger King, while the Virgin brand name has proved less spectacularly profitable for Richard Branson than it did for the Roman Catholic Church. In fact, the only point of my buying a corporation is that its non-tradable assets should turn out to be more valuable to me than they have been to its existing owners (since it is this latter value that will determine the owners' reservation price). To put it another way, the deal creates value through asset specificity. In the nature of things that is a gamble on untried circumstances.

5. Many corporate transactions are structured in ways that reflect requirements associated with creating additional value through the non-traded assets. No less than 48 per cent of transactions notified under the Merger Regulation in the last decade have been joint ventures. It is inconceivable that all of these transactions have been motivated purely by a wish to escape a regulatory prohibition on full merger. On the contrary, most firms have chosen this form because, in spite of the coordination difficulties that attend all joint ventures, the form has compensating advantages. These consist principally in the ability to bundle non-traded assets together within the firm while protecting them from potentially damaging interaction with other parts of the business. A research department can be given autonomy to pursue its projects without a few initial successes turning it into a cash cow for the rest of the corporation. Staff and assets can be transferred to a production joint venture with a guarantee that the venture will end and they will be transferred back to the parent. A speculative venture can be held at arm's length so that in the event of its failure the reputation of the rest of the firm is not damaged, and so on. Understanding the role of and the vulnerability of non-traded assets is crucial to understanding why such deals take place at all.

Loosely speaking, we can think of mergers and acquisitions as arrayed on a spectrum from those in which the prospective gains consist solely of improvements in the value of the assets in their existing combination (in short, where the target firm is an underperformer) to those in which the prospective gains are likely to be realized solely through combining the existing assets in new and imaginative ways with the assets of the acquiring firm.[15] The distinction between performance-correcting transactions and synergistic transactions is not a hard-and-fast one, of course: we are more likely to consider a particular firm an underperformer if an improvement in its performance could be achieved by many possible alternative management teams, and not just one with a particular flair. Conversely, if it would take the special know-how of one particular alternative owner to make the most of the acquired firm's current assets we are more likely to consider any improvement in performance as the consequence of a synergy rather than the correction of a failure.

Since performance-correcting transactions do not yield acquirer-specific gains, the principles of auction theory tell us that virtually all of the gains from the transaction should accrue to the owners of the underperforming firm. Gains to the acquiring firm depend on its ability to exploit informational imperfections which are not only likely to be small in relation to the overall assets but also counterbalanced by elements of the 'winner's curse', the phenomenon whereby the likelihood of success in a common-values auction increases in the degree of over-optimism of the bidder. This asymmetry between gains to the acquirer and gains to the acquired is indeed a perennial theme of the now-large empirical literature on the benefits of merger activity.[16]

While agreeing that any benefits are asymmetric, that literature has had much more difficulty reaching a consensus on whether the benefits are positive overall.[17] The points just made help to explain why this uncertainty is unsurprising. First, since mergers and acquisitions are so highly risky, we should expect empirical studies to be characterized by high standard errors on all the parameter estimates of interest; finding statistically significant results will be intrinsically hard. Second, even if, on balance, it were to appear that mean returns were significantly negative, this could itself be due to the high variance of returns in the presence of limited liability constraints. Limited liability would lead managers of acquiring firms to chance their arm at a number of transactions with negligible or even negative expected gains provided the upside potential were large enough: there is no need to invoke stupidity or testosterone to explain the phenomenon. Third, the difficulty of defining the appropriate counterfactual for comparison[18] is compounded in this case by the fact that, in synergistic transactions, merging firms are likely to be different from their non-merging counterparts (which is why they merge at all): consequently the performance of their non-merging counterparts may be an inadequate control for how the merging firms would themselves have performed without the merger. Fourth, the high value of intangible assets at stake in M&A transactions, coupled with the very fragility of those assets, means that the acquisition process may involve a degree of turbulence that itself threatens the value of the very assets by which it is motivated. This creates a problem of endogeneity that makes evaluating such studies peculiarly difficult. Finally, distinguishing empirically between mergers that do and those that do not enhance market power will be made harder by the significance of intangible assets: a rise in prices after a merger could indeed indicate that market power had increased, but could instead be due to the improved value of the product or service that the new brand or service quality had created.[19]

It would at least be valuable if empirical studies gave us some kind of insight into the ways in which synergistic transactions (those based on new combinations of productive assets) could add value. This is important for policy, since we know that sometimes transactions add value to the firm while diminishing value to society, since they create market power (for example by concentrating non-reproducible productive assets into the hands of fewer producers). The more we know about the other benefits from synergistic transactions, the more comfortably we can identify the particular asset combinations that create market power and evaluate them against any other benefits of the combination.

This is not the place to try to evaluate all the empirical material bearing on this large question. What I want to do instead is more limited: to look at some lessons from a very important literature that has sprung up almost entirely in the last decade, and which examines the causes of productivity growth on the basis of detailed census panel data about individual economic establishments. Once again I shall be illustrative, not comprehensive.[20]

I illustrate using findings by Jonathan Haskel and various co-authors, particularly from a paper by Disney et al. (2000). Table 9.6 shows the results

Table 9.6   Decomposition of UK productivity change, 1980–97 (%)

Study	Years	Growth	Within plants	Between plants	Net entry
Labour prod.		% points p.a.	% of total	% of total	% of total
DHH (2000)	1980–92	4.53	48	3	49
DHH (2000)	1982–89	4.75	64	–7	43
BH (2000)	1994–97	1.01	67	–4	38
TFP					
DHH (2000)	1980–92	1.06	5	41	54
DHH (2000)	1982–89	2.46	38	23	39

Note: DHH = Disney, Haskel and Heden; BH = Barnes and Haskel.

of decomposing productivity growth in manufacturing into that which is due to growth within existing establishments (plants), that which is due to transfers of market share between plants (mostly though not always in the direction low-productivity to high-productivity plants on average), and that which is due to the net impact of entry and exit. Several important messages emerge from this table:

- Plant turnover (entry and exit) contributes a large share of aggregate productivity growth, comparable in magnitude to the share of within-plant productivity growth for all periods when labour productivity is considered.
- When total factor productivity (TFP) measures are considered, plant turnover and transfers between plants together contribute virtually everything to productivity growth over the period 1980–92 as a whole, while contributing a little over 60 per cent during the period 1982–87. This corroborates evidence from other sources such as Geroski and Gregg (1997) that, contrary to some wishful thinking, recessions do not induce impressive productivity growth in plants that survive them.
- Transfers of market share between plants contribute substantially to TFP though negligibly to labour productivity in all periods, suggesting that plants gaining market share were generally those that made more efficient use of capital.

Table 9.7, from the same source, then tells us something very interesting about ownership. It compares the contribution to productivity growth of single-plant firms with those of multi-plant firms. The following findings stand out:

- Multi-plant firms accounted for around 80 per cent of both labour productivity and total factor productivity growth over the period as a whole.
- This was partly because such multi-plant firms proved to have a

Table 9.7   Productivity growth, 1980-92, singles and groups (%)

		Within	Between	Net entry
Labour prod.	Singles	0.6	0.1	15.9
(4.53% p.a.)	Groups	44.6	1.1	33.2
TFP	Singles	0.2	0.5	12.8
(1.16% p.a.)	Groups	4.4	37.1	41.1

Source: Disney et al. (2000).

consistently better record of gaining productivity from the closure of relatively unproductive plants and the opening of relatively productive ones.

- It was partly because multi-plant firms were more successful than single-plant firms at raising labour productivity by increasing the capital–labour ratio.
- And it was partly because multi-plant firms were more successful than single-plant firms at increasing the proportion of output produced by plants that used capital relatively efficiently.

Ownership (of multiple plants by a single firm) appears to have been yielding important benefits. Firms belonging to a larger group probably learn from other parts of the group: we know that the transfer of tacit knowledge is one of the most important functions of the modern corporation, but we know to date little about what determines the transfer of tacit knowledge between plants in the same firm rather than within a single plant.[21] In addition, the group appears to be playing the roulette wheel of plant opening and closure with a notably higher success rate than do single firms. Given the hazards of bankruptcy and the difficulties associated with start-up capital, it is perhaps unsurprising that the internal capital markets of larger groups are capable of smoothing some of these market imperfections: what is more surprising, as well as reassuring, is that they actually use this capacity well, rather than dissipate it in a flurry of internal rent-seeking (as the work of Meyer et al., 1992, might have led one to expect).

More evidence on the latter is provided by the same authors' calculations of hazard probabilities of exit in which the year of entry appears as a dummy variable, along with various controls for size and age. Single plants that enter in boom years appear more likely to exit in subsequent years, though plants belonging to groups show no such bias. This suggests that booms may encourage low-productivity entry among single-plant firms, and corroborates the impression that multi-plant firms prosper better on average from the turnover gamble than do single-plant establishments.

So ownership by a group may well be conferring benefits (on average, it should be stressed) to individual plants that those plants are less likely to realize on their own. Is there independent evidence from similar sources of the benefits due to changes in ownership? The relevant analysis has not yet been performed on UK data, but Baldwin's major (1995) study on Canadian industry includes a chapter on the effects of ownership change on productivity, which comes up with a substantially more positive assessment of the aggregate gains from ownership change than is typical of earlier (non census-based) studies based on productivity data (see also the studies by McGuckin and Nyugen, 1995, and Peristiani, 1997, referred to in note 18 above). He stresses a number of other striking facts about ownership change, such as that acquisitions of plants from firms exiting the industry are more likely to lead to output reductions than transfers of plants between firms staying in the industry (if true, this suggests that the failing-firm defence should perhaps be transformed into a failing-firm offence). He supports the view that 'mergers are more successful when they involve the transfer of intangible knowledge-based assets'. He draws attention to the importance of distinguishing between barriers to entry at the level of the plant and barriers to entry at the level of the firm (in many industries it is hard to build new plants but not hard to challenge incumbents by taking over old plants). And above all he corroborates the importance of plant entry and exit for overall productivity change where it is able to occur.

So, to sum up, evidence from detailed micro studies, which has become available only relatively recently, tends to corroborate the importance of the transfer of non-tradable assets in corporate transactions. It also highlights the immense amount of turnover that takes place continually in many industries, whether through entry and exit or the transfer of market shares between existing firms, and demonstrates the importance of that turnover for overall productivity change.[22] Finally, it emphasizes the importance of distinguishing empirically between the levels of the firm and the establishment (or plant). Apparent stasis in the share of firms in an industry may be disguising considerable turbulence at the level of plants;[23] indeed, one of the achievements of firms appears to be that they facilitate more efficient and productivity-enhancing competition between individual plants.

In the final section I want to consider what all this might mean for European merger control.

4. IMPLICATIONS AND QUESTIONS

It is hard not to be impressed by the sheer productivity of the EU merger control procedure, if one measures its output in terms of cases processed, jurisprudence created and major judicial embarrassments avoided. In 1990 the establishment of the Merger Task Force represented the triumph of hope over bureaucratic experience, and for all the remaining questions about the future of the procedure, that hope has been amply vindicated. That it should now be reasonable to pose broader questions about the purpose of the whole process is, in one sense, the best compliment a young institution can receive.

These broader questions mainly concern how accurately the Commission's procedures for evaluating mergers enable it to identify the one case in 200 that, according to its own procedural statistics, really does pose a danger to competition. (By the way, this is not a question specific to the Commission; it concerns the procedures of all competition authorities, which have seen considerable convergence over the last decade.) What we have learned in recent years about ownership and its transfer, theoretically and empirically, implies that analysis of mergers should be more concerned than it has been to date with identifying the specific assets which are transferred in the merger process. Many of these specific assets will also be intangible, although not all (indeed a number of recent cases in broadcasting have concerned monopolization of some specific assets that are very tangible indeed, such as cable networks). Once these assets have been identified it is easier to determine the nature of the specificity that enables the merging parties to gain synergy from the reallocation of these assets. It should therefore be easier to see whether this specificity arises significantly from the exercise of monopoly power rather than some other process that creates value for society rather than merely transferring it away from consumers.

The two key stages of EU merger analysis (market definition and the analysis of dominance) make no explicit reference to the notion of asset specificity but rather allow it to creep in through the back door. In the procedure of market definition, if the merging parties gained control over certain productive assets that can easily be reproduced by others, the notion of 'supply-side substitutability' allows the market definition to be widened in consequence. But this happens in a somewhat mechanical fashion, and can easily miss key features of the assets that are being exchanged.[24] Likewise, when dominance is being considered decisions sometimes identify asset specificity but do not do so in a systematic fashion. This is not to say that the Commission ignores the issue. Indeed, it is striking that a significant proportion of its prohibition decisions (as well as some in which it has imposed conditions) concern the broadcasting, media and information technology industries, where there may be important risks of certain parties gaining control over highly specific and non-reproducible combinations of productive assets (such as the cable distribution systems referred to above). The important point is that its identification of the nature of the assets exchanged needs to be examined openly and systematically rather than as a by-product of the more traditional stages of merger analysis.

This leads to an issue that is more particular to the Commission's own procedures. The Regulation, unlike the competition laws of some Member States, does not give the Commission the explicit right to invoke an efficiency defence. Although there are some reasons to think that this self-denying ordinance is a valuable barrier against the worst kinds of lobbying and special pleading, it has one major cost. This is that the Commission is never obliged to set out explicitly its understanding of the business rationale for the transaction under investigation (it sometimes does so in practice, but always as an afterthought). Everything we know about the merger process suggests that a competition authority that has failed to understand why the parties wish to merge in the first place (as opposed to merely trading physical assets between them or undertaking some wholly different kind of market-based transaction) will have great difficulty understanding the competition hazards as well. This does not mean that competition investigators should play management consultants, merely that it would be good to see a section in every decision labelled something like: 'Why this deal? Why not another?'

Finally, the empirical evidence on productivity change suggests that a great deal of action may be taking place underneath the umbrella of the firm, at the level of individual plants. To some extent competition occurs at that level too. Merger control procedures can be usefully informed by an understanding not just of the market shares of the firms but also of the production shares of the merging parties' individual plants.

It may appear that I am calling for EU merger control to do even more than the already impressive amount it does, to take account of even more information and process even larger quantities of data. That is not so. So far at least I am posing questions rather than providing answers. I expect that our gradually deepening understanding of what drives mergers in a modern economy may make it possible to use more precise empirical diagnostic tools. Quite how that will be possible I do not know, but it provides an interesting challenge for the second decade of EU merger control.

NOTES

1. The Merger Regulation represents the most sophisticated practical application anywhere to date of the reasoning underlying the subsidiarity principle (see Neven et al., 1993, ch. 6).
2. It is possible, also, that a considerable number of other cases have been indirectly influenced by the very presence of EU merger control, in that the deals would not have taken the form they did in its absence. It is evidently hard to get evidence on this phenomenon. Neven et al. (1993, esp. ch. 4) discuss this issue.
3. For perspective, of the 4679 transactions notified in the US during the fiscal year ending 30 September 1999, requests for additional information were issued in 113 (2.4 per cent), and only 76 transactions (1.6 per cent) resulted in enforcement actions: US Department of Justice, Premerger Office. During the fiscal year ending 31 March 1999, the Canadian Competition Bureau received notification of 192 transactions (an additional 222 requests were made for advance ruling certificates). Of the examinations concluded during the year, all but five were approved outright (see the *Annual Report* of the Canadian Commissioner of Competition). The situation is similar at the EU Member State level. In the UK, the Office of Fair Trading examined 425 transactions in 1998, of which only eight (less than 2 per cent) were referred to the Monopolies and Mergers Commission (the 'MMC') for further investigation. Undertakings were accepted in an additional three (less than 1 per cent) in lieu of a reference to the MMC, although others may have been abandoned in response to confidential guidance. See *International Competition Policy Advisory Committee Report* (2000), p. 96.
4. Council Reg. 4064/89 on the control of concentrations between undertakings, 1990 O.J. L257/13; with amendments introduced by Council Reg. 1310/97, 1997 O.J. 1997 L180/1;

corrigendum 1998 O.J. L40/17. See the consolidated version at the Commission's web site: http://europa.eu.int/comm/dg04/lawmerg/en/c406489.pdf.

5. *XXth Report on Competition Policy* (1990), para. 20. See also: 'Mergers may be carried out in the interest of economic efficiency, permitting improved exploitation of economics of scale and the pooling of expertise, and may thus help Community industry adjust its structure to the challenge posed by the integration of the internal market and the internationalisation of the economy.' *XXIst Report on Competition Policy* (1991), para. 5.

6. Recital 4, Merger Control Regulation. See also Joseph Gilchrist, 'Procedures in Merger Cases' (1997), IBA Seminar: 'The Merger Regulation is user friendly. Unlike Articles 85, 86 or 92, it does not begin with an interdiction. Big is not necessarily bad. Although lawyers and business executives who have dealt with the Commission, particularly in second phase cases, may find this a rather hollow statement, the Merger Regulation does not operate in the kind of adversarial setting and system which is often considered to be the characteristic of operations under Articles 85 and 86.'

7. For perspective, the Commission has rendered only around forty decisions applying Article 82 since the EC Treaty came into force in 1965.

8. *XXVIIIth Report on Competition Policy* (1998), p. 89.

9. Case IV/M.042, Commission decision of 12 April 1991 (1991 O.J. L122/48–55).

10. Case COMP/M.1672, Commission decision of 14 March 2000.

11. The Report and more information concerning the review are available on line at http://europa.eu.int/comm/competition/mergers/review.

12. Independent, that is, of the political control of the Commission.

13. Hart (1995) is an excellent introduction to this literature.

14. But may in other circumstances be a trustee or a representative.

15. Holmstrom and Kaplan (2000) suggest that the 1980s takeover wave in the USA consisted primarily of the first type of transaction, while the wave of the 1990s has consisted mainly of the second.

16. See Fridolfsson and Stennek (2000, p. 2); *World Investment Report* (2000, ch. 5).

17. This is particularly true because event studies have tended to find that mergers raise combined gains to acquirer and target shareholders (with acquirer shareholders breaking even), while firm accounting studies tend to find that mergers reduce combined profitability. See Fridolfsson and Stennek (2000) and Gugler et al. (2000).

18. Fridolfsson and Stennek (2000) note that when mergers impose an externality on other firms, then performance relative to a non-merging control group may not be an adequate measure of the absolute benefits of the transaction. McGuckin and Nyugen (1995) and Peristiani (1997) are two studies that note a positive impact of mergers on productivity within given industries and are not vulnerable to this criticism.

19. In effect the quality-adjusted ('hedonic') price would not have risen even though the crude price per unit had done so.

20. However, Caves (1998) and Bartelsman and Doms (2000) provide thorough reviews and discussions of this literature.

21. This is consistent with cross-sectional evidence (such as that of Baily et al., 1992) to the effect that there is a positive correlation between the productivity of individual plants and that of other plants belonging to the same firm. In addition, Allen and Phillips (2000) have found evidence that part ownership of firms by other corporations leads to improved performance and investment on the part of the owned firms.

22. Geroski (1992) stresses that entrants in many industries not only have high failure rates but may take many years to gain high market share. However, this does not mean that entry is of secondary importance for productivity, for several reasons. First, as he himself acknowledges, entrants may be importantly different from the rest of the industry, particularly at early points in the product life cycle. Second, it is entry of plants that matters rather than simply entry of firms. Third, entry and exit need to be understood together (each may facilitate the other) and it is the productivity of the whole process that is important.

23. On the broader role of turbulence in a market economy, see Carlin et al. (2001).

24. In the *De Haviland* decision, for example, it is hard to believe that the market analysis would have taken the same course if the Commission had taken serious account of the fact that

among the most important assets of an aerospace company are its development plans (its potential models) and not just its actual models. This is because many orders are advance orders and many development decisions are taken on the basis of such advance orders. The nature of competition in the industry is dependent as much upon whether there are technologically competent potential developers of new models as on whether models of a particular specification currently exist.

REFERENCES

Allen, J. and G. Phillips (2000), 'Corporate Equity Ownership and Product Market Relationships', *Journal of Finance*, **55**(6), 2791–815.

Baily, M., C. Hulten and D. Campbell (1992), 'The Distribution of Productivity in Manufacturing Plants', *Brookings Papers on Economic Activity: Microeconomics*, 187–249.

Baldwin, J.R. (1995), *The Dynamics of Industrial Competition*, Cambridge: Cambridge University Press.

Barnes, M. and J. Haskel (2000), 'Productivity in the 1990s: Evidence from British Plants', draft paper, available from <www.qmw.ac.uk/~ugte153>.

Bartelsman, E. and M. Doms (2000), 'Understanding Productivity: Lessons from Longitudinal Microdata', *Journal of Economic Literature*, **38**(3), 569–94.

Carlin, W., J. Haskel and P. Seabright (2001), 'Understanding "The Essential Fact about Capitalism": Markets, Competition and Creative Destruction', *National Institute Economic Review*, **175**, January, 67–84.

Caves, R.E. (1998), 'Industrial Organisation and New Findings on the Turnover and Mobility of Firms', *Journal of Economic Literature*, **XXXVI**, December, 1947–82.

Disney, R., J. Haskel and Y. Heden (2000), 'Restructuring and Productivity Growth in UK Establishments', draft paper available from <www.qmw.ac.uk/~ugte153>.

Fridolfsson, S.-O. and J. Stennek (2000), 'Why Mergers Reduce Profits and Raise Share-Prices: A Theory of Pre-emptive Mergers', paper presented at 9th Annual WZB conference on Industrial Organization, Berlin, December.

Geroski, P.A. (1992), 'Entry, Exit and Structural Adjustment in European Industry', in K. Cool, D. Neven and I. Walter (eds), *European Industrial Restructuring in the 1990s*, London: Macmillan.

Geroski, P.A. and P. Gregg (1997), *Coping with Recession: UK Company Performance in Adversity*, Cambridge: Cambridge University Press.

Gugler, K., D. Mueller, B. Yurtoglu and C. Zulehner (2000), 'The Characteristics and Effects of Mergers: an international comparison', paper presented at 9th Annual WZB conference on Industrial Organization, Berlin, December.

Hart, O. (1995), *Firms, Contracts and Financial Structure*, Oxford: Clarendon Press.

Holmstrom, B. and S. Kaplan (2000), 'Corporate Governance and Merger Activity in the US: Making Sense of the 80s and 90s', University of Chicago, mimeo.

McGuckin, R.H. and S.V. Nyugen (1995), 'On Productivity and Plant Ownership Change: New Evidence from the Longitudinal Research Database', *Rand Journal of Economics*, **26**(2), 257–76.

Meyer, M., P. Milgrom and J. Roberts (1992), 'Organizational Prospects, Influence Costs and Ownership Changes', *Journal of Economics and Management Strategy*, **1**(1), Spring, 9–35.

Neven, D., R. Nuttall and P. Seabright (1993), *Merger in Daylight: The Economics and Politics of European Merger Control*, London: CEPR.

Peristiani, S. (1997), 'Do Mergers Improve the X-efficiency and Scale Efficiency of US Banks? Evidence from the 1980s', *Journal of Money, Credit and Banking*, **29**(3), 326–37.

CHAIRMAN'S COMMENTS

Derek Morris

I would like to thank Paul Seabright for a very interesting chapter which I much enjoyed reading. It raises a whole range of points for discussion.

At the broadest level, Paul's chapter reflects very favourably on the ECMR regime; touches on some aspects of the theory of mergers; presents research findings on the determinants of productivity growth and the possible role of merger in this; deduces a key role for the significance of intangible assets; and assesses the merger regime in the light of this result, asking, first, whether the very small number of mergers affected are really likely to be the damaging ones, and second whether there shouldn't be more explicit focus on the role of intangible assets in mergers.

I would like to cover two broad points arising from this nexus of arguments. One relates to the assessment of the European merger regime, the other concerns the empirical results and the inferences drawn.

On the first, in no way would I wish to argue that the ECMR has not been a success, and the European authorities, both past and present, deserve praise for the way in which they have brought this area of competition policy to life in Europe, in what Paul calls a triumph of hope. But it is important not to be carried away by this.

If we look at the numbers of prohibitions – and Paul is of course absolutely right to say that that is a very misleading way of assessing a merger regime – nevertheless if one does, then 13 prohibitions in 11 years across the continent of Europe have been barely noticeable. The real issues are of course the numbers of mergers explicitly affected, which Paul shows is in the 10 to 15 per cent range, and even more important, but unknown, the number of mergers never embarked upon because of the regime. The ten-fold increase in cross-border M&A activity is not very reassuring here, but the main point is that the same yardstick must be used for the regimes with which the European regime is compared. Moreover, a merger has to be of considerable dimensions to fall within EC jurisdiction in the first place, whereas many of the mergers occurring at national level will be very small. That this is the case, and a potential distortion in such comparisons, therefore, is seen by the EC's active pursuit of reform to lower the thresholds for EC jurisdiction, but concerns at the national level that current thresholds should be raised. In short, while the perception that held until quite recently that the ECMR regime was overly benign may have been too simplistic, I think there is no empirical support for it having been particularly more effective than either intended or elsewhere, and it may be that the endorsement of the European regime by many industrialists could reflect that it has not, at least until recently, had much impact on the processes of concentration in Europe.

This is important. The UK and the Australian authorities have both recently concluded major studies to determine the most effective or 'best-practice' forms of merger control. Both independently concluded that the 'substantial lessening of competition' test, which they have each now adopted, was in significant ways superior to the 'dominance'-based test of the ECMR. This is not the time or the place to rehearse the arguments, but both concluded that the 'lessening of competition' test was a significantly tougher control of merger activity and to be preferred on that account. Over time the interpretation of the ECMR may evolve, but the existing case law on dominance and the infancy of the concept of collective dominance suggest that this has some way to run. So my first point is to suggest a slightly more cautious and perhaps more provisional conclusion on the EC merger regime.

My other point relates to the significance of intangible assets in mergers. That mergers might be significantly driven by the desire to acquire intangible company-specific assets such as R&D, brands, intellectual property rights, reputation and so on is very plausible. Where these are important, a company's expansion is typically going to be very difficult if it requires developing one's own innovations, reputation and brands and then using these to drive down and out those of pre-existing competitors. Mergers will typically be a much more cost-effective mechanism. Mergers may of course be cost-effective where tangible assets are primarily involved, but there will typically be much more feasible alternatives in this case, that is, purchase of equivalent tangible assets. So Paul is right I think to focus on this.

But I have three points to make in this connection. First, the evidence, plausible as the thesis is, seems to me rather thin. It is based as far as I can tell on two things. One is that the industries in which most European mergers have occurred – telecoms, oil and gas, banking, automotive, food and publishing – all exemplify the significance of intangible assets in the creation of value. There is no question that some parts of each of these industries include companies with significant intangible company-specific assets, but there seems an element of faith:

(a) that this is more so in these industries than in many others; and
(b) that merger activity in them reflects this characteristic rather than other elements of global competition that have characterized these industries.

The other basis is the single quote from Baldwin's Canadian study. How compelling this is I cannot say, though I note that he sees intangible assets as a factor in the success of mergers rather than in explaining their incidence (and in mergers, above all else, we know that these two do not necessarily equate).

My second point is that the interesting empirical evidence in the chapter on the determinants of productivity seems to point in a rather different direction. By way of context, theory originally viewed mergers as primarily occurring either in pursuit of market power, or in pursuit of synergistic gains which would lower costs, improve competitiveness and so on, or some combination of these; and it should not be forgotten, much as analysis has moved on, that these are still the main battlefield in many merger cases.

Since then a mass of empirical evidence of many sorts – pre- and post-merger comparisons, comparing raiders and targets, share price analysis, and the like, have undermined the predominance of these at least as motives for merger, in favour of four other explanations:

- opportunistic exploitation of stock market misvaluations;
- so-called 'hubris' models – the continuing belief that one can do better than others have done despite the absence of any statistical support for the proposition;
- defensive merger for retrenchment, capacity reduction and the like, to mitigate what would otherwise have been bigger falls in performance; and
- merger as the most cost-effective way of pursuing corporate development strategies and managerial pursuit of rapid growth.

My point is this. The 'intangibles' argument seems to me to fit well with the view of mergers as effective ways of pursuing corporate development strategies where assets are very specific; but the productivity analysis, in line it has to be said with earlier productivity work in this area, rather tends to support the defensive retrenchment model. As Paul points out, the contribution of between-plant shifts to productivity gains is in fact very weak in the period 1982–89. It only predominates when the recession period up to 1992 is included. This is not unanticipated – it is typically in recession that low-productivity plants will close (this being entirely consistent with the later result that such plants are encouraged by a boom), but this is very much the retrenchment model and doesn't seem to me to relate much to the intangibles theme. Moreover it is (I presume) a presumption that mergers have played a role in the creation of the multi-plant companies where such gains are seen. Presumably the same could be true of multi-plant companies that had grown internally.

My third and final point is this: Paul directs attention to the need for competition authorities to look more closely at the role of intangible assets. Notwithstanding the points above, this is very sensible advice, though, without obviously naming any current or past cases, I am fairly confident that a trawl through merger cases in the UK in recent years would show that considerable attention had been paid to all manner of intangibles, including R&D assets, development plans, brands, and the like. My point, which I'm sure Paul would agree with, is that the authorities do and inevitably will face much the same dilemma here as in the analysis to which I referred earlier. Will the merger result in unacceptable market power through joint control of such intangibles, or is the merger a cost-effective and flexible way of achieving corporate growth and development and an important element in the perpetual restructuring of asset disposition – in this case intangibles – which characterize many competitive markets? These point are, I hope, pertinent to Paul's stimulating paper.

Index